Dear Ahmedbhai,
Dear Zuleikhabehn

# Dear Ahmedbhai, Dear Zuleikhabehn:
## The Letters of Zuleikha Mayat and Ahmed Kathrada
## 1979–1989

Compiled by
Goolam Vahed &
Thembisa Waetjen

First published by Jacana Media (Pty) Ltd in 2009

10 Orange Street
Sunnyside
Auckland Park 2092
South Africa
+2711 628 3200
www.jacana.co.za

© Zuleikha Mayat and Ahmed Kathrada, 2009

All rights reserved.

ISBN 978-1-77009-753-7

Cover design by banana republic
Set in Ehrhardt 11/15pt
Printed by CTP Book Printers, Cape Town
Job No. 001041

See a complete list of Jacana titles at www.jacana.co.za

'The very sense of loss keeps alive an expectation. How easy it is to lose sight of what is historically invisible – as if people lived only history and nothing else!'

– John Berger, *And Our Faces, My Heart, Brief as Photos*. New York: Vintage books, 1984. p. 63

# Editors' Introduction

IN THE AGE OF email and cell phones, when communication across distance has been rendered at once immediate and ephemeral, letters are enjoying other lives as literature and social history. As tactile artefacts that also tell stories, they can be newly esteemed for the magic they have always wielded. Letters are time-travellers, collapsing space, generated out of absence. They pass through prison walls, transgress national borders and private thresholds; they evoke passions from afar. What they convey to their unintended readers – be they archival scholars or readers of a published collection like this one – is both inscribed on the page and implicit in the very physicality of paper and ink. Between the corresponding acts of a letter's writing and reading lies a world of contingency: postal infrastructure, time and sudden events, and the friendship, enmity or business that may be confirmed or transformed. In letters, we encounter afresh the agency of words and the continual acts of faith that make dialogue possible.

The seventy letters published here chronicle the development of a friendship between a political prisoner and a self-described housewife during South Africa's tumultuous last decade of apartheid. Their correspondence begins accidentally. Ahmed Kathrada, convicted of treason and serving out a life sentence on Robben Island, writes to his former Johannesburg flat-mate, Abdulhak "Bis" Bismillah. It is a letter of condolence following a road crash that claimed the lives of Bismillah's sister, Sakina Bibi Mall, and brother-in-law, Dr. Mohamed Mayat, a gynaecologist from Durban. What happens to Bis's own reply is unclear but in the meanwhile his widowed sister, Zuleikha Mayat, responds.

A freelance writer, community organiser and editor of the best-selling cookbook *Indian Delights,* Mayat initiates a conversation with Kathrada that endures until his release ten years later.

Through observations about familiar and remembered aspects of everyday life, these writers bear witness to a changing South Africa. Their discussion ranges widely, from food and poetry to apartheid and gardening, children, racism and Salman Rushdie. Yet, always, Mayat and Kathrada are together pondering the question of what belonging means in a nation-state dedicated to division and exclusion. Their conversation, in its mix of ordinary and extraordinary, offers an important perspective on South African social history, as well as on the more global themes of Muslim diasporic identity and the nature of epistolary friendship.

Strangers at the outset, the writers quickly find that there is much to talk about based on the background they share. Both are Transvaal *plattelanders*,* hailing from the highveld of the former Transvaal (Kathrada is from Schweizer-Reneke; Mayat from Potchefstroom), where the region's mineral wealth and growing mining industry opened opportunities for immigrant merchants in the late 19th century. As progeny of Gujarati families who crossed the Indian Ocean to risk a new life in territories (not yet a nation-state) hostile to them, each grew up with segregation as a prominent social, as well as personal, reality. Each inherited the formidable kinship and clan networks that had been so crucial to the success and survival of previous generations and which, therefore, constituted overlapping social circles. Such a combination of heritage and geography, seemingly culturally insular, rather produced in each of them a firmly cosmopolitan orientation. Childhood in a Muslim

---

\* People from rural areas, "countrymen". Kathrada describes Mayat as a "fellow *plattelander*" in his letter of 10 April 1988; he uses this Afrikaans self-description also in a letter to Paul Joseph, dated 3rd of October 1989, the month of his release. MC AKC 8.3.27

shopkeeper household meant growing up at the multicultural vortex of otherwise partitioned municipal spaces. The shops, busy family enterprises, drew in customers of all colours and backgrounds by offering low prices, needed goods, odd job employment, tasty snacks, and a place for sharing news. This social complexity is also reflected in the linguistic and idiomatic repertoire that Mayat and Kathrada may claim: both were raised in Gujarati-speaking households, studied Urdu and some Arabic in Madressa as young children, utilise English in most of their correspondence and are also native speakers of Afrikaans. Their letters reflect, and reflect upon, the colloquial expressiveness of all these languages.

The paths leading out of the towns of their respective childhoods took them to different places and different lives. Zuleikha Mayat moved to Durban as a new bride in 1947; a year earlier, living in Johannesburg, Ahmed Kathrada had dropped out of school to engage full time in political activism. When their correspondence begins, with Mayat widowed and Kathrada in prison, their circumstances would appear to reflect lives that could not be more diverse. Yet there are significant points of convergence, not only in their continuing social networks, but in what they value and hold to be essential. Each has devoted their life to civic involvement, yet in this commitment – as in the face of loss – they draw from distinct wells for inspiration and for courage.

Ahmed Kathrada is, of course, well known as a hero of the struggle against apartheid, though the story he relates in his own *Memoirs* reveals a man with a genuinely modest sense of himself, desiring to consider his mistakes and uncertainties as well as achievements.[†] When his life sentence began on Robben Island in

---

† Ahmed Kathrada, *Memoirs*. Cape Town: Zebra, 2004. See also *A Simple Freedom: The Strong Mind of Robben Island Prison, No. 468/64*, written with Tim Couzens. Wild Dog Press in association with PQ Blackwell, 2008.

1964, he was thirty-five years old with more than two decades of concerted political work behind him. As a boy, in the late 1930s, Kathrada moved to Johannesburg for his schooling. Here, at a remarkably young age, he came under the influence of political thinkers like Dr Yusuf Dadoo and I.C. Meer and was drawn into political activism, performing volunteer work for various organisations. At the age 16, he gave up his education altogether to assist with the African mineworkers' strike in Johannesburg and Indian Passive Resistance Campaign in Natal. The growing alliance between the African and Indian Congresses brought him into close contact with people like Nelson Mandela, Oliver Tambo and Walter Sisulu, some of whom would become his co-accused and cellmates. Kathrada participated in the Defiance Campaign in 1952, in protests against the Bantu Education Act and forced removals, and was among those charged in the treason trial of 1956-61. With several thousand other activists he was detained when a state of emergency was proclaimed after the Sharpeville massacre of 1960. He went underground for the best part of the next year but when Mandela was arrested in August 1962, Kathrada came out into the open to launch the "Free Mandela" campaign. The apartheid regime responded with a banning order on 22 October 1962, confining Kathrada to his flat, and denying him visitors at nights or over weekends. He was arrested, along with his comrades, in July of the following year and sentenced to life imprisonment in the "Rivonia trial" of 1963-64. When he began his correspondence with Zuleikha Mayat, he had been on Robben Island for sixteen years.

Zuleikha Mayat had been prominent in the circles of Durban's Muslim community since the mid-century as founder of the Women's Cultural Group, a community organisation, and as an author. Between the late-50s and early-60s, her writing appeared weekly in *Indian Views* as the column "Fahmida's World". This was billed as "Mainly for Women", but "Fahmida" (in Persian it is a name that means *intelligent* or *scholarly*) mused not only on the challenges of motherhood and the modern housewife, but (much to some of her readers' disapproval) on the political, legal and moral questions facing contemporary South Africa, and its Islamic/Indian minorities. In the mid-1970s, the SABC radio carried Mayat's "Weekly Letter" on a programme called *Saturday Mirror*, essays reflecting on her extensive travels in Asia and Europe, or commentary on the art, architecture and traditions of Islamic Asia. Mayat became a household name in South Africa, and overseas, when the Women's Cultural Group produced a cookbook featuring the culinary chemistry of South African Indians. *Indian Delights*, which has to date sold over 300 000 copies and is into its thirteenth impression, has generated hundreds of thousands of rands for the Group's educational bursaries and charity projects in the region.

Like Kathrada, Mayat's early institutional schooling was interrupted. Racial barriers similarly prevented her from attending the local white and African high schools in her home town, but unlike Kathrada, her gender precluded travel to Johannesburg as an educational alternative. She recalls:

> *Obviously we [Indians] couldn't start a high school with such limited numbers, so what they did was, the boys would be sent out of town to Johannesburg or to Pretoria, to the Waterval Institute, or my brothers came to Durban, to Sastri College. But everybody couldn't afford that and where to send the daughters in those days? There were no girls' schools, there was nobody who would board a daughter. I had an uncle in Johannesburg – my mother must have just tentatively suggested to him [that I go there to school] so Mamajee said, "Behn, send the sons anytime, six, seven (we had only three brothers!) but poiree tho pothe hachawanu [the*

*daughters you must take care of yourself] you understand?" Okay. So there was no place that I could be sent and I could only finish Standard 6 in our school.*\*

Thus, young Zuleikha remained in Potchefstroom, studying after her chores were over for the Standard 8 certificate and matric with the help of correspondence courses. It was through distance learning, too, that she obtained a certificate in journalism. Upon her marriage to Mohamed Mayat, like most Muslim brides of her time, she moved into the household of her in-laws. They were liberal in their outlook but they were also part of a community that was orthodox in its faith and conservative in their practices. Her husband, who had studied medicine at the University of the Witwatersrand, had other ideas, however, and was a strong-willed person who "wanted a wife to walk alongside him, not behind him. Wherever he went, he wanted to take me and that was breaking a lot of ground in Durban". Encouraged by her husband and friends in the Women's Cultural Group, Mayat grew in her role as a community intellectual. She did not enter into formal employment or formal politics, but her friendship with sociologist and ANC activist Fatima Meer and other Congress members meant that she kept abreast of Congress movement developments.

In the letters between Kathrada and Mayat, there is little direct political commentary. Rather they reveal something of how the changing national climate was experienced in their distinct circumstances. The 1980s were significant for developments inside the prison as well as the fast pace of negotiations that accompanied the mass democratic movement. The decade opened in the wake of the Soweto uprising, which saw the rise of youth leadership in the

---

\* Interview, 2003, KwaMuhle Museum, Durban. ZM personal files.

fight against apartheid, the boycotting of Bantu Education by black students, and the formation of the broad-based anti-apartheid organisation, the United Democratic Front (1983) following the reformist initiative undertaken by the government as "window dressing" to the hard-line measures of divide and rule. Unlike the 1960s, apartheid repression post-Soweto failed to destroy resistance. The government of P.W. Botha reacted to the virtual insurrection from 1984 by declaring a state of emergency in 1986, detaining without trial thousands, and torturing and killing many others. All the while, recession, the decline in foreign investment and disinvestment led to a serious economic crisis. Apartheid was rapidly becoming untenable and the decade would see it crumble, its political prisoners released, and with talk of free, universal elections.

Indian Muslims were experiencing these and other important changes, some of them emergent from the complexity of local diasporic politics. The reaction of Indians to apartheid ran the gamut from armed opposition to active cooperation with the regime, with its tri-cameral structure. Islam in South Africa, in keeping with global trends, was undergoing political and generational transformation. Muslims have historically constituted around 20% of the Indian population of South Africa, this racialised category 3.3% of the total population in 1980. They are divided along class, regional, ethnic and linguistic lines. In the Transvaal, where both Mayat and Kathrada were born, Muslims were mostly of a trader, as opposed to indentured, background and were economically better off than their Natal counterparts. Ethnic diversity complicated other divisions, with identifiable groups like Memon, Surtee, Mia-bhai, Konkani and Kanamia bringing a range of languages and dialects into the mix: Memonese, Marathi, Gujarati and Urdu. For the major part of the Indian Muslim existence in South Africa, these linguistic and ethnic divisions have shaped strong internally preserved identities. In the 1980s, the growing reconfiguration of Islam towards conservative tendencies strove for religious "purification" based on unquestioning loyalty to a literal interpretation of the Quran and Prophetic authority. In response, many Muslims began to construct firmer boundaries around various points of contact: between men and women, Muslims and non-Muslims, Muslims and the state, Islam and secularism. There was a gradual shift from "Indian" being central in defining existence to "Muslim" gaining ascendancy.

Both Mayat and Kathrada were outspoken against these developments. Through her *nom de plum* Fahmida, Mayat decried the various kinds of segregation being entrenched in the 1950s – and, with changes in family and the roles of women, this included segregations along lines of gender as well as of race or ethnicity. She often chided readers of *Indian Views* for divisions and biases internal to the South African "Indian Community". For example, in the first week of February 1959, she directed her attention to the issue of education, reporting that:

> *So great were the number of [Indian] girls wanting admission to high schools this year that it has astonished the most optimistic of feminists and educationalists. Despite the number of new primary and secondary schools in the central area the numbers turned away are many. It leaves one with the impression that we will never be able to keep up with the demand. The obvious answer is to integrate the schools and thereby assure that every South African has a fair and equal education. I can see that the greatest objectors to this state of affairs will not be the whites but us Indians. Heavens! Already we find it difficult to reconcile to the situation – that is to sit in the same classrooms with different Indian groups – so how gallish the idea of sharing schools with a chow chow [mixed pickle]*

*mess of Africans, Indians, Boers, Jews and perhaps even one or two whose ancestors were aboriginals.*\*

A devout practitioner of her faith within a modernist interpretation of Islam, Mayat invoked religious ideals in her ethical appeal to her public: "God intended South Africa to be a stew pot of many races and cultures", she proclaimed through a fictional character created for one of Fahmida's allegories.† Unsurprisingly, Kathrada's principles on these issues are rooted not in theological but in secular, political ideals. In 1985, with typical wit, Kathrada declared to one of his regular correspondents:

> *[M]y background in public life, and my beliefs, do not readily accept the fragmentation or compartmentalisation of activities on the basis of religion, race or class. Once I accept the Islamisation of psychology, economics, etc., then I must allow for Christian Economics, Hindu Anthropology, Zoroastrian Sociology, Buddhist Psychology, etc. Already I find all the talk about an Islamic Atom Bomb not to my liking... My ideal society would be one where the priorities would be on that which unites people rather than on that which divides. Naturally, I believe in the freedom of religion, but I do not accept that there should be a state religion.*‡

Yet, Kathrada also draws upon his early experiences and the kind of morality exercised by older generations of Muslims living in the Transvaal, and is clearly moved by memories that became thematic in his letters to Zuleikha Mayat. In a lengthier and more personal explanation to the same friend, he confides his worry:

---

\* "Fahmida's World", *Indian Views*, 4 February 1959.
† "Fahmida's World", *Indian Views*, 26 June 1957.
‡ Letter to Dr Goolam Karim, 25 May 1985, (no. 7.9.35, Book 8, p92, NB24).

*[Y]ou mentioned the extensive plans being made to build an Islamic Centre in Lenasia, which would cater for a wide variety of activities. I got the impression that the school library and recreational facilities would be for Moslems only. I must confess it is painful to learn that in this day and age [that] instead of broadening our horizons to encompass more and more peoples and a variety of ideas, we are actively propagating and practising outlooks that tend towards the opposite direction. The philanthropy, the sacrifices, the devotion of our parents for community upliftment is traditional. One needs but to recall that until recently the bulk of the schools catering for our people in South Africa were built with money donated by the community. This applied also to country hospitals and other institutions. Of these, very few, if any, were exclusively for Moslems or Hindus. I remember how very disturbed we were about the existence (or proposed setting up) of Moslem and Hindu sportsfields in Pretoria. I can also vividly recall the tremendous efforts that were made to avoid the splitting of the community on religious lines after the establishment of Pakistan. What is most disturbing about recent developments is that the initiative for sectional projects comes from the younger and more educated people. Could it be that our fathers were more broadminded and farsighted than us? To bring it to a more personal level, in my social circle there were Hindus, Christians and Moslems. (I'm confining myself for the moment to the Indian friends.) Some were intensely religious, others not. We were a very close group and celebrated Eid, Dipavali and Christmas together. I'm just trying to think what would happen if on a Sunday afternoon we were to decide to go for a swim. Does it mean that we would have to split up and go to the swimming pools catering for each religious group? What a tragic situation we would be facing!\**

---

\* Letter to Dr Goolam Karim, 24 Oct 1981 (no. 7.9.11, Book 8, NB 28, MCH 22).

The relative positioning of these correspondents with regard to religion and politics is felt as one reads their letters. Zuleikha Mayat is formally "outside" politics by the same latitude that Ahmed Kathrada is "outside" religion/culture. Yet both are also and simultaneously zoned "inside" religion and radical politics by the way that racial and ethnic classifications operated under apartheid. Mayat hints at the idiosyncratic uses of ethnic classification in her letter of 5 November 1980: "Have the newspapers started circulating around there? Try and get the *Graphic* or *Leader* just to catch up with ethnic news. New word that means different things in our country."

The typically low resolution historiography of apartheid tends to elide the complexity of social divisions as well as some of the surprising solidarities between ordinary people in their daily interactions on the street, in the shops, in churches, on playing fields and in private spaces. Informal transgressions of various kinds of boundaries and their equally informal gatekeeping are often lost in the story of policy and law. By contrast, in their dialogue, Mayat and Kathrada reveal a complicated, sometimes painful and often quirky, unofficial portrait of South African "race-relations". Official race relations in different and tragic ways frame Zuleikha Mayat's loss of both her father and husband and, of course, are responsible for Kathrada's incarceration. These realities are the backdrop from which to identify moments in which the grip of power is less certain, when "samoosa diplomacy" can be employed to appease a white policeman from harassing customers in your shop; or in which the white politician arriving at the jail after your arrest might identify you not merely as a traitor and prisoner, but as the nephew of Mr so-and-so from his own hometown. Neighbours who can be simultaneously loyal friends and loyal supporters of the National Party are one of many bemusing conundrums considered here. Such stories are worthy testimonies to the absurdities of apartheid and the frequent failure of its lawmakers' dreams, due to – Kathrada and Mayat both appear to believe – the intervention of basic human decency. It may explain the stubborn optimism they convey in these letters.

Readers will be aware of the qualifications that must be made to any description of this collection as a "private correspondence". In the first place, all the letters were routinely processed by prison censors. A view to how censorship affected prisoners on Robben Island is documented in a petition submitted to the Officer Commanding, apparently in the 1970s. Among the most vehement of the petitioners' complaints was that:

> *[t]here is an inordinate <u>delay in letters</u> being handed to us after these have been received by the Post Office at Robben Island. At times the delay exceeds a month. This delay renders meaningless the purpose of correspondence and exchange of views and responses to queries. We wait for days before writing in the hope that letters would arrive and we can then reply. Often we cannot wait any longer for fear of forfeiture of a letter because of the question of time. We are therefore compelled to write, only to find a few days later i.e. early in the new month, a letter which reached Robben Island in the previous month.*\*

Evident in this appeal is the immense importance that correspondence holds for political prisoners, and the persistent

---

\* RIM. HP. 2000.05- Prison Regulations Petition. 1970s. p. 6. Undated, but catalogued as "1970s". Letter addressed to the Officer Commanding, Robben Island Prison. This particular complaint was point number 4, under the heading "Delays in Letters Sent."

vigilance required to trace and track their various personal and self-preserving exchanges against institutional controls and disciplinary tactics. According to Kathrada's own testimony, "letters both to and from friends and family are the lifeblood of a prisoner's existence. Because of the restrictions on subject matter and length, great thought and care go into a letter…"[†] Under a separate subheading, the signatories to this petition pointedly demanded clarity, and a revision of logic, regarding the prohibition of certain topics of conversation in letters and with visitors. For example, while they agreed that it was reasonable to prohibit *false* reports about prison treatment and conditions, they objected to the operating "blanket-ban" on descriptions of their world and argued that it should be permissible to provide *true* accounts of daily life in prison. Their specific request was that they "be permitted to communicate with members of our family and visitors in a meaningful manner and be permitted to give them a realistic picture of the lives we are leading."

> *A country like S.A. which prides itself as having amongst the most modern and advanced prison system in the world need have no fear of the TRUTH and contents of letters and conversations should not be restricted save and except on matters affecting the security of the Prisons.*[‡]

In the case of the correspondence between Ahmed Kathrada and Zuleikha Mayat, the censored content appears to have been mainly of material considered either critical of, or relating to

---

[†] Kathrada, *Memoirs*, 299.
[‡] RIM. HP. 2000.05- Prison Regulations Petition. 1970s. p. 5. Letter addressed to the Officer Commanding, Robben Island Prison. This particular complaint was point number 3, under the heading "Censorship of letters and visits."

negative personal encounters with, apartheid legislation. Mayat's memory of her father's death, for example, is removed from her letter. It is only because of her decision, from May 1982, to begin typing on carbon paper that we are in this volume able to include the bits of her letters that Kathrada did not himself receive.

The power exercised in practices of censorship does not, of course, reside chiefly in the removal or permitting of specific kinds of information. While the monitoring of knowledge is certainly one important aspect of control, it is in the fact of control itself that the discomfort ultimately resides, creating the uncertainty and anxiety for the incarcerated. What makes epistolary dialogue possible in normative circumstances is precisely what gives censorship its manipulative intensity: the practical ability of the writer to suspend doubt that in the next letter received (though it may arrive weeks or months from the one just posted) what is currently unclear will be clarified, what has been asked will be answered, and that the story begun will be the same story continued. The optimism of a letter-writer is sustained by sequence, its rhythm and reliability. Against the impersonal nature of bureaucratic efficiency, imprinted onto each of these letters by an official stamp with the date of processing handwritten onto it, Kathrada secretly laboured to preserve independent control over his correspondences by keeping careful records of author, content and dates – both written and received – of all his many correspondences. More overtly, he begins each new letter by dating the last one received from the addressee. Additionally, both Kathrada and Mayat occasionally remind the censors of their awareness and abhorrence of their official processing and of its political nature. Mayat also challenges regulated communications through queries about missing letters, as well as through persistent but mostly doomed attempts to send Kathrada culinary treats and books – including the famous *Indian Delights*, which threads its way through this ten year correspondence as a sub-plot of its own. As demonstrated in some of the letters she wrote to prison authorities, also included in this collection, Mayat is not above bringing a tone of acid irony in her appeal to Christian decency, while styling herself as a meek do-gooder. Responses to her queries by officials convey their frequently disappointing answers in polite tones, often with the courtesy of a brief explanation about "regulations", but seemingly without real effect on her determination.

It is testimony to her concern with historical memory, a concern shared by Kathrada, that Zuleikha Mayat kept copies of all these letters in a personal file (as indeed she did for most of her many correspondences). Letters missing from this file have been retrieved here with the kind help of staff at the Mayibuye centre. Attempts have been made to find the missing final page of one early letter – a gap *not* explained by censorship – but we have not been successful, a sad matter which underlines the importance of continued protection of these historically crucial materials. In compiling this collection, we have opted to maintain the correspondence true to how it was written and how it unfolded. This means that the inevitable repetitions, the abundant personal details that may at times seem laborious for the outsider, are – we feel – essential aspects of these letters and to the experience of reading them. Readers may wonder why, given the cast of characters and place-names that appear, we have not edited or more heavily footnoted. Our idealistic view is that there may be a certain value, even pleasure, in the curiosity that is generated when answers are not immediately forthcoming. Life with *Google* has ensured that unfamiliarity, and the mental work it enjoins, are increasingly short-lived experiences. Feeling oneself to be an outsider to a conversation, as all readers of these letters must certainly be, may (we think) be preferable to the banality and interruption of continual footnotes. (If you don't know what *mithai* is, you can find out on Wikipedia!) More importantly, one of the remarkable aspects of this correspondence is that – in most cases – it rewards the patient reader with eventual clarification. Mayat and Kathrada are generous in their explanations and, therefore, much that may initially puzzle is explained as one moves further through the text. In this way, the reader's ability to tolerate delays of meaning re-enacts the anticipation that the original correspondents were obliged to exercise.

Of course, not all questions are answered. As outsiders, we are as inclined (and, indeed are tasked) to read between the lines for what is not said, for evasions and other clues to meaning. This brings pitfalls as well as revelation, but the uncertainties that are standard fare for historians and literary critics become a means to derive provisional answers to the questions that we – reading this exchange also as the story of two people – inevitably come to care about. Such questions may include: What do the writers think (or feel) about each other? Of what importance is this correspondence for them? How does that change over the years? How did they experience each other once a face-to-face encounter became possible, after almost ten years of correspondence on paper?

In the twenty-first year of his incarceration, Ahmed Kathrada confided "I suppose somewhere deep inside me, there must be a hidden wish that somehow time should have stood still so that I could one day see the kids again just as they were when I was jailed." To read these letters is to encounter the problem of the experience of time; the emotion of anticipation; the feeling of time lost; the time lived in memory. Although they are presented here in a single volume, these letters yet never permit a reader to forget that they were composed by individuals who wrote and received them in distant places and circumstances and at intervals of weeks or months. Time is always an agent in their progressive construction, letter by letter, in a paper chain of meaning. Literacy, and the social infrastructure that can carry a sealed envelope over land and sea, means the ability to communicate across space and time, and to communicate with strangers as well as with friends. The authors of these letters wrote them as a personal correspondence yet, by granting permission to publish them, they have enlarged the circle of those who may benefit from their message of courage and consolation.

*T.W. and G.V.*

Where a portion of the text has been removed
by censors, we have indicated it:

[text removed by censors]

A.M. Kathrada
Robben Island Jail
14<sup>th</sup> April 1979

My Dear Bis

It is distressing that this – my very first letter to you – should be on the occasion of a tragedy. I, as well as those of us here who knew him, was shocked when we heard the SABC news item two weeks ago which announced the death of Dr Mayat. My thoughts immediately went out to you, in far-away Canada. This morning I learnt in a letter from my niece that the tragedy also took the life of your sister – the wife of Dr Mall. My niece tells me that you had come home for a holiday; and I'm addressing the letter to Potch<sup>*</sup> in the hope that it will still find you in the country.

What does one say on an occurrence of this nature? In your profession you virtually live with death day in and day out. You see death in almost its every conceivable form. You've experienced the death of relatives, friends, acquaintances, and hundreds of persons unknown. One tends to think that doctors sort of become immune to the effects of death and suffering. But it is not so. It just cannot be. I feel certain that it is precisely because of their close contact with human suffering that doctors stand out as among the more sensitive of beings.

Bis, is there anything I can say that may help to lesson the grief, except to assure you that I share your loss and sorrow? I cannot claim to have known Dr Mayat well. But, over the years I've been hearing about him every now and then. I have followed with admiration the progress he had made in the field of medicine and his rise to the very top. You will excuse me, but I'm essentially

---

\* Potchefstroom

a political being and I am inclined to look at most things through political glasses. When Dr Mayat, yourself, Cas, and an ever-increasing number of fellow Blacks reach top positions in various fields, it does my political heart a lot of good. Every time I hear of some outstanding performance or achievement by one of them I feel very proud and happy. And when one of them is snatched away untimely by death, I feel a deep sense of sorrow. Even more so in a case like this because he was so closely related to someone I've always held very dearly. Bis, please convey my heartfelt sympathy to your family and to the families of Dr Mayat and Dr Mall.

Now a word about you. Many years have passed, and so much has happened since the good old days of "Flat 13". Only recently a young colleague here was asking me how come I knew so many doctors. Without thinking I simply answered "Flat 13". It may not have been an adequate answer, but it was very true. And I reeled off the names of medical students who stayed at the flat and of friends who used to visit them; and with whom I also became acquainted. Last month I was telling my niece that if I were to write a book on the flat it would make a very interesting "who's who". I was thinking of you and of so many others who have done well in their professions.

I still remember how you and Cas used to "pressurise" me to write my matric. Eventually I did so; in fact I used your car to go to "Western Native Township" to go and write. I didn't quite make it in one go, but succeeded the following year. How thankful I was to be to have got over that "hurdle"! When I started studying at Robben Island in 1965 I was so happy I did not have to bother about matric. This led to my being the first prisoner to get a degree here. (I'm not counting the ones who already came in with degrees.) I hope you'll excuse my immodesty; but now that I've told you of this "achievement", I might as well complete the story by telling you that I was also lucky to be the first prisoner to get my second degree here. And I was busy with my third one when it was interrupted. I'm no longer studying.

I'm afraid this is where my boasting has to end. Somewhat dizzy with success, some years ago I decided I should venture into fresh fields and acquire a bit of culture while I'm about it. So with the incipient determination common to novices, I struck out to add a few accolades to my "achievements" and had a go at music. You may recall how "well" I used to acquit myself on the dance floor at the "Gem"! Anyhow, to cut a long story short, my flirtation with The Muses was brief and disastrous. Having learnt to make some intelligible sounds on the melodica I experienced fleeting thoughts of success. But I was soon disillusioned, and, after having stored the instrument for some years, I gave it away. The staves and octaves and whatnots were not for me.

I fared slightly better in the field of sports. I'm able to play a bit of tenniquoits, bridge, scrabble and one or two other things. I wish you had succeeded in instilling in me some enthusiasm for tennis. We have a court for the 30 of us. About 20 play; and it is by far the most popular game. This in spite of the cost of balls and equipment. I tried volleyball, but gave it up after breaking a finger. You know in our section we have all the time in the world. We don't work and can play all day. Yet I don't utilise the time fruitfully and feel terrible about it.

Healthwise I'm fine. Only a few minor ailments, the worst one being a touch of arthritis or something in the back. This gives me occasional trouble, but not really bad. I've also got a very slight touch of emphysema. It was discovered by accident and does not give me any trouble – yet.

I said "lets have a word about you"; and then proceeded to write about myself. Isn't it terrible! I hope you and Joan (and the kid/s??) are keeping well. The last time I met you was 1962 or so when you were in SA for a brief visit. I have an impression that you were going to specialise in paediatrics. Am I right?

There is so much I'd like to ask you, but I'd better call myself to order. This was meant to be a letter of condolence and look how I've gone on. I feel as if I've exceeded the bounds of propriety. If so please forgive me.

I know you must be extremely busy and I should not burden you with having to reply to me. But if one day – even when you are back in Canada – you or Joan have a few moments to spare, do scribble a few lines to me. I would really appreciate it. And if you feel inclined, please send some photographs of yourselves and any mutual friends.

I understand Moms has also moved to Canada. I don't suppose you ever met up with her. There are so many other folks in Canada I'd like to ask you about, but I better stop here.

Once again, my heartfelt sympathy to you and the families of the deceased.

    All the best to you and Joan
      From
        AMK

Durban
19th May 1979

Dear Mr Kathrada

Perhaps I should address you as Kats or Kathy for that is the name I knew you by – in the days when I was young. Perhaps I should tell you first that I am Zuleikha Mayat, wife of late Mohamed Mayat and that I am writing to you in response to the letter of condolence you wrote to my brother Bis.

Unfortunately, Abdulhak had already left for Canada, and my brother Sadik took the liberty of reading your letter, posting it to me with instructions to pass it to Bis after perusal. I take this opportunity of writing to you for even though Bis and Joan will reply to you, how can I ignore your letter so full of concern over the tragedy that struck us?

I am not trying to preach religion to you but just in case you have in your isolation forgotten the classic prayer of our prophet and his companions and which is virtually incumbent on all Muslims to recite every now and again "And forget not the ones detained – but remember them in your prayers and with zakaat!" I will have to look up the books for the exact words but let the above loose translation suffice.

[text removed by censors]

Just see how spiritually sustaining it was for us to have received your letter at a time when our world just crumbled around us? In your case, letters would mean even more. There is a fundamental law in Islam – the Fard E Kifaya – which insists that at least some or one member of the community must perform certain duties or obligations and this will exonerate the entire community from that

23

particular responsibility. For example, the Janaza Namaaz. It is not incumbent on all the community to attend the funeral prayers but some <u>must</u> do so.

[text removed by censors]

You understand the meaning of Arabic words I use but just in case someone thinks I am writing in code, I give the English equivalent:

[text removed by censors]

My late husband would laugh at this letter. He always said (I am an inveterate letter writer to the press and let me boast I was weekly correspondent for *Indian Views* for 8 years and for *Graphic* for nearly a year) that I always come to the point by many a devious route. He always corrected my articles, at my insistence, but when he struck out at my peculiar style and phrase I accused him of "personality assassination".

So far I have not mentioned my grief – the death of Mahomed after a 32 years innings, filled with action that left no time for boredom with each other or with life – is going to take my lifetime to forget – whatever there is left of it. But for the sake of his belief and for the motto that he lived by, that "problems are meant to be solved and if you allow them to get you under then you are truly lost", I just have to pick up the threads and carry on with both his unfinished aspirations and mine.

At the moment I am (interrupted till I get out of my plaster cast on 4$^{th}$ June*) busy on a super deluxe edition of *Indian Delights*. I am also trying to persuade Virginia Gcabashe and Siko Mji (two friends very involved in community upliftment) to help me bring out a "soul food" cookery book based on peasant Indian cooking,

---

\* Zuleikha Mayat was injured with a broken leg in the same auto accident.

like khitchiri and khuri, pumpkin and potato curries, lentil dhals etc combined with traditional African dishes – that is Indian manner of cooking porridge (bhurkoo) and the African puthu! Similarly the different manner of cooking pumpkin, samp mealies, mealie ria, etc etc. All this for funds for African baby crèches.

How sadistic – talking of food to you! May I compensate by sending you [the] current copy of *Indian Delights*? Is this allowed?

Did you know Goolam Hoosen Pahad is married again? I.C. Meer attended his wedding when he visited India last year. I.C. is so taken up with village life in India that he swears there is nothing like it – I retort he has not even been to Dabhel (the village where we Bismillahs hail from) where all my peasant cousins (male ones) are muftis and moulvis besides being farmers –both vocations they learnt in Dabhel, at the Darul Ulum (Theological College) and in the fields respectively!

Kathrada Saheb, how are you for religious literature? You know how it is when we get older, besides our walking sticks we need extra "crutches". Some very enlightened Islamic literature is available these days so if you want to catch up, do let me know.

[text removed by censors]

Very sincerely yours,
Zuleikha

12 Leander Cresc.
Westville 3630
6th Aug. 1979

Dear Kathrada Saheb

I have asked our agent to post you a copy of Urdu/English dictionary and a prayer book compiled by us.* I was just wondering whether an English/Urdu dictionary would not be more useful. Please let me know.

For the Island Library I have posted a copy of our by now famous *Indian Delights* (world-wide reputation and orders come in from India/Pakistan as well). They say surgeons are sadistically inclined and my association with Mahomed of 31 years must have absorbed some of this, therefore I repeat this fact [that] has given me much satisfaction: Often on our travels we met with people who had a copy of our book and invariably the husbands would say that it was their favourite bed-time story book, since they read themselves to sleep on *Indian Delights*.

When we were in Samarkand and Bukhara some years ago, we were delighted to see samoosas, biryanis, naans, pilaaus etc. This should really have been no surprise for, after all, our Moghul dynasty of India are descendents of these Turko/Mongol races, and India was but an expansion of their rule.

Ramadaan is really play-play this year. The weather in Durban being mild and the days so short, no one feels like complaining.

Zuleikha Mayat

---

\* The publication is *Quranic Lights*, published by the Women's Cultural Group of Durban.

AM Kathrada
Robben Island Jail
8th September 1979

Dear Mrs Mayat

I must start off with two apologies; for my delay in replying to your letter, which arrived on 16th June; and, for having got you to take all the trouble to send the dictionary and literature, only to find that the material was returned by the Prison authorities. I hope my guilt for the delay in writing was somewhat mitigated by the indirect acknowledgement via my niece Zohra, as well as the phone call from Mrs Fatima Seedat. As for the literature, I was quite surprised to learn that it had been returned. There has been some misunderstanding. I shall be discussing the matter with the Commanding Officer and hope it will be resolved. You are quite right in thinking that an English-Urdu dictionary would be more useful. But my primary aim in trying to obtain an Urdu-English one was to help me understand the Hindi records, and, in the process brush up my Urdu (which I learned at Madressa). In any case, I had thought that the English-Urdu, Urdu-English would be in one volume. I shall persevere with my efforts in the meantime to get the authorities to change their minds and will let you know. I am sorry to have bothered you with my little problem.

    I find Urdu a very beautiful language and am really sorry I've forgotten so much of it. One reason for this of course is that I've hardly had occasion to speak it after leaving Madressa. Secondly there must have been an unconscious persistence of a childish revolt against the Arab teacher, whose strictness we mistook for cruelty, and consequently came to "hate" even the things he taught us. But fortunately, in spite of this, a little smattering of Urdu survived, together with the ability to read the Arabic script, though not very fluently.

To get back to your letter, or letters (your second one arrived on 1st September). I must confess when I read that Sadik had passed on my letter to you, at first I didn't know whether to be pleased or embarrassed. I was afraid I might have said things and referred to experiences which, if read outside the circle of close friends, may cause a few blushes. But having read your letter I was thankful that some of my frivolous recollections did not cloud my main purpose – to condole with all of you in your tragic hour. It is satisfying to know that you found my words "warm" and "spiritually sustaining". Even if Bis is unable to write, at least I know that my message has reached one who is most closely affected by the tragedy. I am grateful to Sadik for passing the letter onto you.

I must say I admire your courage and the determination with which you have come to grips with the new reality. I hope you have succeeded in persuading Siko and her friend to join you in producing the book on "Soul Food". Incidentally, when you see her again, please pass my warm greetings to her, her husband and family. I hope their son is keeping well.

Yes I heard of Goolambhai's marriage, but did not know I.C. was present. I suppose you know that the late Amina Bhai was my "second mother". I had spent more years with them than with my own folks. I am curious to know who has taken her place. I.C.'s fascination with India is something I would like to understand. Only this morning I had a letter from a young girl who spent a short holiday in India and also found it attractive. So many others have written and said the same. One day I'd like to know what it is that makes India attractive to young people in particular. I suppose the best way is to go and find out myself. But there is the little impediment of a life sentence. I did not know you had visited out of the way places like Samarkand and Bukhara. It must have been interesting.

I have to end now. Please remember me to the children. Also to I.C., his wife and kids, and to all other friends. Best wishes to you from, not "Saheb" please, but Kathy.

AMK

Salsabil
Westville 3630
28th September 1979

Dear Kathrada

Your letter arrived earlier than the returned books. With the latter was a covering letter intimating that literature was not accepted from friends and relatives. My mistake really in wanting to pounce on the sawaab, for in the past our Islamic Propagation Centre had handled books for prisons etc. However when Mr Vankar of the Propagation Centre was told of your needs, he indicated that the Centre would include Robben Island in the future. I hope he is successful.

Urdu is one of the most elegant languages and in my opinion far exceeds French and Persian which too are languages of great finesse. Like all of us I had forgotten my Madressa Urdu, and when Mahomed and I were in London throughout 1962 I availed myself of the opportunity of doing a course in Islamics at the School of Oriental and African Studies. Since a classical language was essential, I chose Urdu and my professor was Ralph Russel. It was quaint to hear a Lancashire accented Urdu but this was redeemed by one of the lecturers. A female doing her doctorate in Urdu literature in London

[text removed by censors]

On my return to

[unreadable due to imprecise pasting by censor]

I continued studying under Farooqui Mehtan and soon he had me contributing poems to the local Mushaeras.

Have you ever attended a Mushaera? In so far as audience

participation is concerned, it has to be total, otherwise it becomes dead pan. Mahomed and I used to arrange mushaeras at our home. [Mushaeras are a] gathering of the bards where each poet either reads his or her own composition or gets one of the professional reciters or singers to do it. Seated on the floor in good old nawaabi style the reader asks for permission from the Mir E Mushaera, and here Safee Siddiqui, of Radio Truro fame, is tops. Incidentally his poetry too is tops. When the Mir and the audience concedes him the permission, then the poet proceeds couplet by couplet waiting for the awful silence or the high acclamation of "Wah Wah" or "Do Baare" or "SubhanAllah". When thus encouraged, the poet proceeds and draws the audience into the orbit of his own imagination, allegorical and symbolic meanings or sheer eloquence of word play. At times, the Majlis is so carried away that some of the excitable ones go into a Haal (state) and the couplet has to be repeated over and over again till the emotions are pacified again. Are tapes allowed on the island?

Siko was jubilant to get the news and salaams from you. She was overcome when you mentioned her son. In return, she sends greetings to you and friends around you. Her son will sit for his finals this year I think.

Goolam bhai married one of the Lockhat girls from Kathor. Some of the Kholvadians were not too happy. According to I.C. she is very much like late Amina Bai and a wonderful cook. How can one not be captivated by India? Sadck had toured India and the East before he arrived in Europe and he says everything was so flat and lacking in punch. You see, in Europe people go around wearing masks – that is, all their sorrows and joys are carefully cosmeticised. In the East you see every wrinkle and wart of society. Its riches and poverty lie bared for all and sundry to see. Its craftsmen work on the pavements creating the most artistic of articles. Storytellers; professional beggars who can narrate history and stories that they pass on from generation to generation but always taking into account contemporary trends, so that the tales have no stale smell clinging to them; jugglers; fortune tellers; letter writers taking instructions from the one who wishes to write to his dear ones in a far place – everyone around free to listen in – all this and much more takes place on the pavements and in the alleyways. The best dentures are made on the streets of Karachi and the price 10 times cheaper than the dentist in his posh rooms across the road.

On our tours Mahomed had a knack of photographing people and life as they lived it, and when we showed our slides he had the audience rocking with laughter or going numb at the poignant stories – no, India and the East takes you by the throat. No visitor can be indifferent.

[text removed by censors]

Salaams
Zuleikha

The Commanding Officer
Prisons Department
Prisons Command
Telegraph address "Prisoners"
Private Bag ROBBEN ISLAND
7400
Reference 1/4/3/3
4 September 1979
Enquiries Major JW Harding
[original in Afrikaans]

Mrs Z Mayat
WESTVILLE
3630

Dear Mrs. Mayat

DONATION: URDU DICTIONARY AND RECIPE BOOK

With reference to your letter dated 6 August 1979 in connection with the above mentioned books, I wish to tell you that no books from family or friends for prisoners are accepted. The "Urdu into English" is therefore being returned to you.

Because of the fact that prisoners on Robben Island have access to the Provincial Library, there is not a prison library and the recipe book is also therefore not accepted.

Your interest in the prisoners and their welfare is however appreciated and I regret that you have entered into unnecessary cost and effort.

Yours truly,
J.W. Harding Major
On behalf of Commanding Officer
Enclosures

A.M. Kathrada
Robben Island Jail
21st June 1980

Dear Mrs Mayat

I am afraid I have to once again begin my letter with an apology. Your letter of September arrived a long time ago – on 27th October in fact. The best part of a year has already gone by and I suppose you had never expected to hear from me again. But, like the proverbial penny, I make my appearance once more. Many years ago when I was still at high school, we got I.C. to be an adjudicator at a meeting of our Debating Society. In his words of advice to aspirant speakers he said we should not start a speech with an apology. It was good advice, and, in my opinion equally applicable to letter-writing. But, for some reason or other it eludes me almost every time when I've been negligent about replying. Well, the apology has already been written in this letter, and I just have to carry on. As Omar Khayam said "The moving finger writes, and having writ moves on…". Incidentally this reminds me of the old days again. It was either I.C. or Yusuf who would now and then decide to render Khayam in the original. In retrospect I think he only knew one verse which he would quote over and over again (please don't tell him that). But he succeeded in imprinting it in my memory, so that even today I am able to recall "karima bê baksha…" Etc.

I'm just rambling on, am I not! In prison talking about the past is one of our favourite occupations, so please forgive the lapses. Before moving away from I.C., I suspect they are grandparents by now. Please congratulate him and his wife, and of course the parents of the baby. I hope they are all well. A recent photograph of I.C. gave us the impression of a somewhat ungainly protrusion in the midriff region, and we couldn't help but smile. We wondered if the photo had not been a bit unfair! His wife looked lovely. Unfortunately there were no photos of the children.

I took up the matter of the literature and dictionary. As far as the dictionary is concerned, I was assured there would have been no difficulty had it been posted by the bookshop, to the Commanding Officer, with a covering note that it was for me. This might seem to be unnecessary red tape, but we are dealing with civil servants, and almost all their actions are governed by regulations. It can be quite frustrating for the public. Perhaps Tolstoy can be forgiven when in desperation he exclaimed that civil servants had regulations instead of hearts.

As for literature, I think this is now being taken care of. Since the beginning of the year we have an Imam from Cape Town visiting us monthly. He belongs to an Islamic body of which a Dr Kotwal is an official. They are trying to make the necessary arrangements. Lest I give you the wrong picture, I should make it clear that I am not really religious. But I do have an interest in developments in the religious world, and of course I respect the beliefs of all people. In jail I have been attending Christian services, as well as those conducted by a Hindu priest. And now the Moslem. I have a great regard for the sincerity of all these people, and gratitude for the interest and sympathy they so unfailingly display towards us. Among them I have met some wonderful human beings.

A bit on the lighter side, I must confess I fully enjoy the special goodies we have for X-mas and Easter. For all these years we also used to have lovely Dipavali parcels, but since Mr Govender took ill, these have come to an end. We've tasted samoosas, chevda, various sweet meats, and even mince curry and Packo biryani! Not exactly recipes from *Indian Delights,* but delicious in our circumstances. You know we are also allowed to spend R17.00 a month on toilet articles and foodstuff, such as biscuits, peanuts etc. I often buy

Packo's mango pickles, and believe me, they actually taste nice in jail. Also the chilli sauce.

You've probably read in the papers that we are going to be allowed to study again. I haven't quite decided on what to do, but will most probably enrol for History Honours. Soon we are also going to be allowed to have newspapers. This will be most welcome.

I must end now. I suppose Siko's son has qualified by now. My fondest wishes to them all. How are Joan and Bis? Please remember me to them as well, and to all other family and friends.

Best wishes and regards to you, from
AMK
Tho a bit early, Eid Mubarak to you all.

5th November 1980

Dear Kathrada

We all have to start with apologies for there seem to be long delays between receiving and answering correspondence these days. My excuse will be *Nanima's Peti* or *Nanima's Chest*. This is a new publication which I am doing for the Women's Cultural Group. It all revolves around an old peti belonging to one of my distant aunts. Suddenly everyone remembered similar chests belonging to their grannies. We have been able to collect sufficient material, that is, old embroideries, kurtas, sadaryas (do you remember the jeek embroidered velvet waistcoats and matching topees little boys and girls used to wear on Eid days?) in fact a fabulous collection of old costumes, Kashmiri shawls, etc. In the book it looks very impressive with Dennis Bughwaan's colour photography, Andrew Verster's art work and layout of the book and naturally (very modestly I assure you) my text based on old and ancient memories.

We hope the book will be out before Christmas sales rush. It will sell at R9.50 and, if all goes well, the Natal Society of Artists hope to launch it at their gallery. An exhibition of the clothes will be held at the same venue simultaneously.

I smiled when you assured me that you are not religious. Anti religion or "indifferent to religion" attitudes have gone out of style. It is no longer something to be ashamed of if you are bent towards it. Perhaps the Hari-Krishna and Buddhist cults have something to do with the change in attitudes. The very "in thing" is to belong to the Tableeg Jamat at least, if not to the Zikar Groups etc. And what applies to the Muslim world also applies to the Christian and other beliefs. Your respect for others' beliefs is very very Islamic. The

Quran says "Revile not other religions…" Islam also insists that religion is nothing new and all the different dispensations going under some name or other are the same given to Abraham and before him to Adam and Eve. Provided there is no fanaticism, the world of the spirit is absolutely fascinating and full of adventures both in the realms of the physical world as well as in the world of ideas or concepts.

Have you read Juluddin Rumi? He explains that the foetus in the mother's womb, however intelligent, will never be able to form a concept of the world that lies just outside the womb. It has to be born and exercise its senses etc. before it can realise what this world is. Similarly we, with our finite minds, cannot form concepts of the Life Hereafter. One will have to be literally reborn and experience that life before illumination can dawn.

A hurried letter like this cannot convey deep philosophical concepts and my own knowledge is so limited I should not even try, but don't put curbs on your mind, let it take you into realms that you may sub-consciously have been blocking till now. Be assured the world of the spirit is not limited like that of our Maulanas. It is full of adventure, especially when it allows man to find himself. That is some discovery! If man can ever find God, well the Islamic God is so abstract, the Concept so… I don't know what word to use, but Islam says that the finite mind can never encompass the infinite. Well, that's it.

There is some wonderful literature around. It is not ephemeral and other worldly, it is all [so] very realistic and relevant that one wonders why we were never given it before. Possibly the Maulanas had to garb it in funny concepts so that we don't find out the truth. You know the Brahmins used to put lead in the ears of the poor sudras who happened to hear some of the eternal readings by chance!

I must be getting old. Just see how I have rambled on and on…

Forgive me for not being able to achieve something with respect to the dictionary etc.

Have the newspapers started circulating around there? Try and get the *Graphic* or *Leader* just to catch up with <u>ethnic</u> news. New word which means different things in our country.

Bakri Eid has just been; Muharram is around the corner and soon Xmas will be here. Greetings for all these.

Salaams,
Zuleikha

A.M. Kathrada
Robben Island Jail
17<sup>th</sup> January 1981

Dear Mrs Mayat

Thanks very much for your letter, which reached me at the end of November. It is always nice to hear from you, for your letters usually have some bits of information that remind me of the bygone years. I don't know when last, if ever, in the 17½ years in jail I thought of the contents of Nanima's peti. Your letter brought to mind the little boys and little girls with heavily embroidered clothing – the waistcoats, topees, velvet dresses etc. However, if I'm not mistaken, this sort of clothing was more prevalent among people of certain gaams. The Dabhels for example. I cannot remember anyone in our little hometown with Kholvadian and Lachpurian families sporting such garments. Naturally the petis were there but I cannot recall ever peeping into the contents of the ones at home. Tho I cannot forget – I must have been about 25 – when my mother sent me a lovely godra, made in India. She must have had it in her peti for years. I don't know if there is an English word for it, because I don't think the word eiderdown quite describes that beautiful and warm godra. I was very fond of it. You know in 1963 circumstances obliged me to leave my flat in a great hurry – at a few hours notice in fact. I found it very difficult to leave that godra behind. But I was going into a new kind of life, a completely different environment. I was expected to undergo a metamorphosis, a change of customs, habits and ethnic grouping, and assume a new identity.\* The godra would have been a giveaway. It was too obviously Indian. On many a cold winter's

---

\* Kathrada is referring to his Portuguese underground alias, "Pedro Perreira".

night in my cell I think of that godra. I wonder of what use a godra could be in a village like Lachpur. Does it ever get cold there?

A significant thing was that at that time mine was about the only godra around. I never came across another one at the homes of any of my friends. It was such a rarity already. As for the clothing of our childhood years, I suppose one would only be able to find them tucked away in a peti of an ancient family member. I am sure your book and the exhibition are bound to arouse interest. Who knows, some of these items may come into fashion again. After all, some of the long dresses, trouser suits and other clothing that white women wear these days, are they not really a variation of the sort of things worn by our mothers and sisters? Only they call it by some fancy name and it bears the stamp of a Paris fashion house! Incidentally when it comes to women's clothing and food, I may be accused of being an Indian chauvinist. To me there is nothing more beautiful than the sari and the type of clothing worn by our young girls these days. Photos of these are about the only redeeming feature of *Fiat Lux*.†

We have been allowed to buy newspapers since September. I've been reading the *Daily Mail, Die Burger, Cape Times, Argus, Tribune, Sunday Times, Express, Rapport*. It is difficult for me to convey what this has meant to us. Apart from being away from our near and dear ones, this is a deprivation we have felt most: It is so good to be able to feel a part of this world again. I notice there is a proliferation of Black journalists these days. At the time of our arrest there was hardly a single one working on the white papers. From the old timers of the *Post* and *World* only a few are heard of: G.R. Naidoo must be occupying a leading position in his paper, after all these years in the field. Yes I am going to try to get the *Leader* and *Graphic*. There should be no difficulty.

---

† A monthly magazine published by the apartheid government's Department of Indian Affairs – essentially a state propaganda publication.

About studies, they seemed to have changed their minds as far as post-graduate degrees are concerned. I have received no answer to my application to do History Honours. I may have to abandon the idea altogether.

Health and spiritwise I'm fine. Let me take the opportunity of wishing you the best of everything for the new year.

Kindest regards to you, the family and friends

    From
        AMK

Salsabil
Westville 3630
14th February 1981

Dear Ahmed

*Nanima's Chest* looks great and much credit must go to the photography but especially to Andrew Verster, one of our leading artists who put in a great effort with the designs and layout. I had written to Brigadier Harding at the Island asking whether a copy could be sent to you. He suggested that I send a copy for approval to the commissioner of prisons in Pretoria and ask that it be sent to the Island library. This I have done and I have also sent a copy of Muhammed Asad's translation of the Quran. It is most readable and sounds like good sense – which is what the Quran is, of course. If you come across it, try to read it. I like the way he has translated Taqwa of God not as fear, but consciousness, of God.

You can't miss *Nanima's Chest*. It's bound in Coolie Pink cloth with the title and screen chest in gold foil. Let me know what you think of our young models. I am sure the shapes have changed since you last saw them or their version of young girls. The very beautiful one opposite the mendhi designed hand died in a car accident just a week before the book came from the publishers. Her Mona Lisa smile haunts me. For one so young she was so serious, soft spoken and reflective by nature. She appears on pages 12, 57 and 73. Bushra Ansari, granddaughter of Maulana Ansari of West Street Mosque and, from her mother's side, granddaughter of Maulana Siddiqui (Safee Siddiqui of Radio Truro's sister's daughter.)

The godra or padded quilt has an old history in China as well as in India. Even in the Gujarat it gets cold enough on winter mornings to warrant a godra but its use is so – what shall I say? –

versatile. When there are more guests than beds, then you strew a few down on your floor and they are more comfortable than mattresses. For the palangris or kathlas of India (wooden frame thonged with ropes which serve as beds and sofas) and over these one has to put a godra or two, otherwise a limb might soon protrude through the ropes. When ladies go visiting from gaam to gaam in India, then the floor of the bullock cart is lined with godras and others are placed for them to lean against.

The unginned cotton from your own fields is given to the Pinjaras who come around with their contraption to beat it into waddling which you then use to stuff your own godras with. How cheap and how convenient.

Do you remember Moosa Essop Mia? He was married to a Parsee lady and they had this huge home in Bree Street opposite the New Town school? Well, Moosa writes to me sometimes just to share his knowledge of Urdu poetry with me. I wonder why we underestimate our own people. Moosa's knowledge of Indian music, poetry, history and family genealogies is vast. Another wealth of information is Dr Krishna Somers: ex Durbanite, who for many years was Professor of Medicine at Kampala University (Makarere) till ousted by Idi Amin. Lately he is head of medicine at Perth University. Somers again knows more of Gujarat history than specialists in the field. What he knows of Indian jewellery, textiles and styles could fill books. Whenever these two write, my children also read the letters (as they do yours of course) and laugh. They say these letters could write another book for me.

I may be cutting into your quota of letters. Please, I will understand if you cannot reply soon, but do let me know if the books make it to the library at Robben Island.

With Salaams,
Zuleikha

A.M. Kathrada
Robben Island Jail
11th April 1981

Dear Mrs Mayat

Thanks a lot for your letter, which arrived on the 28th February. Thanks also for posting the literature to Pretoria. It has not yet reached our library but I expect Pretoria to okay it soon. I shall take it up with the local authorities. I am eagerly looking forward to seeing *Nanima's Peti*. It was a pleasant coincidence just the day after I posted my last letter to you to see a write up on it in [the] *Tribune*. A few weeks thereafter there was an article in the *Daily Mail* supplement. What a delight to see the lovely young models. I assume these days one can find Moslem girls who are professional models. Many years ago, Mrs. I.C. brought along a musical show to Jo'burg. If I remember correctly it was advertised as "Maglis-e-Rung-o-Raag", and included a Mannequin Parade headed by Miss Priscilla Rowley, I think. There were no Moslem ladies among the mannequins: I suppose at that time it would have been too radical an expectation. One of the reviewers of *Nanima's Peti* thought there would be an adverse reaction among some "radicals" to such a "sectional" venture. I'd be interested to hear what sort of criticism, if any, was levelled.

It was tragic to learn of the death of one of your models in an accident. My sympathies to you and to the bereaved family. You mentioned her uncle who is connected with Radio Truro. Unfortunately I've never heard of him. This radio station is of more recent origin. The radio programmes we have are almost exclusively Springbok and SABC. Am I correct that Radio Truro broadcasts from Swaziland? Somehow I have that impression.

I notice that the Cape Town Film Festival has included the

Indian film, "The Outsiders" by Mrinal Sen, in its programme. Have you perhaps seen it? The short review in the papers was interesting. I will suggest to our chaps here to try to get it. Did I tell you that we have weekly film shows here? We do see some good ones occasionally. The documentaries from the Provincial Library are almost invariably good. We've seen Odessa File, The Fifth Offensive, Holocaust, Belle de Jour, The Champ etc. At the end of the month we'll be seeing Kramer vs Kramer. Some weeks we have 2 or even 3 films. The extra ones are hired by individual prisoners. Films are a pleasant diversion in our otherwise monotonous existence. However, I must confess they're getting a bit too much for me. These days, unless there is a particularly good film, I rather spend the time reading newspapers.

You mentioned Moosa Mia and Dr Somers. I know both of them. In fact Moosa's stepmother was a close relative of ours. But having grown up in Jo'burg and away from the family I failed to maintain contact with relatives; and many of them, not surprisingly, regarded me as a "black sheep". I wasn't aware that Moosa was so well versed in Indian poetry, music and history, but I'm not surprised any more. Over the years I came across a number of people, some in the most unexpected places, who turned out to be extremely knowledgeable in these fields. I have often thought of them and wished I had spent more time with them in order to benefit from their wisdom. This type of regret one feels acutely when one is wasting away the years in jail. In one of his books, Nehru wrote that among his prison colleagues there were men who were recognised experts in every field of knowledge. What an experience it must have been!

I am surprised to learn that Dr Somers is such an expert on Gujarat. I take it this means he is Gujarati speaking. You know I always knew and admired him as an outstanding medical man and never categorised his ethnicity. If I were to have attempted it prior to your letter I most probably would have said that he was Hindi speaking. Even more surprising, considering his profession, is his interest in jewellery and textiles. Anyway, one never stops learning. If you are in touch with him, please convey my greetings. He may remember me – we were on nodding terms.

A bit of good news is that I was given permission to do History Honours. I have registered and am waiting for my lectures. It's going to be a bit tough to get back into the routine. Otherwise all is well. Hope the same with you and the family. Best wishes and fondest regards to all of them, especially Joan and Bis, and Sadek and the folks in Potch.

All the best to you from
AMK

Salsabil
Westville 3630
18th June 1981

Dear Kathrada

A letter was received (accompanying the copy of Asad's translation of the Quran and *Nanima's Chest*) stating that the books were returned since a library is in operation at Robben Island. I wonder whether residents of the Island can request books for their very special library? If so, Islamic Propagation Centre and Taj Company can supply books not available from other sources. My disappointment was great when the books were returned 9 weeks later!

Do you get the *Graphic* and *Leader*? *Graphic* has always been ultra moderate but of late it has taken a sickening stance on most issues.

Kris Somers is Hindustani – actually Bihari. His knowledge of things Indian is cosmopolitan for he would know more of Gujaratis and Memons and Tamils than the person belonging to these groups. He has declined offer of post of Rector at Durban-Westville [University]. In so doing (I think) he has increased his life span by a decade, for the students there can keep things at a hop!

Did I tell you I have two grandchildren? Jihaan is two years plus and is the daughter of my daughter. Jaleel is 3 months minus two – belongs to my son Nasim who used to play soccer for Berea-Durban during his years of medical studies. He had to give up soccer after he broke a leg – Well, Jaleel dribbles and kicks remarkably well, but then he has his Dadima's lounge for his soccer pitch! What an activist... Jihaan on the other hand dissipates her energy in exercising female wiles and her vocab is astounding. Some time ago she had a nappy rash and in her agony she cried out – Nanima! Burning, burning – Fire! Fire!

Ramadaan is two weeks from now – but I have started a little practice run and must say that I very much like having breakfast at 5am and supper at 5pm. Sort of sweet!

Eid Mubarak – with Salaams,
    Zuleikha

10th July 1981

Dear Ahmed

I hope you don't take it amiss but please accept enclosed money as Eidy. One of my most precious memories remain – that was also the occasion of Eid and a newspaper report said that eight detainees (all or most Muslims – and that's years ago) would not be allowed any parcels from outside. I discussed this with one of our leading Maulanas and he agreed that no one dare be left out on Eid day – so with Maulana and some other leading Jamaat officials I went to local detention quarters. After much pow-wow to the credit of the authorities, permission was granted for me to take Eid hampers for all of them.

*Nanima's Chest* is selling steadily. Juta's from Cape Town are regular buyers, but of course this book is no *Indian Delights*. The current edition [of *Indian Delights*] is sold out and we have orders for a couple thousand. I am working all hours of day to get the new edition out by September. In your last letter you had mentioned that Muslim models were just not available years ago. Even now professionally this is rare, but for cultural and charity shows we have had no problems ever and I am going back some 20 years in time. However, Saira Essa (Memon) has opened her own theatre and our conservative sensibilities are outraged, for her theatre tackles some very controversial plays!

With Salaams and Eid Mubarak to all of you,
    Zuleikha

A.M. Kathrada
Robben Island Jail
5<sup>th</sup> September, 1981

Dear Zuleikhabehn

I hope you don't mind my addressing you this way. I think we know each other well enough now for me to stop using the formal "Mrs Mayat". I've been debating with myself whether to use Zuleikhabai or Zuleikhabehn, and opted for the latter. You see we only have one behn in our family. My bhabhies are "bai", as are the wives of a number of friends. I thought I could unilaterally declare you "behn",[*] and join you among a few friends whom I address in this manner.

Having settled that, I hope, I must thank you very much for your last two letters which reached me on 25<sup>th</sup> July and 8<sup>th</sup> August. In particular, a big thank you for the "eidy". It was very thoughtful of you. Far from taking it amiss, I really appreciated the gesture. It set me thinking and took me right back to my childhood days. For that is the last time I can think of that I received something for eid which was specifically referred to as "eidy". Over the years family members and friends have never failed to send cards, and money, but I cannot recall anyone saying it was "eidy". In fact it must have been many years ago that I even thought of or used the word. You know I have found that no matter how old one may be chronologically, he almost invariably retains something of the child in him. Some little bits of childlike responses, emotions, interests, expectations. Perhaps I am more guilty of this and am projecting my own feelings by generalising. Be that as it may, but I must confess to experiencing a delightful, albeit childish, feeling of joy

---

[*] sister

on receipt of the "Eidy". I suppose, being in jail has something to do with it. Escape into the past is part and parcel of a prisoner's life. Pleasures of reminiscence take the place of the uninviting and disagreeable features of the present. And what can be nicer than childhood!

Perhaps related to this is the tremendous feeling of deprivation one experiences at not having children in our midst. Occasionally we do see, and in a couple of instances some of us have actually touched, a child. I cannot describe the exhilaration and excitement of these occasions. In the absence of this, one wallows in reading about children in letters and books, in talking about them, and in films. Films such as Heidi, The Champ, Kramer vs Kramer, iLollipop proved to be among the more popular ones.

You will have guessed that your brief references to Jihaan and Jaleel made enjoyable reading. There is a growing army of little ones at home – children of nephews and nieces – and it is delightful to read about all their antics, prances and utterances. Of course dadimas, nanimas and kids are mutual favourites. A record here talks about grannies being "one of them love-machines", and in an amusing but effective way it shows the affection of the singer for gran'ma. I'm sure the two little ones must be bringing you endless pleasure. Incidentally, a niece of mine has just brought forth another grandchild for me. She is married to Dr Ahmed Bhoola, and they live in Gaberone. You may know the Bhoolas of Meyerton. I have an idea they are Dhabelians, so you may even be related. Is Nasim in private practice?

You once mentioned how knowledgeable Moosa Mia is about genealogies. Having lived away from home all my life, my knowledge of my own ancestry, I'm ashamed to say, is nil. And I so much would like to know, but alas, I don't know who to turn to.

I'm very sorry about the books being returned. We do have a sub-depot of the Provincial Library, but they have nothing like *Nanima's Chest* etc. I will pursue this further, and let you know. It's good to hear that both your books are selling well. Congratulations.

You also mentioned Saira Essa. I have since read a long write up about her, with photo and all. Her Upstairs Theatre sounds most interesting. I liked her forthright views, and am looking forward to seeing a review of her play on Gandhi.

I must end now. Fondest regards to all the family and friends.

Everything of the best to you, from
AMK

Ministry of Justice
Hendrik Verwoerd Buildings
Parliament Street
Cape Town
Phone 45-6429
1981-10-27

Mr. Mahmoud Rajab
President's Council
PO Box 1891
Durban
4000

Dear Mr. Rajab

DONATION OF BOOKS

Pursuant to my letter dated 9 September 1981, I wish to inform you that I had [sic] now the opportunity to consider your request.

The South African Prisons Service does not accept donations of books for use in prison libraries as they function as sub-depts of the various Provincial Library Services. It is therefore regretted that your offer cannot be accepted.

The librarian at Robben Island Prison is however negotiating with the Cape Provincial Library Service to obtain the two books in question.

With kind regards
H J Coetsee MP
Minister of Justice

M. Rajab
Rajab Centre
85/89 Victoria Street
Durban 4001
Rep. of South Africa
PO Box 1891
4000
Phone 315141/5

Mrs Zuleikha Mayat
Westville: Durban

Dear Mrs Mayat,

I am sending you herewith for your information a copy of a letter received by me this morning from the Minister of Justice, and which is self-explanatory.

   Kind regards,
     Yours faithfully
       Mahmoud Rajab

December 10th 1981

My dear Ahmed

How lovely to be addressed as behn by you. Let me share with you a few anecdotes about the terminology bhai and behn. You know after Haj, fellow Hajees address each other as Hajee Bhai and Hajee Behn and after they have shared a ship voyage it becomes Jihaz Bhai – hence the surname Jajhbhay. Traditionally people put so much store by this sharing of Haj and voyage that the relationship at times is stronger than that between blood relatives. Modern air travel has thrown this latter categorising overboard for imagine Air India passengers calling the hijackers – I beg your pardon, the alleged kidnappers – as jajhbhais. You may know the Bhoola family of Durban. Ahmed Boola is a lawyer. Anyway his mother (she must be in her 90s now) has always been very specific about these things. Many years ago she was on her way to a funeral to Bloemhof and they must have stopped at our home (completely strange to her) for the usual cup of tea, wudzu and toilet, for Indians not having hotels or inns [allowed to them] in those days, were forced to stop off at fellow Indian homes (they still do). When she heard after my marriage that I was a daughter of the Bismillahs where she had stopped for this short while, she came to pay a visit and assured me that I could count her as an aunt. For had my mother "not called her Behn while she was a visitor at our home"? To put it into colloquial Gujarati "Are dikri mane behn kari bolela"?

> [The remainder of this letter appears to have gone missing in the archives, as it is clear from the next letter that Kathrada did in fact receive it intact. Repeated attempts by the editors to locate the missing text have been unsuccessful.]

A.M. Kathrada
Robben Island Jail
20<sup>th</sup> March 1982

Dear Zuleikhabehn

Your letter was among the first that I received this year, and I am sorry I could not reply earlier. I think I mentioned to you before that we prisoners have a predilection for transporting ourselves into the past. Your letter not only contained valuable bits of information of which I was totally ignorant, but it invariably evoked a host of memories about people, incidents, places and events. Take for instance your reference to Potch and the removal of the folks to the group area. It reminded me of my visit to your place. It must have been 1949 I think. I had come to Potch with Mrs Fischer; we had spent the day there, so were invited to have lunch at your place. I almost think the lunch was at Bis's. Anyway I still remember the beautiful houses. In fact, the Bismillah houses were widely spoken about all over the Transvaal. You'll remember at the time the land problem was already acute and it was not uncommon to find two – and even three – generations of family members crowded under one roof. Do you mean that the group area was declared elsewhere and the community had to move from the place you all occupied? What happened to the shops in town? Do you happen to know the Gabrus? My niece, Sabera, is married to one of them. At least I think the name was Gabru. But I'm sure she is in Potch. Incidentally a few years ago Minister Le Grange visited the jail. When I was introduced to him he said "O ja jy is van Schweizer-Reneke", and for a few minutes we were parochial Western Transvaalers and indulged in talk about our respective places. You know of course that he is from Potch.

    I liked the anecdote about Ahmed Bhoola's mother. In every

country town there would be a family or two whose houses had to serve as stop-over places for travellers. The old people used to derive great pleasure from these visits. Our place was also like that and I can still remember a number of interesting visitors. As you know my father took his religion very seriously and he taught us as children never to turn away people who stop for refreshment, rest or shelter. Let me recount a little anecdote. I'm told that during the depression years large numbers of poor white people walked from place to place in search of employment, shelter and food. Often they'd be with their families. One such man – Mr T – wandered into Schweizer from the OFS,* completely destitute. As you know Indians were never allowed in the Free State; and as a result there existed all sorts of myths about Indians. Mr T went from one white farmer to another, looking for work, but he was unsuccessful. Hunger drives a man to desperation. Full of fear, Mr T at last entered my father's shop and explained his plight. The old man immediately took him in, fed him, gave him clothing and some cash, and told him he was welcome to call again until such time as he can find employment. This was the beginning of a relationship that developed into warm friendship, which lasted until Mr T's death in the seventies. There was a period when Mr T suffered ostracisation and punishment as a result of this friendship, but he remained steadfast and loyal. Of course this is a very brief account of a story that could fill many pages, and circumstances oblige me to relate only the bare bones. But I'm sure the story of Mr T, with interesting variations can be told a thousand times over by the country shopkeeper. I started writing about Ahmed Bhoola's mother, and wandered away onto

---

\* The Statute Law of the Orange Free State (1891), one of four provinces brought together under Union government in 1910, prohibited Indians from living or trading in the region. Indian businesses were forced to shut down by 11 September of that year, and owners deported without compensation. This remained the case after Union.

something else. Yes, I knew Ahmed, from the time he was staying at the Bharoochie's in Fordsburg. I've also been to their place in Mansfield Road. Is Ahmed still a columnist for the *Leader*?

I must thank you very much for providing me with the background information about our ancestry, and in particular about the derivation of our surname. It is most interesting. I hope that something is being done to preserve and enlarge on the type of information Moosabhai possesses. It is invaluable. The Maulana Margoub you mentioned was my father's brother. Someone once told me he had been Mufti of Rangoon. He visited South Africa in 1935 or thereabouts and I have vague recollections of a man with a reddish beard. The story goes in the family that he found my recitation from the Koran quite promising, and he wanted to take me to India in order to become a Molvi. But apparently my mother threatened to go on a protest hunger strike, or some such thing, and I stayed. Fatoo Mala was my aunt. I stayed with her when I came to school in 1938, until 1945. She was quite learned, but we found her very strict. There were a number of Akhalwaya families in the neighbourhood, one of whom (Ismail Akhalwaya I think) was married to a Bismillah lady. Their daughter used to be my neighbour in Kholvad House right up to the time of my arrest. The Daya who wrote Urdu poetry is my cousin – my father's sister's son. She was never in South Africa. This Mehmud Daya is still alive and well. But I don't know if he still writes poetry. He lives in Lenasia. There is another quite learned man – Goolam Husein Ismail – in Schweizer. Moosabhai knows him as he used to manage the Mia shop in Schweizer.

You know over the past few months I've been wondering how one addresses a female who has been to Haj. My sister in law was there last year. And so was Fatima Seedat from Durban. And I didn't know how one should address them. Now your letter has clarified this.

We've been hearing quite a bit lately about the rivalry, and even violence, between the "Tabliqs" and "Salaamis". I'm afraid I'm at a loss. A brief explanation from you will be welcome.

Since my last letter to you I had a discussion with a Colonel Scott from Prison Headquarters, Pretoria, in connection with the reading matter that was returned to you. He is in charge of this aspect of things and was surprised to hear what I related. I explained that it was not possible to obtain books such as *Nanima's Peti*, *Indian Delights* etc. from the Provincial Library, and also complained about the fact that even a Koran and dictionary were returned. He suggested that in future such matters should be directed to him. So one of these days if you can find the time, I suggest you should write to Col. Scott and take up the matter afresh.

I was very happy to learn that Nasim, Aslam and Rashid are so advanced in their professions. It is also interesting to hear of Razia's hobby – pottery. I come across articles now and then on pottery but generally ignore them. I shall pay more attention to them.

Do you remember Vallabh? I recently had a letter from someone who said Vallabh has been having quite a bit of trouble with his eyes.

I was sorry to hear of the death of G.R. Naidoo. I was never aware that he had a serious heart ailment.

This will be all for now. Life goes on as usual. Luckily we now have our studies to keep us occupied. I may have told you I'm doing Honours in History. I'm hoping to do it in two stages. I had my results last week and was lucky to get through. I hope to register for the remaining 3 this year.

Fond regards to all the family and friends. Everything of the best to you.

From
    AMK

[Undated but received by Kathrada on 8th May 1982]

Westville 3630

My dear Ahmed

Not knowing whether you are restricted to number of incoming-outgoing mail, I had just taken my place in the queue (mentally) when replying. But the memories you have evoked, it also being a Saturday (no chores except for clearing desk) and the fact that there is a steady drizzle which means no gardening, I am replying promptly.

I was busy with some writing yesterday and as usual my grandchildren were playing around the table. I heard Jihaan saying "Bhailoo (where she has picked up this term of endearment for Jaleel, I don't know) you see Nani's face is not old only her hair is old." The silver on my head is so lush that even the babes notice it. Anyway, reason for recalling this bit of a gem is that at my age memories and recollections have a big place. Since I mean this letter to contain a lot of these I am duplicating the letter in the hope that some grandchild will one day find the contents newsworthy.

First of all, congratulate me. The new *Indian Delights* is out and it is a beauty. As my children say, it's no longer housewifey but professional, meaning thereby that Andrew Verster who had been responsible for the arrangement deserves the credit for appearance. The public that had patiently been waiting for this new edition has just overwhelmed us with orders and that has not given us time to launch or publicise it yet. Price R10.95 + GST.

*[[In 1945 my father broke away from the traditional habit of

---

\* Double bracketed text here indicates censored text, i.e., that Kathrada did not receive.

Asians to have living quarters behind their shops. This started a trend and soon most merchants in the Asiatic Bazaar in Potch started to build separate homes. Those merchants who were in the central business area were discreetly told to move their residences and their business rights would not be trampled. Over the next few years they too had settled around us. Meanwhile the mass removal of Africans from the location across our shops (where they had lived before the place was named a location by the new rulers of the country) was accelerated and soon the Coloured population had to give way. In the interim, the roads that went past our shops to the rich farming regions of the South were re-routed and now even the farmers bypassed us. Business was slowly strangled. Since the threat of removal of business was there, the shop-proud Indians were no longer improving their properties. Then comes along Minister Le Grange accompanied by local big shot Indians, for an inspection in loco. The minister in most scathing terms said that the shops were a disgrace to the good name of the town and the poor committee accompanying him did not have the courage to say that the threat of a non-renewal of the lease hold permits was the cause of the state of the premises. Meanwhile the municipality had already erected a plaza for Indian shops way out in the back parts of the town. As had been happening all over the country the Indians were forced to sell their premises to the Group-Areas Community Development and move into the new shopping area. An entire Community who had owned their own shops all along were now made rent payers, and what exorbitant rent too! My father, though long retired from business, refused to sign away his residence rights. Again and again the officials came. The last time they came, my father was very weak from let's say just old age, and he told them in good old Afrikaans, "Kyk hier, ek is klaar met die lewe. Ek trek niks verder nie. My plotjie grond het ek klaar bestel dit is waar my kinders, my sal uit dra".* Three weeks later he died and his son Sadik and son-in-law Mohamed Mayat carried him to the plotjie in the graveyard. At the funeral many town dignitaries were there. The one bank manager consoling Sadik said "You know your father never had an overdraft at Barclay's Bank throughout his association with us (My grandfather had started the business in 1886). "Fat lot of good it did him" retorted Mohamed "For all his clean civic and commercial record he was hounded through the twilight years of his life."

No, Ahmed, all the shops in Potch were demolished, including Dabhel House and as for the beautiful homes we owned, persons of the White Group now occupy them. They got it dirt cheap. The new one has cost us five times more but what hurts my mother most is that her sweat in the orchards and gardens cannot be enjoyed by her grandchildren.

You are right. The story of your father can be multiplied several thousand times over and it will still not measure to the contribution of Indians in this country. When Sadik and family had to move, my article in the *Rand Daily Mail* under the heading of "When Pioneers Move" highlighted some of the achievements and hardships of our people.

Haji Behen refers only to that female who was on the same Haj trip as yourself but Hajiani is applied to anyone that performed Haj.]]

Ahmed Bhoola no longer writes for the *Leader*. A team of correspondents take turns in doing the editorials. Nowbath still writes "Talk of the Bazaar" under the pen-name Fakir.

Moosa Bhai is too much of an eccentric and recluse and refuses to write anything for publication. What a store of anecdotes lost as a result.

---

\* 'Look here, I am finished with life. I'm not moving another step. I've already ordered my plot of land; that is where my children will carry me out.'

The Akhalwayas too have been scattered around. The Fordsburg shop still operates but is under threat of Group Areas. They buy *Indian Delights* in lots of 500 at a time.

I recall you were engaged to a [Newtown girl].

From the earliest of days of his Mission our Prophet forbade the creation of a priestly class saying that every Muslim must be a propagationist for his religion and so every trader, traveller or tin maker undertook the propagation of Islam wherever he went. (Never by the sword as the Orientalists would have us believe.) The Arabic word for such propagationists or teachers was Tableegh. Up till the Second World War, Tableegh was undertaken by individuals but since then they formed themselves into bands that went around re-teaching born Muslims a New Awareness of their Faith and conducting classes for converts. A movement then came into being and it is now world wide. Each year over Easter weekend they hold a rally in South Africa called an Ijtima or gathering of the Jamaat (Community). This year the Ijtima will be in Ladysmith and giant tents will provide sleeping, eating and namaaz facilities for some 7 to 8 thousand persons.

Young people have taken very strongly to the Tableegh movement and one is struck to see the young age of the congregationists in Mosques throughout the world. If you have studied the History of Islam, you will notice that the Sufi movements had their greatest periods of growth when under political stress or persecution. When we were in Russia in 1974 we found the Naqshabandi Sufi movement very much alive even though the authorities keep a strict surveillance. When off duty every second male was seen to wear the black caps embroidered with white cottons which was the occupation of this great spiritual giant when the Mongols were bent on eradicating Islam.

You will also know that a political split started very early in Islam and those that wanted Hazrat Ali to assume leadership split after his death into the party (Shia) adherents of which over the years came to be known as the Shias. Most Iranians, Yemenese, the Aga Khanis etc are all Shias. Those – and this is the majority of the Islamic world including all of us – belong to the Sunni group meaning those that follow the way of the Prophet. The Tableeghis are absolute Sunnis so this split between the Tableeghees and Sunnis is such a farcical and misleading term. However you will remember that the Urdu speaking population of South Africa (Mia Bhais, Hyderabadis etc.) were always great believers in the Moulood Un Nabi Festivals. It is a festival commemorating the birth of the Prophet. Nothing wrong in that but the purists (currently meaning the Tableeghis) maintain the Islamic fundamental law that nothing man made is to be added to the religion as Revealed by God for in these accretions one goes off the right path, it causes controversies, it makes the load of Living Life even more difficult. What the Tableeghis also find objectionable is that when the Salaami is recited (you do remember "Ya Nabi Salaam Alaikum" don't you?) the listeners are under obligation to stand up for that time. The Salaami Group maintains that the soul of the Prophet comes to the gathering to accept the Salaams. This according to Islam is uncondonable for only God is Omnipresent and not the Prophet or anyone else. So the split is really between the Salaami and the Tableeghis and not between Sunnis for we are all Sunnis and in South Africa apart from a few Aga Khanis and a few Daoudi Bhoras in Durban no Shias are around. The Aga Khanis have quit, and the Bhoras have intermarried into the Sunni group.

Since the books were returned to me I have made further efforts to get them to you and I shall certainly be writing to Colonel Scott.

Valabh Jaga remains a very good friend of our family and he is virtually a brother. At one stage my father remarked that Valabh enquires deeper into his health than any of his other sons. His retinas have been giving a lot of trouble. Several operations have been performed and he is just left with sufficient sight to go about his daily work. Driving a car or reading is out!

All luck with your honours course. If ever possible, try to read the great Theologian philosophers like Imam Ghazzali, Jalaluddin Rumi etc. Some excellent translations are available in English. They make such a sense of religion. Literature for study purposes – how is this obtained? I know one year when we were going to London the Meers had asked us to obtain some very special manuals for Nelson but these were at the time unobtainable even in London.

There is a tremendous Indian Festival in London this year. All the museums have special exhibits of Indian art, jewellery, costumes, objects etc. laid on. Then there are the dance and music festivals in so many parts of Britain. All this during April up till September. Two years ago the Festival of Islam in Britain proved highly popular and the Indian government is doing its thing this year.

Jaleel has a baby sister whom we have named Nureen. (Nur meaning Light of God). She is adorable and Jihaan mothers her no end. Jaleel is of course put off since she claims so much of his mother's time.

You will forgive me if I do not take time and care when writing letters. Your letters are an absolute delight to read. Beautifully phrased and neatly written. I just bang on my typewriter as the thoughts come but with my correspondence course matric English – well...

With Salaams to you and your friends,
    Zuleikha

Prison Headquarters
Pretoria
30th June 1982

Dear Colonel Scott

I have tried during the past two years, to send some books to one of the prisoners at Robben Island. Viz; Ahmed Kathrada, but have met with no success.
The books are:
1. An English translation of the Holy Quran.
2. *Nanima's Chest* which is a book on Indian Antique costumes in the possession of Indian South Africans.
3. *Indian Delights* which is a cookery book on Indian Dishes.
The last two books have been edited by myself.

I have personally never met Mr Kathrada although I know of him through paper reports during his trial. But three years ago when my husband died in a tragic car accident Mr. Kathrada wrote to sympathise. My late husband was a well known gynaecologist and community worker and apparently Mr. Kathrada had known him while my husband was studying at the Witwatersrand University. Since that letter I have been corresponding with Mr Kathrada. My motive for doing so and for wishing to send him the books is based purely on compassionate grounds. I too am deeply involved with community work and being a Muslim my Faith enjoins that compassion should embrace prisoners as well as free citizens.

You will gauge from the titles that the books are not of a political nature. Is there any way in which you can assist in this matter? If required I can post the books to you for censoring before forwarding to Kathrada, or it can be sent through the Red Cross or any way that you suggest.

Colonel, your help will be greatly appreciated and your reward will be with the Compassionate God in Whom we all Believe, even the misguided ones during their years of folly.

    Thanking you.
        Sincerely yours,
            [signed] ZM Mayat

[hand written]

8<sup>th</sup> of Ramadan
30<sup>th</sup> June 1982

My dear Ahmed

Sorry it seems that my typing ribbon has gone on strike – I forgot to purchase replacements in time! Ramadan is so easy this year, it's virtually like having breakfast and early dinner at 5:10.

I am enclosing a subscription card herewith – if the authorities will allow it, fill it in and send it off and I will pay the subscription. That, I would like to give you for an Eid present. *Arabia* covers the whole Muslim world – its minority problems, economics, politics, development, so forth. [[The January issue had chosen as its prisoner of conscience a Mr Ahmed Kathrada, and others in this series were prisoners in Moscow, Pakistan etc. Please don't think that this is the reason why I wish to give it as an Eidy.]] *Arabia* is a top class magazine which presents facts thoroughly researched and objectively unlike most Islamic orientated magazines which are heavily biased and prejudiced – thus clouding issues.

My mother who is 84 fell while watering the garden in Potch. She fractured her thigh and I thought this is the beginning of the end of a wonderful example of Indian womanhood. I underestimated her and even the doctors were amazed at her quick recovery. Within 3 weeks she was on crutches (it had taken me 6 weeks) and has even begun to go into the shower by herself. You know her motto is "Work and hard work cures more ills than medicines." She has never had time for depression or self-pity. When she was nursing my father through his last illness she started learning Urdu from him – within 3 years she had mastered it sufficiently to be able to read the meaning and exegesis/Tafseer of the Quran. That when she was <u>73</u>.

A Happy and Blessed EID MUBARAK to you and your friends

Zuleikha

P.S. If you are not allowed to subscribe, then do let me know and I will send a gift voucher.

[Note made by Kathrada on this letter: "Not Allowed"]

A.M. Kathrada
Robben Island Jail
10th July 1982

Dear Zuleikhabehn

Your letter reached me a long time ago already – on 8th May to be precise. Thank you very much for all the information it contained, especially the clarification about the so-called "Tabliq-Salaami" dispute. I haven't been reading any reports recently about fresh flare-ups between the rival groups, so I assume that things have cooled down – or at least the violent aspect of the controversy. We certainly can do without these sectional clashes, which merely tend to entrench divisions, and which after all the argumentation, adverse publicity, bloodshed and litigation redound to the credit of neither party, and are harmful to the community as a whole. What makes their religious schisms all the more unfortunate is that the disputants almost invariably become so emotionally involved that they become impervious to reasoned debate and discussion. I suppose you'd say this situation is not unlike the behaviour of politicians, and you would have a point there. It is relatively easy for me to concede this, being away from the maelstrom of everyday political life.

Before I proceed, let me congratulate you on the new edition of *Indian Delights*. I shall not give up hope of seeing it one day, and who knows, I may even have an opportunity of actually trying out some of the recipes outside jail. Once upon a time I used to pride myself on being able to cook a couple of Indian dishes. I don't know whether it was the taste, or sheer hunger that drove my friends to eat my preparations but they did say a few complimentary things about them. At that time there was no question of consulting authorities (tho' we did have a copy of the first edition of your book with the introduction by Fatima) – we were always in a hurry to eat and get it over with. Our best friend at the flat was a broiler. That, of course, required no skill whatsoever. It was just a matter of a bit of seasoning, setting the time and switching on. The broiler did the rest. The occasions for actual cooking were not very frequent. Then there were the wonderful neighbours whose generosity and care knew no bounds. There was a continuous stream of trays from several flats converging on Flat 13. Often we were careless about returning the dishes promptly; they would just pile up, and then we wouldn't know which dish goes where, so they'd remain. Then on a day when we were out, and only the domestic help was there, the good ladies from the flats would slip in and collect their dishes. The position became worse when I was placed under house arrest. I was staying alone and was not allowed to have visitors. The flood of sympathy was overwhelming. Every evening just after six o'clock the ladies would send their little kids – some of them mere toddlers – each carrying a plate or bowl of something or other. They thoroughly spoilt me.

I am thinking of all this for two reason. Tonight, nineteen years ago, was my last night of freedom; we were arrested on 11th July 1963. So I can't help but think back. Then, you'll recall in my last letter I mentioned an Akhalwaya lady who was a neighbour of mine. Well this morning I received my first letter from her daughter, and the whole day I've been thinking of those little kids. She wasn't among the kids as she couldn't even toddle then, but her sister, about two years her senior, was a regular. And she was my favourite. I simply delight in reminiscing about those days. The kids were clever and they devised their own little plans and strategy to derive some benefit for themselves. You see, I started keeping a supply of chocolates and other goodies at the flat, and whenever the kids came I used to give them something. They quickly saw the pattern, and the next thing I found was that on weekends and holidays when I had to be at home, they would start pestering their mothers from early in the morning to give something for uncle. Then I'd hear their tiny knocks and they would troop in – one carrying a roti, one a puri, or samoosa or something. And then they would run off. Now house arrest by its very nature meant among other things a drastic reduction of physical activity. This, coupled with all the food, resulted in a serious weight problem which I was really only able to solve after my imprisonment.

A thought has just occurred to me. I mentioned earlier about trying out your recipes outside jail and I thought I might have given the impression that I may be going out one of these days. I was simply being frivolous and what I said had no relationship whatsoever with recent developments whereby political prisoners are to be given remission, parole etc. As you know I am doing life and we have no information as yet as to how the new dispensation will apply to me, if at all.

To come to something you mentioned. You were right about my being engaged [to a Newtown girl]. There was no formal engagement as such but there was the definite intention to marry. We were seen together at cinema and other functions. As you know at that time it was still most unusual for unmarried Moslem girls to appear in public with their boyfriends. So our being seen together was deemed by the people – and correctly so – to have been an engagement to marry. I think I am glad you raised the question. I've long been wanting to make certain explanations. It is a matter that remains on my conscience and the only relief I get is when I hear that the lady is happily married. I must admit without hesitation that my whole behaviour in this affair was callous and despicable. It was entirely inexcusable. All this happened in 1950-51. What makes it worse is that it was not as if the lady was selected for me by the family. No one influenced me. I chose her myself. Of course the family was very happy. Everything was settled. I started university – and the idea was that we should get married even before completing my studies. Then I had to go overseas. The plan was to continue with studies and marriage after my return. I stayed in Hungary for almost a year, and while I was there I began to have second thoughts about all my South African plans. But I did not have the courage to inform her. And what I did, or failed to do, on my return was worse, if not criminal. I simply stayed away from her. When confronted by my folks I told them. They were on the warpath with me. The poor girl still harboured some hopes for a couple of years, and eventually gave up. In 1957 or 1958 she got married, and virtually each day thereafter I eagerly wanted to hear she was happy and settled. There were many rumours about why I changed my mind. The common belief was that I had met another girl abroad. Now it is true that I had a Hungarian girlfriend – and a very beautiful girl too – but that had nothing to do with it. In fact, if there was any substance in the story I wouldn't have come back to SA in 1952. My real reasons were political, or so I thought at the time. You must remember, I was only 22 or 23 and full of youthful idealism and an exaggerated estimation of my indispensability. And that was about it.

That was the only time I ever contemplated marriage. Regrets? Of course it remains one of my greatest regrets. Well there I have told you what there is. There is much I have left out. But those are details. I'm glad I have unburdened myself.

I wanted to write about other matters but they will have to wait. I hope you received my Eid Card. Since it will be August soon, let me wish you a happy birthday. I too happened to be an August baby. Mine's on the 21$^{st}$.

Everything of the best to you and the family and friends. Lots of love to Jihaan, Jaleel and Nureen.

From
AMK

Salsabil
Westville 3680
14th July 1982

Dear Ahmed Bhai

My family and friends were most touched by your Eid Card to us. Thank you and we all wish you a Joyous Eid at the Island and may some of our happiness extend to all of you over there.

Not having heard from you with reference to the London-based magazine, I am sending you a cash Eidy hoping that you will be able to purchase what you really want.

Days of fasting are nearly over and my Jihaan and Jaleel have already started to open the parcels relatives have sent for them for Eidy. The little brats can't wait till Eid. Jihaan will of course be painting her hands with mendhi on the eve of Eid.

With salaams,
Zuleikha

Prison Service Centre
Private Bag X136
West Block
124 Church Street, Pretoria
Col. I C Scott
1982-07-30

Mrs Z M Mayat
Salsabil, WESTVILLE 3630

Dear Mrs Mayet

Your letter dated 30 June 1982 has reference.

Permission is hereby granted for the following books to be sent, at no cost to the State, to Ahmed Kathrada on Robben Island.

1. An English Translation of the Holy Quran which can be forwarded to the prisoner concerned directly from you.
2. A copy of *Nanima's Chest*.

In accordance with Prison Service regulations, this book must be sent direct from the Publisher or a recognised bookshop to the prisoner.

Permission for the book entitled *Indian Delights* to be sent to the prisoner concerned has not been granted.

With best wishes
Yours faithfully
COLONEL For COMMISSIONER OF PRISONS
I C SCOTT

Colonel I.C. Scott
Commissioner of Prisons
Pretoria
9th August 1982

Dear Colonel Scott

I highly appreciate your help in arranging for permission for the two books to be sent to Ahmed Kathrada at Robben Island Prison.

The translation (English) of the Holy Quran is published in Dublin but is distributed locally. The other book *Nanima's Chest* is published by the Women's Cultural Group which is a non-profit making organisation and all their deliveries are undertaken by Taj Company of 127 Prince Edward Street, Durban.

Messrs Taj Company has undertaken to post both the Quran and *Nanima's Chest* on my behalf and I hope this will be acceptable to you.

With many thanks,
   Sincerely yours,
      (signed) Z. M. Mayat

The Commandant
Robben Island Prison
10<sup>th</sup> August 1982

Dear Sir

I have received a letter from the Commissioner of Prisons (Colonel I.C. Scott) which gives permission for an English Translation of the Holy Quran and a copy of *Nanima's Chest* (book on antique Indian clothes in South Africa) to be sent to Ahmed Kathrada.

    I have requested Messrs Taj Company to send out both these books to Ahmed Kathrada and that they should bill me for the books as well as for the postage charges.

    Thanking you.
        Sincerely yours,
            Z. M. Mayat.

A.M. Kathrada
Robben Island Jail
28th August 1982

Dear Zuleikhabehn

Thank you very much for your letters of 30th June and 14th July, for your Eid card and for the "Eidy". I was unable to use it for an Eid party but I am planning a belated celebration on 5th September which will include the inmates who make up our little community in our section. We will be thinking of your kindness. The Moslem Prison Welfare Society in Cape Town sent me an Eid parcel – sweets, cake, dried fruit – to which we added some biscuits and had a little tea party on Eid Day. From this you will gather that jail life is not all hardship and suffering. It does have its bright moments.

You will be surprised how relatively small things assume such importance for prisoners. It's almost unavoidable and cannot be otherwise. I once read somewhere that the years roll by quickly in jail, but it is the minutes and the hours that drag on at a dreary pace. It is a very apt description of our lives. Ours is a very small world and it is mostly the small things that help to fill the minutes and hours. Small talk, small events, small interests – these combine to make up a big share of our days and weeks and months. Let me give you an example. A few months ago a warder brought a chameleon into our section; and from that day on it has become the focus of much attention. It has evoked a variety of reactions and emotions ranging from pity, love to intense disliking. Very few are indifferent to it. Encyclopaedias were consulted to elicit information about the particular species, its reproductive methods etc. In no time it acquired "parents" in the form of human beings, and they care for it as if it were a little baby. Are you able to imagine a 70-year-old and his younger colleagues making it their business of swatting flies so that the creature is constantly fed? Well, it happens. An opinion exists that it should be taken out and left in the bush, but there is considerable opposition. Someone else, who is troubled by flies in his cell, is thinking of taking the chameleon into his place at night. Others are concerned that if it is left outside, it will fall prey to the butcher bird. And so on and so forth. I suppose it can be said, and with some justification, that the chameleon is really bringing out the parental instinct. I don't know. Personally I hate all reptiles and I can't get myself to even [consider] touching the chameleon, but I do watch with interest some of the activities around it. By the way is "boomla" a fish or a reptile? I used to love the things.

What I would like is a kitten, and lots of flowers and greenery. You know it is terrible, so unnatural, to be surrounded for so many hours at night by cement, and then during the day one goes out into the courtyard where space is largely taken up by a cement tennis court! Luckily someone is trying to grow some carnations and other flowers and I just can't wait until they come up. The other day I saw a field full of daisies – a riot of colour, so beautiful and therapeutic. I'm just trying to recall a delightful book I read some years ago which had something to do with cats. I think it was "Jenny" by Paul Galico. You should read it, that is if you are interested in the feline world.

Let me come back to your letter. At the time you wrote about the magazine, *Arabia*, I was informed it would not be allowed. Now there is a new dispensation which permits us to order all magazines that are available in South African bookshops. I don't know if *Arabia* falls into this category. Could you let me know? But please do not send in a subscription. If it is approved I will order it from here.

I was sorry to learn of your mother's fall. I hope she has fully recovered. Things are fine with me. My studies are getting on very slowly. I think I took on a bit too much and am finding it difficult to cope.

Hope you received my letter of 10th July. Keep well. Fondest regards to you, the children, the grandchildren and all the family and friends.

AMK

P.S. 30th August
This morning I was called and given
(i) The Koran (ii) *Nanima's Chest*. Thank you very much.

Durban
21st November 1982

My Dear Ahmed

I glance at the date of your last letter and it says 28th August. I am conscience stricken and what excuse can I offer? Busy and involved? Yes, that I am but also a lot of time frittered away in a lot of useless little things which bring perhaps momentary pleasure but no lasting satisfaction. However, that is part of life. If man but learnt to use precious time more carefully, then this world would be something else.

Aah, your chameleon as yet has no name? If it has survived the attention and interest shown it, then let's hope you find a mate for it. If you run out of flies let me know.

Boomla is definitely fish and in its fresh form very much like our Kingklip. You could call it the fish biltong of India for near the fisherman's colony in Bombay you see lines and lines of boomla strips drying in the sun. The smell of boomla puts a lot of people off this delicacy. My father-in-law narrates an incident that took place some time in the late thirties. A grocery merchant had run into financial difficulties before his creditors forced the closing of his warehouse. Some weeks went by before the assessors could come around to take stock. These were two elderly Englishmen and they followed Mr Bassa into the warehouse. Veritable fumes of dank smell hit them as they ventured in and the stink was so overpowering that the more agile Englishman ran back into the street but the other nearly fainted and had to be helped out. Some crates of Boomla had caused this and the Englishmen were stunned to learn that Indians ate this commodity!

Have I told you the Durian story? This is a fruit indigenous to the Far East and grows profusely in Malaya, Java, etc. The late Soekarno insisted that it be served for breakfast and dinner. Well this Durian looks like Jackfruit (we Gujaratis call it Fanus) – I wonder whether you ever saw it for I never knew of it till I came to live in Durban. Thick prickly pear-like skin but without thorns on the outside and when cut open it reveals luscious yellow custardy segments of pulpy fruit. But when it is cut open, it exudes a smell that announces the ceremony to the whole environment. During our extensive travels in Indonesia, Singapore, Malaya and Thailand, my late husband got to like durian and he liked the stories about it even more. The best one we heard was related by a Surtee who was managing a steel factory in Bangkok. One year, he was returning to Kathor when his Boss (also a Kathorian) asked him to take two large vacuum flasks in hand luggage for his family back home. The flasks were filled with segments of durian. Mr Vaid obliged and put the flasks near his feet on board the BOAC flight.

The first stop was Rangoon. There was to be a re-fuelling stop of 30 minutes. Vaid Chacha returned to the plane after 20 minutes and he was surprised to see some feverish activity on board [the] plane. There were cleaners, wiping and cleaning and fumigating the place and a very irate crew and captain supervising and urging the cleaners into doing a better job. The cleaners left. Mr Vaid ventured to his seat and found his flasks missing. He reported this to the steward who immediately called the Captain. "So, you are the owner of those offensive flasks? What the blazes is it?" Not understanding what the fuss was all about, Mr Vaid said "Oh, only durian fruit." "Fruit!" screamed the Captain. "Do you mean to tell me that humans eat that stinking rotten stuff?" Mr Vaid was most offended. "I don't want your opinion, I only want my flasks. What right did you have to open them?"

To cut the story short, the flasks were not opened. Cabin pressure on the flasks and the potency of the durian had made them explode and blow off the caps. Vaid was anxious lest his boss thought he had taken the fruit for his own family and concocted the story, so he threatened to sue BOAC for the return of his fruit and the captain was determined that he would not allow them back into the cabin and he in turn threatened Vaid with customs laws that prohibit the carrying of flora and fruit into a country without a permit. Compromise was affected by the Captain writing out a note on BOAC paper testifying as to what had occurred and how he had ordered that the durian be thrown into the garbage!

Ahmed, all the good hotels in the Far East carry large notices reading "Bringing durian into this hotel is strictly forbidden." I never got to taste the stuff for I have a large Bismillah nose but the lovers of durian have described it: "smells like a fisherwoman's basket with rotting fish, old stinking canvas shoes, deteriorating rubber, swampy jungles and the foulest breath all combined together. Tastes like a combination of ice cream, strawberries, marshmallows, peaches, angelfood and all the delicious things under the sun – get past the smell and stick your teeth into it and then you will know why even elephants in the Thai forests get durian drunk on the fruit."

Jaleel my grandson is a lover of the outdoors. He is always in the garden helping Fineas, our garden help, and Fineas complains that his plants are often dug out by Jaleel. I cut some oranges into halves and scooped out the insides clean (ate them of course, with the kids). Then I got Jaleel and Jihaan to pack some soil into the halves and we planted some methi seeds that had been soaked in water for two days. Within days, the tiny green methi leaves emerged and the kids watched with delight the progress each day. Somewhere we got careless and the expected luscious green was not forthcoming. Maybe better luck next time.

You may remember the old Afrikaans magazine *Huisgenoot*. Well, that is still around and as conservative as ever. The two new ones on the market are *Rooi Rose* and *Sarie*. Despite protests from their readers, both magazines are now including articles about us dark citizens of South Africa. Naturally the articles are still very safe in so far as they write more of achievements of black women, their aspirations in the future (skirting around political issues) and so on. *Indian Delights* was reviewed as early as in 1970 in *Sarie* and *Nanima's Chest* in *Rooi Rose*. T.V. literature and theatre has certainly introduced changes in attitude but the slogan "Too little too late and too slow" still holds. Surprising number of women (Indian) are working as journalists these days. Fay Saleh, Leela Naidoo, Reyhana Loonat are some of the names.

*Arabia* magazine wrote to me some time ago asking that I help suggest names of distributors for their publication here. Regret have not done anything about it yet. Will let you know as soon as CNA starts selling them.

I would like your honest criticism about *Nanima's Chest*. Many young persons have felt that Indian roots must be shed in Africa and one should not harp about past traditions and heritage. My view is that we can enrich each other's cultures by absorbing other trends and the prime example is India that has always absorbed into its own traditions, those of other nations. Chinese, Persian, Mongol, Greek, Aryan, Arab, Turk all contributed towards the culture of India and made it the rich product that it is today. Close yourself off like the Afrikaner and you remain with your Boerewors en Jan Pierewiet liedjie. Political assimilation will lead to social and cultural [assimilation] in its own time.

Salaams,
    Zuleikha

A.M. Kathrada
Pollsmoor Maximum Prison
30th January 1983

Dear Zuleikhabehn

Your letter of 21st November was redirected to me from Robben Island and reached me on 2nd December. Many thanks. You've most probably gathered by now that I was suddenly transferred to Pollsmoor Prison on 21st October. The sudden change of environment after 18 years plus naturally meant quite a bit of disruption; but I suppose in a way its full impact was somewhat lessened by my preoccupation with exam preparations. I had to try to adjust as quickly as possible to the new conditions and virtually had no time to assess the pros and cons of my transfer. I finished exams on Friday and immediately got stuck into writing letters. Hence this delayed reply. However, in-between letters, and the normal routine, my thoughts constantly go back to the Island. Apart from the touch of rural life, which I adore, I miss the companionship of the lovely big family which we had become. True, I am with old friends here, but we are only six; which makes a great difference. Otherwise one jail is almost the same as another, and we still lead strictly regimented lives. I am of course absolutely in the dark as to the reasons for our transfer and any attempts to speculate are simply futile. In the meantime I am waiting for results and after that I shall be able to decide what to do studywise. I'd like to do M.A. if I get through, but there is a regulation which stipulates that M.A. studies can only be allowed to prisoners who have two years or less, of their sentences remaining. As you know I'm doing life for which there is no ceiling, so it seems M.A. will be out. I will take up the matter after the results.

You acknowledge my letter of 28th August, but don't say

anything about the one I wrote on 10<sup>th</sup> July. Please let me know if you received it.

Now to *Nanima's Chest*. I'm afraid I'll have to be brief. What I had planned to do was to reproduce comments by a young man who was my neighbour at Robben Island. He was simply ecstatic. His comments were of special significance because he hails from Soweto; he is highly intelligent and articulate; and most important he is young and came to jail after 1976. In fact I had arranged with him to write out his comments. Then, I had given the book to my fellow librarian, and he circulated it throughout the prison. I had just begun to get a feedback when I was removed. Let me assure you that there was not a single negative comment. Not a single person, no matter what his persuasion, made remarks about discarding past traditions and heritage. My own views are best expressed in a passage I read by Gandhi where he says: "I want the culture of all lands to be blown about my house as freely as possible. But I refuse to be blown off my feet by any". I think that more or less accords with your views. My main criterion for judging questions of this nature is whether they promote sectionalism. *Nanima's Chest* should give no cause whatsoever for any anxiety on this score. I should of course like to discuss this in greater detail with the pros and cons adequately slated. But unfortunately it cannot be done in letters where we are obliged to restrict ourselves to a fixed length.

Your regular references to the antics of Jehaan and Jaleel are a source of great pleasure – and amusement. I may have mentioned before that the deprivation one feels most in jail is the absence of children. According to a recent dispensation we are now allowed visits from children. In December I had the thrilling and unforgettable experience of seeing a baby just the other side of the glass for the first time in 20 years! My niece had brought along her 3 month old Leila to visit her godfather.

We now have an F.M. radio, and I've been listening to the

Saturday "Indian" programme. It is lousy. But every now and then there is a bit of information of some person I know, or an interesting interview. Recently there was an interview with Saira Essa which I found informative. Last week – and I hope I have misheard – I thought there was a report of the death of Dr Ismail Sader. Is it true?

I'm afraid I have to end now. I hope you and the family and friends are all well. You haven't [mentioned] Siko for some time. My fondest regards to her and family.

Fond regards and best wishes, from
AMK

A.M. Kathrada
Pollsmoor Maximum Prison
Private Bag x4
Tokai
7966
12th June 1983

Dear Zuleikhabehn

This is going to be just a short note. I haven't heard from you for some time and am wondering if my last letter ever reached you. Your last letter was of 21st November, which was redirected to me from Robben Island, and reached me on 2nd December. It arrived in the midst of exam preparations, so I only replied on 30th of January. In this letter I commented on *Nanima's Chest*. I also mentioned that you had acknowledged my letter of 28th August, but don't mention anything about the one I wrote on the 10th July. I fear that two of my letters to you never reached, and I am therefore taking the precaution of registering this one.

I suppose you must have gathered by now that I was transferred to this prison in October last year; by now I'm already a veteran of almost 8 months. I still miss the island all the time. Incidentally today I've completed 19 years of my sentence! That's been quite an innings, don't you think!

My purpose in writing this note was twofold. I wanted to find out about the letters. Secondly I wanted to send Eid greetings to you, the children and especially Jihaan, Jaleel and Nureen. Unfortunately my supply of Eid cards has not yet arrived, and I'm afraid if I wait for them I might be very late. So you'll have to excuse me and accept my wishes through this unconventional means.

I have to write similar Eid notes to a number of folks; and to get them to reach in time I shall have to get them posted without delay.

My apologies again for the shortness of the letter. I hope you don't mind but I also asked my niece and Mrs Seedat to check with you about my letters. I just wanted to make doubly sure.

Otherwise life goes on as usual. We are only 6 of us here, and that does make us long for the big happy family we were on Robben Island. Luckily the loneliness is mitigated a bit by our studies which keeps us quite busy. Yet there is nothing to compensate for all the other facilities we enjoyed there. What we do have is our own FM radio, which is very useful. I listen in to the Saturday morning "Indian" programme, which I find thoroughly lousy. Every now and then though I do hear about someone I know, and that makes it a little less intolerable. I'm also getting the *Graphic* and *Leader*, and find them worse than they were. Does Nowbath still write the Fakir column? What cynicism! I notice there's [a] book at CNA *Indian Cooking* by Lalita Ahmed. Do you know it? When you write back tell me something about the new Isipingo hospital put up by Indian doctors. Also about the film "Gandhi".

This will be all for now. I was lucky with my results, and managed to complete the Honours. The Prisons won't allow me to do MA; so I'm doing another Honours, in African Politics.

Keep well. Everything of the best to you, the family and friends.

From
AMK

22nd June 1983

Dear Ahmedbhai

I certainly did not receive the two letters you mention and it seems that the one I posted to Pollsmoor Prison did not reach you for your niece had notified me of the change of residence. Who do I complain to? The post office here assures me that any letter not delivered is returned to the sender marked "addressee unknown" or whatsoever may be the case.

I was in the Transvaal last month during the course of my mission (I will mention this further in the letter). I went to see your eldest brother in Lens and he has promised me help. However, I asked him if there was some reason why you were not communicating with me and he said that your family was very much disturbed for they too had not heard from you. The authorities kept reassuring them that you were well but there were no letters from you. They were busy renovating their home and I was there for just 30 minutes or so. The family was well.

My mission? I am doing or hope to do so someday – if granted long enough respite by Allah – something on the contribution of Transvaal Indians in South Africa. Knowing of the contribution of the Dabhelians – that's my home village in India – I saw fit to start with them. The Mias, Gardees, Akhalwayas, Surtees, Mintys, Bismillahs, Saloojees, Nanas are all originally Dabhel. I have for quite some years now been corresponding with Moosa Mia (son of Essop Mia who was one of Gandhi's colleagues) and although APOLITICAL the man is so knowledgeable about culture, history etc. that I started off with him (except that I have already much of the Bismillah history from my parents). The contributions of the Mias in the field of commerce, industries, education (you do remember Mia's Farm or Waterval Institute don't you?) has been so massive that they are truly the Barney Barnato, Oppenheimer and Rhodes – Indian version!

Moosa gave two tapes full of information and I will see him again later. However he insisted I meet a few more persons to get away from the Dabhel field and hence my visit to your brother for they were the pioneers in Northern Transvaal and later in Schweizer-Reneke. Your brother mourned over the breaking down of all that they and other Indians had built in S.R. and I mourned the equally tragic demolishment of the Potchefstroom Asiatic Location where in 1886 my grandfather took out his license for a General Merchant trader. The story is sad. Equally sad is your immolation of 19 years and my sympathies and prayers are all I can offer.

Incidentally during the interview with Moosa, Moulana Marghoob's (your uncle's) name cropped up. When the Dabhelians helped erect the Theological College in Dabhel, Moulana Marghoob played an eminent role and his name is among the Board of Trustees when the Trust was drawn (1906).

Your long silence I attributed to disappointment or anger with *Nanima's Chest*. It must appear so ridiculous for one in your situation to see persons like me still dabbling with memories of the past and a culture so far removed from Africa! I am not apologising for this anachronic bit of literature. For me the past makes the present and that together goes to the future, to preserve VALUES. Look, I still want your criticism and while it may hurt I have never lost a friend who gave it well-meaningly.

Our first edition of 25,000 copies of *Indian Delights* was sold out within 10 months. The second impression copies have just begun to arrive from the printer and already 5000 copies have been sold. From the profits of the last edition (55,000 Rand) we gave 20,000 (twenty thousand) to Natal Cripple Care and R5500 to Golden Gate school for handicapped children. From our Trust Fund, 30 university students' academic fees were paid by us (two students at Medunsa Medical College which is a new institution). Allow me this little boast, the girls have worked hard to get so far along without the active help of males!

I am enclosing R16.00 for Eidy. Please try and purchase a copy of *Indian Delights* from CNA (Johannesburg, Durban or Cape Town branches. The address of the Johannesburg Branch is P.O. Box 10799 JHB 2000). This should be enough for the book plus the cost of postage etc. I may have seen Lalita Ahmed's cookery book and will go and see it again, but if you are thinking of ordering, try and obtain *Indian Cook Book* by Charmaine Solomon, Souvenir Press, London. It is the second best on the market, the best of course is... *Indian Delights*. Souvenir Press is negotiating with us for them to print our book and for selling rights, which is a compliment and it just shows how well known we are.

I buy the *Leader* and the *Graphic* occasionally these days. Mohamed used to bring it home regularly and often it left us more angry than anything else. Nowbath is now the editor of *Graphic* and as far as I know he is still Fakir, for no one else has that drinking problem! Despite his shortcomings I have liked him as a person but his history of not quite making it in journalism, law or education has made him cynical and open to influences – and many people use his talents to get their point across!

The film "Gandhi" to start off with made me proud of being an Indian. This colossal bit of work was just three hours of cinematography at its best. The crowd scenes, the philosophy of India were superbly projected. Now, and I am sure you have read all the reviews that I have – the story was not of the Congress movement, nor of India's struggle for independence, nor historically or biographically accurate, and in actual fact all Gandhi's warts and shortcomings and mistakes were not only hidden but shown as beauty spots and achievements. The Congress movement in India was on very sturdy feet by the time Gandhiji came along. Shaukat and Mohamed Ali, and all those early movers who formed Congress are just not there. Jinnah (and I was never an admirer of him) has been portrayed like some cynical and deformed creature – dubious, sly, self-motivated and so forth! After all that in the words of the producer it was a picture of Gandhi and not of Congress and not of history but of Gandhi the man as the producer saw him. Well the producer saw him as a saint and I was happy to be an Indian seeing it and not a Pakistani, nor British!

Jihaan attends a nursery school in Pine Street where madressa plus nursery is combined. The first time I have ever seen a child enjoy the religion part of education. Her Arabic duas are as clear and full of understanding as are her little recitations. Of course, the Apa throws in a bit of Jehannum and scorching fire but it does not seem to have scared her, in fact she shows great pleasure in telling Jaleel that if you use that word (and he knows some words!) God will throw you into the fire! Jaleel and family have rented a cottage at La Mercy Beach so he attends a nursery in that area. His water sketches by far outshine Jihaan's masterly art and it rankles both Jihaan and her mother. Nureen started to walk at 10 months plus (first birthday in March) and has now begun to make two-word sentences. "Car keys" she started saying before she could say daddy and this hurt Nasim so much he actually sulked. They all call me Nanima although I am Dadima to Jaleel and Nureen but this is because Jihaan was first in the field and like monkey see monkey do. They just crawl over Nani and when they are in an impish mood they say "Naan where are you?" I always retort by saying "Naan is at Mullahs or Manjira's café or Naankhataay is in the biscuit tin but if you want me say Nanima". My greatest regret is that Mohamed is not here to enjoy this cream on top of the milk (malaai) or this (Rupiya Noo Viyaj) the interest on our investment. The feeling of being wanted and needed that one's children and grandchildren give you – there is just no other warmth (excepting that maybe of a wife or husband) on earth like that.

This is the month of Ramadaan. After Sehri at 4.30am I normally sit for an hour or two praying, meditating and tilawat of Quran. After that I pick up a pen or start typing. I started this letter at 6.15am and it is now nearly 8am so let me say Ramadaan Mubarak and Eid Mubarak to you. Let me assure you that even if your letter had not reached me yesterday I would still have written to you before Eid as I would have to do for all those relatives and friends of mine who are overseas. May Allah's Grace fill our Lives and thoughts wherever we are. May He continue to give us the strength to retain our principles and to bear our burdens. "Ameen".

With all good wishes,
Zuleikha

A.M. Kathrada
Pollsmoor Maximum Prison
24th July 1983

Dear Zuleikhabehn

I was very pleased to receive your letter of 22nd June; it reached me on 11th July, together with the Eidy, which, incidentally was R18, and not R16 as you state in your letter. I did not receive the earlier letter you posted to Pollsmoor. If you can spare the time I would suggest that you write to the authorities here and ask them about it. They will of course tell you it must have got lost in the post. I must confess I find it very strange that the "inefficiency of the post office" coincided with my arrival here! As you gathered from my folks they too have either not been getting my letters, or getting them many weeks late. Fortunately they now allow me to register my correspondence; but that of course does not solve my incoming mail. Unless it comes registered. This type of thing had happened for many years on Robben Island too, but for the last few years the letters had been reaching – both ways. Except for the occasional one, like the one to you of 10th July. I never thought my letter problem would recur. But there it has. And with a vengeance. Zohra tells me that folks from London have also complained about my "silence". And yet I've been writing. Anyway, enough about letters. Let's just hope things will go better from now.

Do you know what: the day I was transferred from Robben Island, among the things that were given to me were two items that surprised and pleased me. One was a letter from my brother Solly, written to me in 1964! And the other was an Urdu-English dictionary. I can't remember now whether it was you who had sent the dictionary. If it was, my thanks to you. If it wasn't you, it must have been Professor Ramfol of Westville University. In which case

I'll appreciate it if you could phone and tell him about it, and pass my thanks and regards. I am curious to know what items I am still likely to get one day when (and if) I am released!

Let me recap what I had said about *Nanima's Chest*. What I had planned to do was to reproduce the verbal comments made by a young man who was my neighbour on Robben Island. He was simply ecstatic. And I am not exaggerating. His comments were of special significance because he hails from Soweto; he is young, highly intelligent and articulate. His interest in the book surprised me; (I used to tease him that I had thought all he knew about was bombs and guns). In fact I had arranged with him to write out his comments. In addition to that I had given the book to my fellow librarian there, and he circulated it throughout the prison. This also surprised me, as I never thought there would be any interest in a book on Indian women's clothing. I had just begun to get feedback when I was removed. Let me assure you there were no negative comments. Not a single person, no matter what his persuasion, made remarks about discarding past traditions and heritage. My own views are best summed up in a passage by Gandhi, where he says: "I want the culture of all lands to be blown about my house as freely as possible. But I refuse to be blown off my feet by any". My main criterion for judging things of this nature is whether they promote sectionalism. I do not believe *Nanima's Chest* should give any cause for anxiety on this score. My comments are too brief, but unfortunately I cannot do better because of the restriction on the number and length of letters.

I must confess, however, that I do harbour some fears that this type of thing can be overdone, especially if tackled by people whose outlook is narrow; and the consequences can be undesirable. I believe in the promotion of the ideals of a common South African culture; while at the same time allowing "minority cultures" to flourish freely.

This brings me to your project about Transvaal Indians. I assume you will be concentrating on their contributions in the field of business, education, culture, sports etc, and not politics. Having in mind some of the names mentioned, a discussion of their role in the political field can be controversial. On the other hand some of them have made such valuable contributions in other fields that the book won't be poorer if their political life were to be excluded. I hope you won't regard it presumptuous of me if I sound a word of caution. Try not to make too much of the "gaam" aspect; and I hope you will not be confining it to Moslems.

I must congratulate you on the wonderful success of *Indian Delights*. I never imagined the extent of its success, both from the point of view of circulation and revenue. The scholarships and welfare contributions made by your group are truly magnificent. My congratulations to you and the ladies.

I don't think they will allow me to purchase *Indian Delights*. When you wrote to Prison Headquarters in connection with *Nanima's Chest*, did you not include *Indian Delights*? When it was not included with *Nanima's Chest* and the Koran I assumed it had been refused. However, if Colonel Scott happens to come here I shall raise the matter with him. In the meantime, the Eidy will be used for the benefit of our little community – perhaps for Bakri Eid or some such celebration. We will of course remember you with gratitude.

We had a lovely Eid, by way of eats. But the best thing for me was that I was actually able to hold and cuddle a little child, even though it was only for a minute. It is the first time in 20 years that such a thing happened to me and I was beyond myself with excitement. I just couldn't get over it. That little girl really made my Eid. I think I have mentioned to you before that the deprivation one feels most in jail is the absence of children. Now that I think of it this is one of the things I wrote about in my letter of 10ᵗʰ July, which didn't reach you. One of these [days] I'll try and relate the incidents to you – it remains one of my favourite stories. Do keep writing about the antics of Jihaan, Jaleel and Nureen. It makes lovely reading.

I was pleased to hear over the radio today that there has been some rain in Natal. Let's hope it continues.

I notice that there are a whole lot of Indian professors these days: Ali Moosa, Coovadia, Seedat, Bhugwan etc. I'm of course not forgetting Fatima.* It must be a great feeling to be unfettered again. I believe she is going to do something on women, and revise her "patriots".† My fondest wishes to her and family. When did you last see Siko? I hope she is well.

Could you send me the address and the subscription rates for *City Post*. Also tell me if it is worth subscribing to?

This will be all for today. Hope you and all the family are well. Do try and tell me a bit about Bis and Joan. And pass my regards to them.

Best wishes from
AMK

---

\* Meer
† He refers to her *Portrait of Indian South Africans* (1969).

Westville
3630
21st September 1983

Dear Ahmed

It is a relief knowing that the irregularities in your post have been ironed out. I shall still register this letter just in case! It had been my intention to complain to the officer at Pollsmoor but leave a matter overlong and it never gets done. Like the ditty we sang at Madressas "aaj ka kaam kal per na choro".*

Not having learnt to say a simple NO, I am finding it difficult to phase myself out of activities and get to sit down and write, as was Mohamed's and my intention once he retired from his medical work. I did enjoy my week in the Transvaal chalking up interviews with old Pioneers. One Mr. Patel residing on a small farm store near Potgietersrus was on my list and I was told that him being 90 years old I had better hurry. What a sprightly 90 years young old man. I found him writing letters for the society with which he is still involved. How can I then talk of phasing out? The old man was in a spotless white kurta; his trimmed silver beard and neat silver hair was an excellent accessor[y] to his very slightly wrinkled ivory skin. There was a slight stoop but this could be more because of his height rather that his age. Among many varied information on life in the Transvaal he said that he had looked after a shop in Schweizer-Reneke for a year in the 30s. He gave me some information on the Kathradas of whom he spoke very highly but naturally he was critical of Ahmed Kathrada for having chosen an ism rather than Islam – I hope you do not mind my conveying criticism.

---

\* Do not postpone today's work for tomorrow (Don't procrastinate).

I am going to Johannesburg for 10 days in October, ostensibly to promote *Indian Delights* and a masala that I have formulated. This is a paste made of ginger and garlic with all the spices necessary for a good tarkari in it and a tablespoon per kilo of meat gives you a dish like mother used to make. I will of course also do the interview of several families and if in the beginning these are all Dhabelians it is because knowing them makes it so easy for access. Unlike researchers with degrees to back them up I cannot just walk into homes and ask for interviews. This was one of the drawbacks of *Nanima's Chest* – that it is based on clothing that belonged to families whom I know.

Zubeida Barmania [is] daughter of A.I. Kajee's eldest daughter and, of the late A.I. Kajee's progeny, the only one that is extremely talented. She graduated at Aligarh and her classical education and knowledge of Urdu literature is tops. She is also a sitarist and singer of gazals. Zubeida then went to Lebanon and received her masters in Islamic studies from the University of Beirut and thereafter she went on to acquire a LLB from Wits. For some years now she practises Law in Toronto but whenever she comes back home someone or other grabs her for a talk or a ghazal recital. Fatima phoned the other day to say that Zubeida would be singing at her home and I should attend which unfortunately I could not do. I.C. phoned next day to enquire why, since it was the first time after some years that they were entertaining at home. He also conveyed the news of Mr Dadoo's death which he had just received. You will have heard from the media that prayer meetings or other may not be held in and around Durban – this to prevent Dadoo being honoured. Incidentally Abu Hurayra sends his salaams.

When I applied to send you books only the Quran and *Nanima's Chest* was acceptable. *Indian Delights* was returned. Of the dictionary in Urdu I remember having asked Taj Company to send it but I think that too was returned. I still have to ask Dr

Ramfol whether it was his effort that was successful.

Your remark that there are very many professors these days. Well Medical School has a very big quota and of course so does Durban/Westville. But the whole scene has changed from the fifties which you may remember. Every office in the biggest of White owned organisations is now filled with Indian staff – so are banks, laboratories, etc. When I was organising the fete and also when I approached supermarkets for the handling of the masala (gorima's magimasala) inevitably I had to speak to the P.R.O. or the head buyer or the manager and these were all Indians. This is of course the Durban scene but I believe that Johannesburg etc too is catching on fast. The last secretary of the head CNA branch in Johannesburg who phoned to enquire about a composite account for various store branches was a Mrs. Pillay. Superintendent of Stanger hospital is Dr Fatima Motala.

Jaleel is only four and much too young for a BMX bike – "You know, like the one ET was given a ride on" he said, when he requested one for his birthday. But Jaleel has so much energy and ability sportswise (you know his father used to play professional soccer and only gave it up when he broke his leg in the $5^{th}$ year of his studies) that I bought him one. Whereas Jehaan still has to use the two small side wheels of her two wheeled cycle, Jaleel drives merrily up and down the driveway on his BMX. There has been one nasty fall but thank God nothing broken. Naseem likes outdoor life so has moved out to La Mercy and is renting a cottage at the beach. On his plot he has chicks, rabbits, bantams, 4 dogs, a cat and three horses which friends stable there. My whole family are excellent horsemen. The first thing Mohamed taught me was to ride a horse and he used to be very annoyed when my horse won a race on the sands of Brighton Beach where we had a cottage. The other day when Naseem was on holiday he took Jaleel to school (nursery) on horseback. The little fellow was greatly disappointed for he arrived too early and his colleagues had not witnessed the state [of] arrival.

I am not sure if you are familiar with Durban. I keep on mentioning areas and people and it may all be Dutch to you.

With Salaams,
Zuleikha

A.M. Kathrada
Pollsmoor Maximum Prison
Private Bag x4
7966
16th October 1983

Dear Zuleikhabehn

Thanks for your letter of 21st September, which reached me on the 4th Oct. I think it's still early days to say that my correspondence problems have been ironed out. My outgoing letters do reach, because I register them all. But I can't be too sure about the incoming. I can just hope that things will run smoothly.

By the time this reaches you, you will have returned from the Transvaal, hopefully loaded with a wealth of material for your new book; and lots of orders for your new masala. I read in the papers, and also heard over the air that you'd been giving demonstrations in the art of preparing Indian dishes, at the Shades of the East Trade Fair. There have been no reports so far about the success, or otherwise, of the fair itself. By all accounts there were massive preparations. Was it an entirely commercial venture, or was it in aid of some charity?

Your meeting with 90-year-old Mr. Patel must have been most interesting. It must have been the first time in all his years that he is interviewed by an Indian woman author! I don't know him at all. But I can remember my father speaking about his friend Rasool (Patel??) who had settled somewhere near Pietersburg. Could it be the same man? I am looking forward to the book, for I feel sure, among other things I shall learn a lot about my own father; and his friends and contemporaries. I may have mentioned to you how ashamed I am of my ignorance about my father and his generation. You will be helping to fill a huge gap in my knowledge. And I'm sure I'm not the only one in this position.

I realise that my comments on *Nanima's Chest* were not only insubstantial but couldn't have been much use to you. I did try to explain the danger of making comments when one is restricted in length and content, of such works. I do, however, hope that I did not offend you in any way.

I was so pleased to hear about Bis and Joan, and the children. I had no idea that he was the father of 4 kids. When next you write please pass my fondest regards to them. Have you already visited them? Canada must be having the second largest settlement of South African Blacks, after England?

I have a vague idea that I briefly met Mrs. Barmania – way back in 1963. It was at the office of Advocate Mohamed. I wonder if I am correct. I never realised she was such a talented person. The musical session at I.C.'s place brings to mind the late Doctor Dadoo. As you probably know he was a great lover of such sessions, and would have enjoyed them tremendously. His death has been a great blow. I wish I could describe to you what he meant to me. He was father, brother, guardian, colleague, mentor, confidante – and much more. In the same week two other persons died, to whom also I was quite close – Rev. Michael Scott and Advocate Berrange. I should so much like to pay my own tribute to them (and to many others) as I knew them. If ever I get a chance one day to implement a project I've been harping on for some years now, I shall use the opportunity to say a lot about them. I'm sure I couldn't have missed mentioning the project to you. It will be a book based on Flat 13, Kholvad House and in it I hope to write about the scores and scores of interesting people, of all walks of life, who have either lived there, visited, or passed through. When I think of it, even I get surprised at the wealth of information that can be encompassed in such a work. For the present my plans will have to remain a distant dream. The climax to my story would have been in 1962-63, when I was placed under house arrest, thus putting an end, officially, to visitors. At that time I was living alone, and even my mother could not visit me. Unofficially, the visitors continued of course. In my next letter I must tell you about the little kids who used to bring me food when I was under house arrest. Incidentally on 22$^{nd}$ Oct it will be 21 years since the house arrest orders were imposed upon me by the late Mr B.J. Vorster!

This will be all for today. Do you know what bit of information surprised me most in your last letter? The news about having been a horse rider! A Moslem woman of my generation riding a horse! I just couldn't imagine it. One never stops learning.

All the best to you and the children. Also to Abu Huraira and family and the Mjis, ie all three of them. I didn't know which one you referred to.

From
    AMK

Westville 3630
21st November 1983

Dear Ahmed Bhai

My friends who accompanied me to the Transvaal were overwhelmed at the hospitality of our people. Durban has a reputation of snobbishness as well as a tinge of superiority complex. Something of the nature that we gaam people always alleged against the Kholvad crowd.

The families that I visited in between other commitments – well some of them – were people whom I knew of through the anecdotes my parents had narrated in childhood years. Some of these families had no connection or rather had lost contact with the Bismillahs for some decades and yet when I went in unannounced, they had no difficulty in determining whose daughter I was and they just swept me off my feet with their love and warmth. May I just tell you of one old lady who was not even on my list.

I stayed with Ismail Mayat (S.A.I.C retired) and family in Ophirton. I was surprised that despite the Group Areas there were some 70 families still in the area and Mrs. Mayat then named some of the families. When she mentioned the Durveish family my mind started flashing stories of Maulana Durveish who was one of the persons instrumental in establishing Dabhel Darul Uloom (Theological College) and who was among the very early Maulanas in Johannesburg. I asked that Ishmail Bhai drop me off at their shop two streets away. On entering I salaamed and told the elderly woman (my age) who was in the shop with her husband that my name was Zuleikha Mayat and immediately she responded – Oh Amina Khala's daughter. Do you see how our community keeps contact? We had never met each other but she knew where my mother's children had married.

On explaining my mission she said "my mother in law stays with the Maulana's son behind the Newtown Mosque but no problem we will take you there". Both husband and wife then took me on a busy shop day to their mother. Old Granny Durveish is, according to the son, 96 but the old mother calculating by the Islamic calendar says that she has turned 100. Very active she was wiping the table in the kitchen when we arrived, hearing and eyesight as keen as her mental alertness. As for memory she started raconteuring of days gone by as if events had happened yesterday.

She filled in missing gaps of Dabhel, of life in Johannesburg, of the drop in ethical and moral standards among all groups of people. I enquired about the strange name Durveish and she chuckled. "Ha", she said: the name is really Pandor but when he (referring to late husband) was young and the family was poor, he and two friends ran away in search of learning. They made their way from Madressa to Madressa till eventually they arrived in Deoband. You do know, Ahmed, that in the Islamic system a scholar was never accepted at an institution on account of the fees he could pay. Rather the candidate had to prove to one of the ustads that he was mentally capable and determined to improve that faculty. If convinced, the question of fees and lodge never came up. You were taken on as a disciple of so and so.

In this manner all three boys from far away Gujarat obtained their sanads (degrees) from Deoband and returned home. Coincidentally all three young men had Ahmed for their first names and in order to identify them the college came up with nicknames. The one with the most pious bearing and flowing beard became Maulana Buzrug, the second who was a sternly Righteous person (ask my late brother Abdul Hay and he would testify that his sternness bordered on cruelty) became Maulana Bhagat and the one who was inclined to give away even his own shoes to the beggar who accosted him became Maulana Durveish – "Child, said Granny, "He never came home for meals without dragging someone along with him to share it."

What a lovely story. Truth is stranger than fiction someone has said: I am about to scream with frustration for I want to get started with my fictionalised history or whatever it is called but how to phase myself out of activities and involvement...*

At the moment I am working with young persons who are trying to start a private school. Children of nearly all our so called leaders (and so many of professional people's children) are now attending private White schools. I should not talk for we sent our son Aslam to Waterford in Swaziland. The proposed private school will be for all that can pay the fees and Islamics will be part of the curriculum. African neo-converts are with great difficulty being accommodated in Indian Govt schools so perhaps this school will help in that area.

To the contrary your comments on *Nanima's Chest* were highly satisfying to me.

I forgot the Johannesburg trip had a sad ending. One of my colleagues – Amina Moosa – a member of the Group for 22 years suddenly collapsed and died. I thought my own experiences of traumatic deaths had inured me but each death has its own poignancy especially when that human life could have contributed so much more to its environment. Amina served humanity as well as our circumstances here permit. And she will be able to meet her Maker with a clear conscience.

Behind every man there is a woman, so often we hear that. Behind me was Mohamed Mayat who really taught this country bumpkin everything he knew and he, unlike most of our society,

---

* A part of Mayat's research is now published as *A Treasure Trove of Memories: A Reflection on the Experiences of the Peoples of Potchefstroom.* Durban: Madiba Publishers, 1996.

allowed me full expression for whatever talents I may have had. When I refused to learn swimming he built a pool with no shallow end and together with the children I was forced to take up the challenge and show that I had overcome my fear of water. Horse riding was so much of our life that my son Nasim lives out at La Mercy where on his plot there are 3 horses of friends. He has the pleasure of looking after them and teaching his wife and children to ride. Jaleel, just turned four, was taken to nursery school on horseback one day and to [the] utter disappointment of Jaleel he was too early and very few of his friends saw him arrive in so stately a fashion.

If the lady you saw in Adv. Mahomed's office was rotund, short and jolly then it was Zubeida's mother, but if she was petite, vivacious and thin then it is the lady herself and there was a story going around of a marriage in those regions, but never got off the ground. May I relate a lovely bit of gossip. At Fatima's home a musical recital was arranged for Zubeida on one of her visits. The Barmania's had invited some of their friends as well and among them was advocate Saheb. Many of the ghazala were aimed at him and the last one left none of us in doubt on that score. Zubeida ended her repertoire with Ghalib's famous "Jo Wayeda kiya tha Nibhana parega". "The promise made will have to be taken care of". Which brings me to Flat 13 Kholvad House. It was associated with another of Ghalibs couplets "Jub muft haath aye to is me boora kiya". (If it comes of its free choice into your hands who are we to complain – this is a loose translation but more in keeping with intention than an accurate literal translation.) Maybe you can add this to your book. My brother Abdulhak was naughty enough to relate that bit!

Somehow they all came to Potch. The Cachalias, the Rev. Scott, Pahads and so on. Dr Dadoo never made it there but once when he was visiting the Meers he came with them to a dinner at our home in Durban. Besides dinner we had laid on some Indian dancing by P. R. Singh and party and rendering of ghazala by Maya Devi and you know how Dadoo enjoyed Quawwalis etc. What I also remember was that though he enjoyed the pigeon biryani, he just drank jugsful of dahi* saying that in prison he came to love it.

Rasool Patel is your father's friend. Oh yes in Johannesburg I also looked up Choti Khala Bhayad, now living alone at Zohra Mansions. Bedridden and with her son and family in Canada she looked depressed. News of Dadoo's death had just reached her so that may have added to her depression. I was always in awe of Choti Khala.

As for Indian participation in 3 tier Govt; a foregone conclusion. That quality of leadership that can take a people to great heights is no longer around.

Let me end here for I am not sure whether my letters are allowed.

Salaams,
Zuleikha

---

* Spiced yoghurt

Pollsmoor Maximum Prison
Private Bag x4
Tokai
7966
11th December 1983

Dear Zuleikhabehn

What a delight to read your letter of 21st November, which reached me on 5th December! Your observations about some of the community's senior citizens; about Transvaal hospitality; about Bis, and Ghalib's couplet; about Deoband university, etc revived many old memories and experiences. And, as prisoners through the ages have been wont to do, I revelled in a veritable orgy of nostalgia. Needless to say, no schoolwork was possible that night; the mind simply rebelled, and books, pen and paper had to be tossed aside, making way for a few hours of bliss. How I longed to talk to somebody about it all, somebody with whom I could relive the days that have gone by. Why don't I turn to my colleagues, you may ask. After all I know some of them since the mid forties. True. And, jail being a great leveller, there should be no problems. However, many will be surprised to know that there are one or two things that jail does not level out. Chief among these is the generation gap. When I want to give over to nostalgia and reminiscence I want to be free from inhibitions or any form of constraint. This, to me is only possible when I am with friends of my age group. We do often talk about the old times with my colleagues here. But when it comes to certain experiences, especially some youthful indiscretions and the like, the age barrier immediately intervenes, and conversations have to be trimmed accordingly. Are you surprised? I don't suppose you are. If I may venture a possible explanation for my predicament I would suggest it has something to do with the essentially peasant backgrounds from which my colleagues and I hail. The young people may say that we are not yet fully liberated from "old fashioned" customs, traditions and values. That may very well be. But I personally would want to cling to <u>many</u> allegedly "old fashioned" practices and values in preference to some of the things we get in the name of "modernity". Please note that I have underlined "many", for I don't want to give the impression of being puritanical or an old fashioned prude. Or a "square", as the young people of a decade ago would have said. But I do deprecate the withering away of many good old ways and habits in the face of urbanisation and westernisation.

The need, and perhaps inordinate desire, to recall old times is of course a form of escapism. Anything to get away from present burdens and deprivations. What can be easier than to talk about the past, and speculate about the future!

I shouldn't give you the impression that there were no reminiscences that I could share with my colleagues. In fact there was quite a bit. It was good to hear that the traditional Transvaal hospitality still prevails, and sad about Natal's snobbishness. It was great to hear about old Chotikhala Bhayat, or "Ouma", as we affectionately knew her. I can understand her depression, with so many of her family and friends, either dead or settled far away. I often wonder why she chooses to stay on at the flat. I remember the names of the three Maulanas – Buzrug, Bhagat and Durveish. I should have known Maulana Durveish personally and have been trying to picture him. But I've been unsuccessful. I know the house and can remember he had at least one son. My memory stops there. Deoband University I can remember, but am no longer certain whether it is in India or Pakistan. Weren't Moulvis Saloogee and Cachalia also products of Deoband? Ismail Mayet and I were at school at the same time but already since those days we had been treading along different paths. He is also known to a colleague of mine, who, much to my surprise, had actually been to Ismail's house! I didn't think such a thing was possible. Ismail's great friend used to be Moosa Mia's younger brother Mohamed. I wonder where he is. I suppose one of these days Ismail will be an MP, or rather, an MD! Although we did not see eye to eye we never quarrelled.

During the 20 years in jail I've always found December a rather difficult month to get through. This is because it is festive time, and we're right in Cape Town, but cannot join the festivities. You may remember that my very first visit to Cape Town was in December 1948, with Bis, Cas and Hoosein, all 3 medical students. Enver had already qualified as a doctor and came along in his Cadillac. We had a most wonderful time, and made quite a few friends. I've been back many times since. I can agree with a friend who has travelled the world many times, that there is no place to beat Cape Town for hospitality and warmth. This line you quote from Ghalib, I don't know in what context Bis related the story, (or stories) to you. But, with our pitifully small repertoire of Urdu poetry, this particular couplet was used over and over again. On our Cape Town trip it was recited many times. Some occasions we can look back to with amusement, while there may be one or two we'd rather forget. Coincidentally the word Durweish features in the line just before the one you quoted. Do you remember it? If I'm not sure Abu Huraira will remember it. If I'm not mistaken we originally learnt the verse from one of the two Yusufs.[*]

I suppose music lovers will have flocked in their thousands to Swaziland to the Lata Mangeshkar show. Will you be going? I notice Peter Tosh will also be performing there soon. I was wondering if, given the choice, which of the two I'd opt for. I think

---

[*] Mayat sketched out lines from this Urdu verse, and a rough translation, at the bottom of this letter from Kathrada. See plate.

I'd go for Peter Tosh!

My sympathies to you on the death of your colleague Mrs Moosa. I can imagine how hard it must have been for you. Did she die in Jo'burg? On 5th November I also received some bad news. My second eldest brother, Ismail, died after a heart attack. It came to me as a shock, as we are generally a healthy family.

This will be all for today. I hope you will have enough material by now to start writing your book. So many old veterans have already passed away, and no one has written anything about them. I'm thinking of the late Nagdeechacha, the two Saloogee brothers, Dr Moosa Patel's father, old Essakgeechacha, Fakirbhai, Suliman Jada etc etc. There are many more.

I noticed that "Person Mayat" and "Person Ntombela" were mentioned in the Fakir column. I assume he is referring to you. Not knowing the background to the story I cannot comment.

My health continues to be fine. I hope the same goes for you and all the family. I'll be writing exams in January.

Keep well. Fondest regards to you and all the folks

from
AMK

Westville 3630
13th June 1984

Dear Ahmed

I may have to register your letters again since I haven't received a reply to my last one. That way at least I will know that the mail has reached you. Or did I upset you with all my religious fervour? It's the <u>in</u> thing you know. There are the <u>born again</u> people and their equivalent in the Tableegh Jamaat among us.

Ramadaan is child's play this year. Sehri is around 5am and breaking fast at 5pm and since it is not so cold in Durban one hardly feels discomfited. I am enclosing Eidy for you herewith. I am not sure what you may be allowed to buy or not buy but I do wish you Eid Mubarak.

With your transfer to Tokai, people around here were expecting a release order. Especially with all the Release Mandela campaigns, is there no chance?

Did I tell you that Jihaan has a baby sister (2 months) named Humayra? There is a russet feathered bird among the Arabian specie named Humayra and Bibi Ayesha* was nicknamed Humayra. However our Humayra has brownish hair like Jihaan so her only hope is to sing as sweetly as the bird (which is another one of its qualities) in order to live up to the name. Big sister dotes on baby and helps look after her. Jihaan finishes her first sipara† at the nursery-cum madressa she attends and she insists that her nanima hand out sinni to all her classmates. I am sure you remember the naan khataays or julebis that used to be given at Madressa when children finished their Quran. Well the new generation want to

---

\* Wife of the Prophet
† First of the thirty parts of the Quran

hand out at end of siparas as well.‡

Nureen "can sit all by myself" on their horse and is insisting that daddy put on side wheels on Jaleel's old two wheel bike so that she can chase her brother around. Something has gone wrong with the line spacer of the type writer and I have to remember to turn the thing manually.

We live in most violent times. A friend who lives just a street away from us was murdered in her home in the evening. Her husband had just gone to the Mosque and when he returned it was to a wife that was dead and a house burgled. Burglar alarm and security services are doing a roaring trade these days.

I went to give Paulina (my late sister's housekeeper who had been pensioned off a few years before Bibi died but who still lives on the premises) her Eid parcel. When she saw the jersey she said Thank you in her nicest Zulu "but the blanket you gave me is 5 years old and there is no warmth in it any longer". You know, one wants to creep behind a bush when you hear an old 80 year old faithful to have to tell one that you have been neglecting her. She is no longer mobile and I with the car cannot look her up to give her even such eventful news as the birth of Humayra.

With Salaams,
ZM Mayat

---

‡ It is traditional to hand out something sweet after completing all 30 parts. Now, Mayat points out, the kids want to get something after each part.

A. M. Kathrada
Pollsmoor Maximum Prison
Tokai 7966
8th July 1984

Dear Zuleikhabehn

Thank you very much for your letter of 26th June, and the Eid card, both of which reached me on 4th July. When I didn't get a reply to my letter of 11th December I began to suspect if there wasn't going to be a repetition of our experience before we started registering our letters. My suspicions have proved right, much to my distress. You know one feels so helpless and frustrated because one knows beforehand what the answer to any enquiries will be. As in the past when your, and other letters went astray, I was told this morning that no letter from you had arrived. And I'm afraid there is nothing more I can do about it from my end. I believe you will receive a similar answer from the Commanding Officer. So it seems the only way to ensure that our letters do reach is to register.

By the time this letter reaches I suppose the parcel of mithai will be back with you once more. I was told this morning that the parcel had been returned unopened. I feel very sorry about this, and am partly guilty for not warning you beforehand that they do not accept food parcels from outside. Let me elaborate a bit. Both on Robben Island and here, Moslem prisoners have been receiving Eid parcels from the Moslem Prison Welfare Organisation in Cape Town. For the 1983 and 1984 Eids that I spent at Pollsmoor, applications were made from outside for special parcels for me, which were kindly granted by the Commanding Officer. This time, Shenaaz (Behn's daughter)* made the arrangements, and

---

\* That is, Fatima Meer's daughter.

this resulted, (as I've just been telling her in a letter) in a "total onslaught" on the part of the Meer family – with us at the receiving end. But it was a different kind of onslaught – a most delicious and welcome one. We had Biryani, and chicken, samoosas, papad, roti, kabab, soji, mithai, meat pies etc. We ate for 2 days! Some of the food was cooked by Shenaaz, and Dr Ayesha Arnold, the rest came by airfreight from Behn and Rashida in Durban. Apart from the quantity, quality and variety, the fact that it came from such close friends, made this the most memorable and enjoyable Eid that we've had in jail. I don't suppose the authorities bargained for such a quantity, and for allowing it in they are to be thanked. I must not forget to thank you for your kind thought; I'm sure we would have really enjoyed the goodies.

Let me complete the story of Eid. I'm sure you've heard of the Babla Saloojee who died such a cruel death in 1964.[†] He stayed at the flat for many years, and I regarded him as my little brother. His widow, Rokeya, came to visit me on the day after Eid, and she brought along a whole turkey and a pot of biryani. But this too was turned down. To think of the trouble she took. She went all the way to Klerksdorp, where she has a brother, to get the Turkey. And then she flew with it to Cape Town, only to be disappointed. At least in her case I was allowed to get the visit. With Shenaaz and her mother I was told their visits would not be allowed.

To get back to your "lost" letter. When I recall some of the

---

† The official version was that Suliman 'Babla' Saloojee committed suicide by jumping from the sixth floor of Greys Building and landing on a parapet. Dr Mohammed Moosa Moolla, a longtime friend of Balbla told a Human Rights Commission in Dar Es Salaam in June 1967 that Babla did not display any suicidal tendencies. Given the torture of prisoners like Mac Maharaj and himself around that time, he came to the conclusion that he was killed by the police and his body thrown out of the window as a cover-up story. The first question posed to Dr. Moolla upon his arrest was 'Where is your friend Kathrada?', who was on the run.

things I said in my letter of 11th December I'm sure your replies and comments would have been most interesting. As I've told you before, your letters are generally very informative, and I feel quite bad when they go astray.

I had a letter recently from Dr Karim (of Bethal), who told me that you two had shared a platform at a Moslem Youth Conference. I saw a photo of yours in either the *Leader* or *Graphic*, which I think was taken at the same conference. Incidentally do you know who writes the Sadiq Ali column in *Graphic*? He seems to be carrying a huge chip on his shoulder. I just can't imagine why people buy the *Graphic*, or the *Leader*, for that matter. Surely there is room for a high quality newspaper catering for the same readership?

My congratulations to Humayra's parents – and of course to Nanima. I'm sure Jihaan must be fussing over her sister. Reminds me; a few months ago a visitor brought along her little daughter, Shameez, who is two years old. It was one of the nicest visits I've had. Although we were separated by a glass panel, that was the first time in 21 years that I was so near a child for such a long time. And Shameez is very lively and talkative; she talked endlessly, danced, sang and generally performed for my benefit. It was a thrilling experience. Within minutes of the visit she pointed to a warder and said "police". She followed this up later by saying "I don't like police". I thought to myself "well, here is a left-wing radical in the making". As I was about to warm up to the subject Shameez made a complete about-turn and declared "I don't like Papa" (that was me!), "I don't like Mama", "I don't like police". However, she finished the visit on a happier note.

I'm sure you must be very busy with preparations for the wedding. My congratulations to the couple. If Joan and Bis are present please pass my fondest regards to them; and their children and friends in Canada.

This will be the lot for today. Things are much the same.

Luckily we have our studies, newspapers and radio, and of course visits and letters, which all contribute towards preserving our general wellbeing. Otherwise we'd be utterly bored with this type of existence.

Keep well. Everything of the best to you and all the family, and friends from

AMK

P.S. 9th July 6:40am

I'm just listening to Radio Today. Right now there is an interview with Professor Yacoob Seedat, who has returned from Finland. He seems to be quite a top man in his field. Did you know he also passed through Flat 13? It was nice to hear him.

15th July 1984

Dear Ahmed

To our great regret a parcel of mithai (as Eidy) sent for you accompanied by the enclosed card was returned with a note "Gevangenis nie geregtelik om pakkie te ontvang nie!"*

Yesterday (Saturday) Shireen Dlo chota motala married Fuad Soomar and at the reception in P.M.burg† virtually everyone you can think of was there. Young couple both committed persons. At reception Hassan Mall asked about the welfare of my family, then enquired how many grandchildren? My reply "four at the moment but InshaAlla 6 by September". He wanted to know how that was possible and I said that all three units of the Mayat Family are producing – Razia delivered Humayra in March and daughters-in-law Nadya and Shameema are expecting in September. Grandchildren make you feel young not old!

A nephew from Canada currently staying with me gets married at end of month. This week my mother, aged 86, arrives with the first batch from Potch and slowly friends and relatives will trickle in – I pray all goes well.

Salaaams,
    Zuleikha

[enclosed card:]

Jaleel, Jihaan, Nureen and Humayra hope that you will enjoy the home-made mithai and they do pray that it will reach you safely

---

\* "Prisoner not entitled to receive parcel"
† Pietermaritzburg

without much hassle. It seems that my last letter did not reach you and I will have to register all my post to you again. With all the best that Eid can bring,

    Zuleikha

Westville 3630
29th August 1984

Dear Ahmedbhai

It's back to typed, duplicated and of course registered letters to you even though the postal clerk gives me a sharp look when she notes the address. For your information we get served at the same counter with Whites since Westville is one of the forward areas. Incidentally your letter dated 8th July, censored on the 11th, only reached me near end of July when I was in the midst of wedding arrangements.

To remind you of what our weddings are still like – being the hostess for the groom's party (Jaan wallahs) naturally the entire Bismillah clan landed at my doorstep – some as early as two weeks before the wedding for some had come from Montreal, Toronto and Fergus in Canada. Bis and family could not make it. Two days before the wedding houseguests numbered 40 plus and so Nasim in La Mercy and friends and neighbours helped out with sleeping accommodation but they all had to be fed and taken around. Mildred our housekeeper is so good that everyone raved over the variety at breakfast time and the salads that she concocted. In between looking after guests I had to arrange functions where Bismillah clan could meet Kajee clan, and then later exchange of gifts etc.

All this was time consuming work. Why do I do it when all my life I had protested at the waste of time and money for such functions? One of my reasons [was] to impress the Canadian teenagers that here was a Way of Life that has something to offer. The indifference of the Western Way of Life may be cheaper on the pocket and emotions but it can never compensate for the love, care and concern which our Way of Life has to offer. Also, after Bis' departure for Canada and later another sister to Dublin, there was no opportunity for my mother's brood to collect together. At the ripe old age of 86 she had her great grandchildren from Montreal, Toronto, Johannesburg, Potch, Potgietersrus and us Durban wallahs all under one roof. The last time we tried such a reunion it ended in the death of my sister Bibi and Mohamed. This really was the only way to say thank you to an old lady with great principles and a lifetime's service for not only her family and her community, but Chinese, Coloureds, Africans and Whites. They all came to her for advice, help and succour in times of need. All done in the soft self-effacing way of modest Muslim women.

To answer some of your questions. Sadiq Ali of the *Graphic* is none other than brother Pat Poovalingham at one time your cell mate in the 60s (so he informed us over S.A.T.V. last night when he won the Reservoir Hill seat for Solidarity). Pat the self-made man who early in life came under the wing of Paul Sykes of FOSA fame, and who rose from humble beginnings to President's Council Fame and now Tri-cameral Parliament will understandably have a chip on his shoulder.*

For years Mohamed and I tried to get a high quality paper off the ground. The demands put by interested parties put me off.

---

* The South African parliament was modified in 1984 to give limited political voice to Coloureds and Indians while Whites retained political power in the Tricameral Parliament. Africans were excluded from the new structure. The Indian chamber, or "House of Delegates", consisted of 45 members, and had control over education, social welfare, housing, local government, arts, culture and recreation as they affected Indians. The August 1984 election was opposed strongly by the United Democratic Front (UDF), an umbrella organisation of community organisations and trade unions formed to coordinate the boycott of the election. The House of Delegates election consequently had a very low voter turnout, around 16%, leading to a credibility crisis.

The Muslim sponsors wanted it to be a pro-Muslim sort of paper but we have already some of that type of papers around and they are read by Muslims only. The business class sponsors wanted it to steer clear of all political affiliations – and what sort of paper would that be? – so that was off. After Mohamed's death I was approached again by a few merchants to be part of an editorial team but even though I got along well with people I felt that the personalities would have a hard time rubbing shoulders together. Anyway, the feelers they put out were very vague and I had the feeling that they would never come forth with the money. So we buy [the] *Graphic* paper out of habit if nothing else!

Professor Yakoob Seedat is married to a niece of my husband. I don't think that Flat 13 rubbed off on him though – completely apolitical. Has two sons in a private school (White) and even in their primary standards are showing signs of brilliance. Yakoob has risen far in the medical field and was in the running for dean at Medical School, but was beaten at the post by [a] female. Ahmed we live in a difficult world. When the medical school was founded and Mahomed was one of the early lecturers there, a world of criticism was launched calling him sell out and that sort of thing, that is after a band of them struggled hard to get a private university off the ground. Lack of resources and expertise prevented that at the time. However today medical school is staffed by very forward looking persons such as Jerry Coovadia etc.

We have just seen the farcical poll come to an end with a band of persons (not all of them) from whom one would not buy a second hand car! One gentleman who broke the record with one vote as his total score has two wives and many married children, and his extended family could have easily won him a hundred votes for they all live in his constituency. Some candidates did not have the deposit money but they saw the fat carrot of a salary so they tried to raise loans against that. Another went around promising ten rand notes to those who voted for him – that is if he proved successful. Our boycott has proved very successful but we have landed with a sorry bunch of delegates for the Indian house.

My youngest daughter in law is in hospital awaiting the birth of her first child. I was with her all night and as soon as this letter is over and posted I will be back with her. There seems to be a little complication – will you pray for her and the unborn child?

No, I must add this, in case you have not been informed. Fatima and Ismail left for Haj. Eventually the authorities relented and gave Ismail a passport. Bakri Eid is on Thursday so let me bid you and your friends a Blessed Eid.

With Salaams
Zuleikha

M. Kathrada
Pollsmoor Maximum Prison
Private Bag x4
Tokai
7966
9th September 1984

Dear Zuleikhabehn

Thanks a lot for your letter of 15th, which reached me on 23rd July, together with the card on behalf of Jaleel, Jihaan, Nureen and Humayra. How lovely it would have been had they allowed the accompanying parcel of mithai – instead of returning it all the way to Durban. I wonder if the powers that be ever become aware of the effects of these little hurts. One would imagine that after 21 years in jail there'd be a radical relaxation in the rules and regulations that govern our lives, so that there would be as few deprivations as possible. But, unluckily, it does not appear as if there are any changes in the offing – not for the foreseeable future at least. I must thank you and the children again for your kind thoughts.

I wrote to you on the 8th July, and deliberately delayed this reply thinking that you would write first. Even as I write I am two-minded about posting this letter because I have a feeling that a letter from you is on the way. In my "old fashioned" way of thinking the "ladies first" rule still applies! The other thing that makes me hesitate is that due to circumstances including the lack of adequate planning, I've got myself into a bit of difficulty with my quota. You are aware, I take it, that we are only allowed a fixed number of letters and visits a year. If our letters cross, it is possible that I may only be able to write to you again at the beginning of 1985. But I will let you know via my niece, Zohra. I'm sure you will appreciate my position. I must try to ensure that I plan my correspondence better in the coming year. If you have not yet written I will of course still be able to receive one letter from you before the end of the year. No need to tell you how very welcome your letters are – they're always interesting and informative.

Shenaaz also mentioned Shireen's wedding in PMBurg. By all accounts it must have been a very nice affair. My only memory of Shireen is of a very sweet and pretty little girl of about 4 or 5. With the recent relaxation I've been able to have a number of visits from young adults whom I had last seen as little kids. At times I could just gaze at them in wonder; my mind simply refusing to accept that they were no longer the kids I knew. It was quite an experience. I've often been trying to picture Shireen as she would be today. But my mind keeps harking back to 1962. I suppose somewhere deep inside me there must be a hidden wish that somehow time should have stood still, so that I could one day see the kids again just as they were when I was jailed.

I hope by the time this letter reaches, you will have recovered from the exhaustion resulting from the recent big events in the family, namely the wedding of the 27$^{th}$ July, and the two new additions. I can imagine how very busy you must have been. But I suppose after everything is over, one is left with an overall feeling of satisfaction and joy. My congratulations to Nadya and Shamima, and their spouses.

A couple of months ago I heard Prof. Abdul Mitha on the radio. He was described as President of the Cardiac Society of S.A. Must be quite a top man in his field. Do you know him? I've also been reading about Prof. Ali Moosa, on malnutrition. There certainly seems to be a proliferation of professors!

You remember you once wrote about the Arabic Islamic Review? I've got 4 copies. I've only managed to page through them; there seems to be some interesting articles.

This will be the lot for today. Hope your mother is keeping well. Fondest regards to her, to you and to all family and friends from

**AMK**

7th January 1985

My dear Ahmedbhai

Having eaten into your quota of letters in 1984, I delayed my replying to your last one. Taking stock of the past year I find that once again I have frittered away valuable time and this I can now ill afford. Trouble is over-planning and not getting to grips with what has to be done and also my inability to say NO! Societies, family, friends – they all think this old aunty has lots of time and leisure and a relative passed the remark the other day when she saw a grandchild on my lap "How lovely for you, time passes so quickly with them". Sure, time does pass and I cherish every moment when I am with my grandchildren (score is now six, the latest addition being Javed, brother of Jaleel and Nureen, and Dilshad, only child of Aslam and Shameema) but these are precious moments taken from essential work that remains to be done.

[text removed by censors]

Fatima's brother Dr Ahmed Meer is married to a Foi Bhen of mine. Their daughter (a teacher) married a lecturer in History at Uni. Durban/Westville. All the Meers, Motalas, Bismillahs were there. I.C. and his brother A.C. are now the two senior Meer males for the older generation is gone. In your last letter you asked me about Dr Mitha the cardiac man. Yes I do know him for in our increasing yet small Community we tend to know or know about each other. The Medical school is full of Indian Professors and lecturers, and these are very able persons. Addington Hospital some twenty years ago opened its doors to two non-white doctors (term in usage at that time) to treat its Coloured patients and my husband happened to be one of them. The first week he was called by the Superintendent and told that it would be better if he used the side entrance. Mohamed walked out of course never to return. These days Prof Seedat's in charge of the renal unit at Addington and it treats them all, not only the Coloured patients. My niece-in-law is a clinical psychologist at Addington so you can see how things are changing.

[text removed by censors]

With best wishes for the new year,
    Zuleikha

A.M. Kathrada
Pollsmoor Maximum Prison
Tokai
7966
23rd February 198[5]

Dear Zuleikhabehn

Your letter reached me on 17th January already, while I was in the midst of exam preparations. But that is not the reason for my failure to reply earlier, as I completed my last paper exactly a month ago, ie on 23rd January. The problem is that with your letter we experienced the recurrence of something we thought we had seen the last of in the early seventies, namely the mutilation of letters in the name of censorship. I was given only two strips of your letters – the opening paragraph, plus the lines dealing with the marriage of Dr Ahmed Meer, and the bit about the Addington Hospital. The rest, I was told, is considered to be undesirable! I have been trying to get some idea of what it is that you have suddenly written to warrant such a Draconian step; but unfortunately I have not been successful. I went to the extent of submitting some of your previous letters to the new officer in charge of censorship to give him an idea of the type of matters we have been allowed to discuss in our ongoing correspondence. About the only bits of "politics" in your letters were a few lines on the Indian "elections" and Pat Poovalingam saying something about me on TV. But I'm told that what has been cut out is much worse! Naturally I find such an allegation unacceptable. I am surprised, upset, disappointed and frustrated. There is just about nothing more I can do about it. I even showed the ravaged letter to Lord Bethel in the presence of senior officers. (You may have noticed that Lord Bethel mentioned it in his article). But it has made no impact. One shudders when one tries to comprehend the mentality which can perpetuate such a wanton act without any qualms. It is only a short step away from book burning!

Since I am unable to tell you what sort of things are considered to be objectionable I suggest that you keep on writing about the type of things we have been discussing all these years. After all, they have found nothing wrong in the samples of your letters which I submitted.

Before I forget about Pat Poovalingam, let me just make a slight correction. It is true that we were in jail together; but it was in 1946, and not 1960. I must say I was surprised that he spoke publicly about it; I thought it is a skeleton that he'd have preferred to keep hidden.

I notice that Nowbath is now in "parliament". Do you know if the *Leader* is still being published? I've only received a few issues since November. I have written to them.

While still on the media, I read a few months ago that Radio Truro has been taken over by some businessmen, including someone called Saffi Siddique. What is the significance of this development? We unfortunately cannot catch the station on our FM radio. I hope we are not missing much.

Sometime in October last year I read a bit about you in *Rapport*, in Tant Anna's column, I think. You were mentioning the pride and love that goes into the preparation of a pot of biryani. How true. Can I ever forget the suppressed excitement at the moment the dough is removed and the wonderful aroma that fills the house? Do the young girls these days still use the same method?

Remind me. I received some wonderful photos of Shireen Motala's wedding. She has grown up into a beautiful young lady. It was nice to see some of the older folks too. Do either of your sons resemble the father? Sitting at one table is someone who reminds me very much of him. Unfortunately, I don't know any of the others at that table. One of them could possibly be Farouk Meer, but I can't be sure. Sitting on the opposite side was a lady with a bit of skin problem. My description can't be of much help, but if it was your son he may remember.

Things are fine with me. The Red Cross arranged for us to be given an annual medical check-up. During the week I was taken to a specialist in town, who examined me thoroughly; he said I was okay.

My exam results will be out in a week or two. I may have told you that I was writing my finals in African Political Studies. If I get through, it seems that I may have to stop studying. I applied to do M.A. [History] but the Prison Authorities have refused permission. Only prisoners with two years of their sentence left are allowed to study beyond Honours. So this doesn't apply to me. You probably know that the so-called offer of release by Mr Botha was not accepted by us.

Keep well. Best wishes to you and all the family and friends, from

AMK

Westville 3630
26th March 1985

Dear Ahmedbhai

Fortunately I keep carbon copies of all letters to you. On checking I find that nothing that was written in the censored one constituted danger to the state or anyone or anything. Some comments on social changes – cosmetic and otherwise – were made, and remarks on the antics of some of our tri-parliament MPs (Indian ones). I can see, on reading the letter over again, that the social scene comments would have hurt the feeling of some persons for the truth does hurt.

None of my children look like their father but in characteristics, sense of humour, etc. they are certainly his children. The grandchildren again – both grandsons and one granddaughter (Nureen) have dark eyes. Razia's two daughters and Aslam's daughter all have what we call Manjri eyes, not quite the colour of Mohamed's but ranging from grey to green.

You guessed correctly. The person in Shireen's batch of photographs is Farouk Meer. The lady with the skin condition is Jessie Waghmarae married to Vallabh Jaga. Vallabh is a protégé of the Bismillah family. An orphan, he spent most of his holidays with us in Potch, though his parental home was in Bloemhof. We all accept him as an extra brother and when my father was sick during his last few years, Vallabh made regular trips from Nigel where he practices, to attend to my father, change his medicines and so forth. My dad remarked that a son could not take more care! The person with them who you think resembles Mohamed is Jessie's cousin Heman. He is very fair and does have light eyes.

The release offer from authorities and its rejection was well covered by world media. Passing comments on this might hurt sensitive toes so I shall pass the temptation. But I will say this: the refusal made its impact. What it must have cost you all, one can imagine.

Biryani just does not smell like "them days" anymore. For one, the saffron is too costly and dough sealing is not done even by the old ones, for they find that modern utensils seal well. Even the biryani cooked in the big degs, is sealed with foil these days. I am constantly devising shortcuts and passing these on in recipes for with wives holding jobs outside the homes and with domestic help a costly luxury and difficult to obtain, we all hunt for labour saving methods.

Last month I had a family gathering. I cooked Khitchri, Khuri, vegetable curry with moothias (dumplings) and chicken stuffed and trussed properly like dadimas used to do. With papad, everyone thought it was a delicious meal. It was a long time since the Mayat clan were served such farm fare at a family get together!

*Leader* and *Graphic* are still published. Nowbath's volte face was expected. So many have grabbed the chance. Am I treading on thin ice again?

Radio Truro has been taken over by Zakaria Siddiqui or Safee as he is popularly known. Izzie Kirsh who owned it sold it to Safee who had been associated with it right from the beginning.

[text removed by censors]

He is the son of late Maulana Basheer Siddiqui and the entire family are very cultured and talented. Safee is one of our top Urdu poets and his sister Sayedda (whose daughter is photographed in *Namima's Chest* and who with her sister died so tragically in a car accident) is another top poetess. The Kirsch Group being one of those conglomerates could easily let Radio Truro go, but to Safee it is a dream come true for now he has a free hand with the programmes. Not so free really, for there is competition from Radio Lotus and Safee sees to it that he does not enter any controversial areas. Capital Radio based outside the Republic is free of restrictions.

If you like Urdu and Hindi then you are missing a lot for Radio Truro plays all the latest hits from India and Pakistan, and covers local talents fairly well.

My mother phoned to give me news of the death of Mariam Bai Durveish. When I last interviewed the old lady (15 months ago) she said she was well over [a] hundred. I am told she died at age 107. What is remarkable is that except for the last two months of her life, her hearing, speech, memory, coherence, etc. was that of someone in their 40s or 50s at most. I found her wiping the mess of[f] the kitchen table, walking unaided to the lounge, offering me supari and sharing her memories in the most delightful way. They just don't make such models any more in this throw-away age!

With Salaams,
Zuleikha

M. Kathrada
Pollsmoor Maximum Prison
Tokai
25th May 1985

Dear Zuleikhabehn

I'm sorry for not replying earlier to your letter of 26th March, which reached me, intact, on 9th April. I have hopes, for the time being at least, that there won't be a recurrence of the type of mutilation which was perpetrated against your January letter. Touch wood. So I don't think you should allow yourself to be inhibited by that experience. Just continue to write the normal type of letters that you have been writing all these years. Whenever you're in doubt, use your "womanly intuition"! Okay?

Thanks for the information about some of the people on the photographs. I still curse myself for not having recognised Jesse, whom I know so well. I feel sure that if I'd been aware that she'd had a skin condition I would have recognised her without any hesitation. In fact the face was so familiar, and I looked at it several times before putting it away. I'm sure Jesse will be pleased to know that she still looks exactly the same as she did when I last saw her. The years appear to have made no impact on her youthful appearance. I am aware of Vallabh's close relationship with the Bismillah family. I first met him in 1943 or 1944, and we remained good friends ever since. He is a very fine person. I was sorry to hear that he had virtually lost his eyesight. Is he still able to practice? I understand his son was also doing medicine; how far is he? Do you happen to know anything about Jesse's brother, Dinny? I don't think I've heard about him for almost two decades. If you happen to be in touch with Jesse, please pass my fondest regards to her, Vallabh and the family.

I hope you have been finding some time to devote to your book. I am worried about the rate at which our community's senior citizens are passing away; and I'm thinking about the large number who have already gone, without their rich experiences having been recorded. While I was doing History Honours, as well as the Honours in African Politics (which, incidentally, I have now completed), I had to consult numerous text books which touched on recent history. It was amazing to discover the huge amount of factual inaccuracies and distortions. A lot of these are as a result of the dearth of source material; but perhaps an equal, if not <u>the</u> real reason, was the failure on the part of many authors to interview men and women who had first hand information about events during the period dealt with. I am not now referring to only political matters, but to the entire spectrum of activity. Many feature articles in newspapers are much worse. The *Graphic* is bad enough (and the *Leader* not much better), but one doesn't think of these when discussing competent journalism. There's a chap called Ameen Akhalwaya (I think he is Ahmed Akhalwaya's grandson) who worked for the *Sunday Express*. He showed a lot of promise and one always looked forward to his articles. But every now and then he'd write a feature on sports or education, etc, covering the last 20-30 years and I'd be most disappointed to see the inaccuracies. I recall an article of his on the Central Indian High School (with which I was closely involved), and I was saddened by the factual errors, which marred an otherwise good piece of work. I almost wrote to him to correct the errors, but I feared that he may take it amiss. The trouble with this type of thing is that, in time to come, researchers will use such newspaper articles as their primary sources – and in the process they will perpetuate inaccuracies.

The thought has crossed my mind that if I am given permission to do an M.A. I'd tackle a thesis on the errors, and resultant distortions, contained in books dealing with various aspects of Black life in post 1945 South Africa. Needless to say that most of the books are written by whites or foreigners. I have strong views on this; I firmly believe that the best and most authoritative works on Black life – cultural, social, political, economic – will of necessity have to come from Black authors. By saying this I hope I don't create the impression that my attitude is based on racial considerations. Unfortunately space does not permit me to fully develop my viewpoint. I wrote an assignment on the topic a couple of years ago, and I think I managed to put across my standpoint therein. My lecturer, tho' not necessarily agreeing with me, appeared to appreciate what I was trying to convey. One day, if you are interested, I'll try and summarise it for you.

If we think that ignorance of our recent history is bad, how much more frightening to wake up to the fact that many millions of people have forgotten, while many more millions have never learnt, of the existence of the Nazi death camps of the 2$^{nd}$ [World] War. I met young people on Robben Island who just could not believe that these atrocities actually took place. I myself would have found it difficult to believe everything had I not personally visited Auschwitz concentration camp in 1951, from where I brought back a handful of human bones, to show people what Nazism meant. I shall never forget that visit – I think 4 million people were killed there.

Let me come to something else. Now that I am not studying I've been thinking of the years that I spent as a UNISA student. Only now do I begin to appreciate the correctness of the statement that the more one studies the more one comes to realise how ignorant one is. One cannot but feel small and humble in the midst of the massive knowledge explosion which stands out as an eternal challenge. We can do no better than to pin our hopes in the children and the youth; to assist and equip them to the best of our ability in order to meet the challenge.

I'm afraid I have to bring this letter to an end. I liked the bit about the gathering of the Mayat clan where you prepared Khitchri, Khuri, papad, etc. I hope you didn't forget some boomla. If I were to come out of jail one day I think those dishes would be my first choice. However, I found that non-Indians did not take to them so easily. They used to prefer Biryani etc.

This will be all for today. Please apologise to Naseem and Razia for my omitting to mention the names of their spouses on the Eid card. Unfortunately I can not recall their names.

Keep well. Eid Mubarak to you and the family
from
    AMK

Salsabil
Westville 3630
10th June 1985

Chief Officer in Charge
Pollsmoor Prison
Tokai

Dear Sir

I am requesting permission to send a gift of food and a book for one of your prisoners namely Ahmed Kathrada on the occasion of our Festival in ten days time (most probably on the 20th of June).

The food parcel will contain some homemade sweets and should you insist on it I can ask the local red cross organisation to pack it for me and send it to you, for handing it over to Kathrada. The same can be done with the book which is a collection of recipes on Indian cookery which was compiled and edited by myself. This book – *Indian Delights* – is a very popular book and has been sold throughout South Africa for the past 23 years. (The current third edition has already sold 50, 000 copies). I realise that Mr Kathrada cannot do anything with a cookery book, but this one is full of Indian traditions and anecdotes with regards to the cooking culture of Indians.

Although I have been corresponding with Ahmed Kathrada for the past six years, I have never met him and I write to him on compassionate grounds. You as a Christian will understand that on festivals such as Christmas one has to remember the sick, the needy, the lonely ones of this earth and it is on this basis that I ask you to consider this request.

May I expect an early answer – for time is short.
Sincerely yours,
Z.M. Mayat

P.S. If necessary I can give the money for the book to the Red Cross Official to purchase from a bookstore and then pack it.

Westville 3630
11th June 1985

Dear Ahmed Bhai

Salaams and Eid Mubarak to you and all your friends from the Mayat clan. The enclosed photograph will show you my six grandchildren and the saddest moments of my life are when I reflect that Mohamed did not live to enjoy even one of them! Since I have not enough hands, Jaleel, the son of Nasim and Nadya is holding his baby brother Javed and his sister Nureen is standing next to them. In my arms (right arm) is Humayra and Dishaad in the left arm. Jihaan (sister to Humayra, and these are Razia and Rashid's children) is next to me in navy dress. Dilshad is Aslam and Shameema's baby. Shameema is, as you may know, niece of Karim and Kader Essack. The other kids belong to Razia's neighbourhood. With three production units on the go I have achieved six grandkids in six years. How's that for population explosion?

I have written to the officer in charge of Pollsmoor to grant permission for a food parcel to be delivered to you via the Red Cross and also a copy of *Indian Delights*. The last 25,000 copies have been sold out within 15 months and it is now in its third impression (the enlarged edition). What a delightful seller is *Indian Delights*. Apart from the thirty students we select for studies at universities each year, we have helped many institutions and persons achieve their projects by injecting vital funds into a development fund and we hope to build a centre for women's activities in the future with this. The land for this has already been purchased. Wish us luck. At the rate we are proceeding we might be able to get Winnie to open it for us. Which reminds me…

You mention the fact that others have been left to write our history books. The person who has just written Winnie's biography is also a rank outsider, but all credit to them for being so well ahead of all us slow coaches. There was a big lament by a historian responsible for writing history books for South African schools. He said these all have a bias for history of whites in this country and they had been written virtually as if ¾ of the population was non-existent, and that these, when mentioned, was only because [they] just could not be omitted!

I picked up a book from a sale many years ago with the title "Africa before they Came" (meaning before the Whites came or rather before colonisation). Mrs Galbraith Welch relies heavily on French books which [are] again translated from Arabic sources. Muslim historians like Masudi, Ibn Batuta, Ibn Khaldun, Es Sadi, Mahmoud Kati etc. are heavily quoted and the writings of these early Muslims show Africa as a very civilised continent with a deep culture and art of its own. Mali, Ghana, Sudan, Niger are well covered by the early Muslim writers and historians such as Maqruzi etc. "Just one anecdote written by a trader to the caliph of the times gives us a picture very vivid and appealing. The trader asks the Caliph to solve a problem about the semi dress of the women of deep Africa and he paints a background picture with words. 'I have travelled over many month's journey over vast areas of land. My life and my goods have never been in danger and I find the people most hospitable to me, a stranger. They show keen interest in Islam and the BOOK and many have readily responded to it. However the women here keep their bosoms uncovered. Even the ladies of the Royal households remain exposed and they prefer to wear only gold jewellery on the upper half of their bodies.' The reply of the wise Caliph was that he should leave the way of dressing, which was traditional there, as it was – later modesty will dawn and the neo-Muslims will begin to wear clothing as is required by Islam." I am quoting from memory but this is more or less the gist of it.

Only recent writings by western authors and anthropologists [mention] these early Arabic sources. I have a feeling that I have written about this in an earlier letter. If so forgive me, but I often quote this book to our narrow-minded contemporaries who have not yet forgotten to pass snide remarks about the cultures of others.

Amin Akhalwaya may be looking for a job since the closing (tragic really) of the *Rand Daily Mail* and the *Express*. Ahmed, since I am on tap to my six little brats and their mothers, I find that a lot of time is being frittered away. But both they and I love the close contact and love play (in Gujarati we call spoiling children "laar karawe") so much that for a time I am quite willing to retard progress of work schedule. However, I am collecting interviews with as many as possible, so in the event of my death some other student may pick up missing links from this. Your letters too are being filed away since some day someone will want to conduct a research of the age of long long detentions.

As for the prison camps of Germany... there is no way the Israelis are going to allow the world to forget these. Constantly books and films are being published to remind the world, the Christian conscience continues to be pricked so that America and Western countries give more and more aid and favourable decisions on behalf of Israel. Let the Arabs stew but poor Israel must not suffer any more. If we have to chalk up atrocities we might as well remember Hiroshima and Nagasaki and American intervention in Vietnam and Korea!

Do you know the story of boomla – this is authentic. During the depression years or later the wholesale grocer and importer (Bassa) closed down. The appointed liquidators opened the premises some weeks later for stocktaking and when they reached the warehouse the two white appointees were overcome by the vaporous smell emanating from the bales of unopened boomla. They could not imagine anyone wanting to eat such stinking fish!

I phoned Vallabh and Jessie and conveyed your regards to them. Vallabh does practice for there are patients who insist on his treating them. A lot of sight yet remains. Dinker Wahmara emigrated to Kenya many years ago and has done very well there. His son is at Wits studying medicine, and Vallabh's son studies medicine in India. It is a strange world.

Two rands [are] equal to one American dollar at the moment. This has resulted in many firms going under. The giant empire of Lockhat Bros has just gone down and when a giant falls it manages to crush and bruise a dozen lesser ones with it. This chain re-action unsettles the whole commercial world. *Financial Mail* records that 16 companies are going under daily in South Africa. And the spectre of Disinvestment looms on the horizon. I wonder what relevance cost of living indexes have on Pollsmoor community?

May your Eid be Blessed.
Zuleikha

A.M. Kathrada
Pollsmoor Maximum Prison
Tokai 7966
22nd July 1985

Dear Zuleikhabehn

Your letter of 11th June reached me on 17th June. Many thanks. Thanks also for the photo; granny literally has her hands full, but it is obvious she is enjoying every moment of it. The recent decision of the Prisons Department to allow children to visit, and the permission to get newspapers have undoubtedly been the most progressive developments in the 22 years of our imprisonment. In December–January I was fortunate to be able to see 6 children – all kids of my nieces. It was a wonderful experience. Unfortunately because of a provision in the Regulations on so called "first-degree-relatives" I could only see the kids (and their mothers) through the glass. Only "first-degree-relatives" may have contact visits. According to their definitions these are restricted to: wife, children, brothers, sisters and parents! Our efforts to persuade the authorities that according to our custom, the family extends much beyond their narrow definition have not been successful. I find the kids of today so much different than we were. They are much more knowledgeable, articulate, self-confident and uninhibited. They were able to converse on a wide variety of topics; I could have easily spent a whole 40-minute visiting period talking to one of them. It's been a most refreshing experience.

When you say that Shameema is Kader's niece, I assume she is the daughter of the late Omar. Am I right? Unfortunately I never came to know Omar very well. He enjoyed a reputation of being a very learned person. Our stops in Maritzburg were always very brief; we spent most of the time with Chota and family. The intention was always there, to meet other friends, but it remained largely unfulfilled. In jail, where we have so much time, we've often talked about Omar and many others who were so talented in one field or another, and from whom we could have learnt such a lot. Unhappily they'll have to be added to our long list of regrets.

The reference in your letter to your efforts to send an Eid parcel via the Red Cross was the first time I got to know of the business. The authorities told me nothing about it. But I suppose the Commanding Officer must have written to inform you that it would not be allowed. Cape Town friends who contacted Pollsmoor were at first told the same thing. A little while thereafter the Commanding Officer called me one morning, and, much to my surprise, informed me that he had reversed his previous decision. So Shehnaaz, Dr Ayesha Advocat Omar and Enver Bharoochi (son of Bharoochichacha from Fordsburg) brought us lots of food; which once again made our Eid day. Unfortunately this time the stipulation was that there was to be no homemade cooked food, so we missed the Biryani, curries etc we got last year. Things like mithai etc would have been allowed only if they were contained in shop or factory-sealed packages, like Dairy Box etc. Fortunately there are places in Cape Town which sell packets of chevda, and other sweetmeats, so we did manage to get some traditional foods at least. And in addition we got Packo Biryani. So all in all we did quite well. I'm very sorry about your parcel, and must thank you for your effort. I should have thought that with your perseverance, by now they would have at least allowed *Indian Delights*. But there's no such luck.

When you say "sponsor" 30 university students from the proceeds of *Indian Delights*, do you mean you pay their entire tuition fees? It must be amounting to a great deal of money. And then there is the Women's Centre project. It's all a bit difficult for us to comprehend. You see, the largest sums of money which we handle are our study expenses, newspaper subscriptions, and the R30-00 per month which we are allowed to spend on groceries and toiletwares.

We heard that the giant Lockhat concern had gone under; the *Leader* carried something on the plight of the poor workers.

Just a word on the question of perseverance. Enver Bharoochi first applied to visit me some years ago while I was still on the Island. He was refused, but kept on applying. Last year in August he was finally allowed to come, together with his wife and little daughter, Nadia. He and I were childhood friends, and it is very nice to see him. However perseverance has not always succeeded. My nephew Enver and his wife Zohra are still not allowed to see me. Zohra last visited me in 1974, and has been refused since then. She must have applied about 20 times! Fatima was also refused again a few weeks ago.

Thanks for phoning Jesse and Vallabh. That explains the Eid card I received from them. I'm glad to hear he has not lost his sight altogether.

I must end now. Our health and spirits remain good. Because I'm not studying, I manage to read a few more books. But unfortunately it is difficult to resist the temptation to get under the blankets, especially on cold nights. With studies one has no alternative but to get up and sit at the table. It's good for discipline.

Keep well. Fondest regards to the children, and grandchildren, and the family.

All the best to you, from
AMK

M. Kathrada
Pollsmoor Maximum Prison
Tokai
7966
18th November 1985

Dear Zuleikhabehn

My instinct tells me that something is again amiss in our correspondence. A quick look at my record shows that you are generally very prompt with your replies, and I have a feeling that you must have already replied to my letter of 22nd July. My enquiries here elicit the standard reply: "Nothing has come…". I nevertheless felt I should write to you to find out. If indeed you have written, please make the usual enquiries from the Post office, and the Pollsmoor authorities.

This is going to be a short note. Yesterday I had a visit from two friends – Enver Bharoochi and Ahmed Allie; quite a substantial part of it was taken up by reminiscences of old times. Allie (or Aggies as he [is] popularly known) is the son of the late Bagus Allie, a well-known Cape Town personality. We met Aggies on our very first trip to Cape Town with Bis, Cas and Housien (in 1948), so naturally we recalled the days we spent here. This was his first visit to me since I've been in jail. All in all it was a really hilarious visit; it was only when it ended that I realised I was in jail. For 80 minutes I was a "free" man. His parting shot was: "We are now going to have our Biryani…", and he apologised for not asking me to join them!

I never cease to be amazed every time visitors come, and tell me of friends who have settled in so many different parts of the world; and I'm saddened when I'm almost invariably told that one or other friend had passed away. Yesterday, for instance I heard for the first time that Dr. Paul Hendrickse had died in Nigeria. (He was the brother of Rev. Hendrickse of the Tricameral Parliament). I first met Paul through Cas, both of whom were to specialise in gynaecology. We became quite friendly; in 1962 he was here on holiday from Nigeria, with his English wife, and we spent a lot of time together. My ban had expired and I had dashed to Cape Town before they could renew it. Those were the days of the Mixed Marriages and Immorality Acts, so husband and wife were obliged to live separately. Paul was a very fine, simple person and very devoted to his profession. He will be missed by his many friends. He has, however, been spared the humiliation of having to live through some of the contemporary tragedies in which his brother is involved.

The news of Dr Moroka's death was also sad. He's had a very colourful life, and I hope someone will write it up. I was his co-accused in the Defiance Trial of 1952; and I last saw him in 1962 when I popped in at his place in Thaba Nchu while I was on my way to Lesotho.

I've been following the series written by A.C. in the *Leader*, and am finding them very interesting. I like the personal angle, and little bits of information which are not generally found in history books. I hope he will publish the series in a book. There are some factual inaccuracies which will have to be corrected.

I was pleasantly surprised the other day, when I opened the *Leader*, to find a photo of the late Aminabai Pahad and some other Transvaal ladies. It was taken at the Gale street camp in 1946.

I suppose the *Graphic* has folded up. My subscription copies stopped coming some time ago, and my letters to them remain unanswered. I'm sure it won't be missed. Have you been seeing the Lenasia paper, "The Indicator"?

I hope you are managing to find time for your book. Oh yes, this reminds me; I'm sure you must have seen the book on Indian food by Mrs Ramola Parbhoo. She seems to be very busy promoting it. The reviews have been generally favourable, though one of them conceded that it couldn't be compared with *Indian Delights*.

This is all for now. We're keeping well. I'm sure you must have been seeing the media reports on the health of our colleague, Nelson. We know more than what has appeared in the papers; we're looking forward to his return.

Could you tell me something about the "Indian Academy of South Africa."

Best wishes and fondest regards to you, the children, the grandchildren and all other family members and friends, from

AMK

Witwatersrand Medical (Indian) graduates, class of 1946,
from right to left: Dr AbdulHak Bismillah ("Bis"), Dr A.I. Limbada,
Dr M.G.H. (Mohamed) Mayat (seated centre), Dr Karim (back row centre),
Dr Ismail Kajee, Dr M.S. Motala.

Zuleikha and her husband, Mohamed Mayat, in Spain, 1962

Ahmed Kathrada, Zuleikha Mayat, portraits from early life

Amina Bismillah, Zuleikha's mother, in her Potchefstroom garden before Group Area removals

An Indian shop ("Gani's shop") on Potgieter Street, in what would become an officially 'white' area of Potchefstroom.

I suppose music lovers will have flocked in their thousands to Swaziland to the Lata Mangeshkar show. Will you be going? I notice Peter Tosh will also be performing there soon. I was wondering if, given the choice, which of the two I'd opt for. I think I'd go for Peter Tosh!

My sympathies to you on the death of your colleage Mrs. Moosa. I can imagine how hard it must have been for you. Did she die in Jo'burg? On 5th November I also received some bad news. My second eldest brother, Ismail, died after a heart attack. It came to me as a shock, as we are generally a healthy family.

This will be all for today. I hope you will have enough material by now to start writing your book. So many old veterans have already passed away, and noone has written anything about them. I'm thinking of the late Nagdeechacha, the two Salooyee brothers, Dr. Moosa Patel's father, old Essakjeechacha, Fakirbhai, Suliman Jada etc etc. There are many more.

I noticed that "Person Mayat and "Person Ntombela" were mentioned in the Fakir column. I assume he is referring to you. Not knowing the background to the story I cannot comment.

My health continues to be fine. I hope the same goes for you and all the family. I'll be writing exams in January.

Keep well. Fondest regards to you and all the folks

from

AMK.

Do good unto others — Good will come unto you. — No more than that is the cry of the Durweish

my life I sacrifice unto you — I do not know what prayer sleep

I understand this (if nothing) else if it comes in you (and free) if you can get it for free — what harm could there be.

Kathrada on the rooftop of Kholvad House (Moulvi Cachalia behind).

Mayat's notes and translation penned on Kathrada's letter of December 1983 in which he makes reference to this couplet by Ghalib. Mayat had heard from her brother that the verse was "associated with" Flat 13 Kholvad House.

Zuleikha Mayat on horseback in South Drakensberg, Bulwer, 1949

Zuleikha Mayat with granddaughter, Nureen, 1984

to Zulekhabehn,

Naeem, Nadya, Zubeel, Nurgen, Javed
Razia, Rashid, Ichuan, Humayra, Iacan
Aslam, Shamima, Dilshaad

Eid Mubarak to you, all family members and friends

from
Omar

Please say Eid mubarak for me to Zehn, IC, and
family

A M Kathrada
Pollsmoor Maximum Prison
7946
May 1988

All that's best
In Eid Greetings
I am sending now to you.
Hoping that you'll find in life,
Real success in all you do
Health, Prosperity and Peace
May all these blessings
Never cease

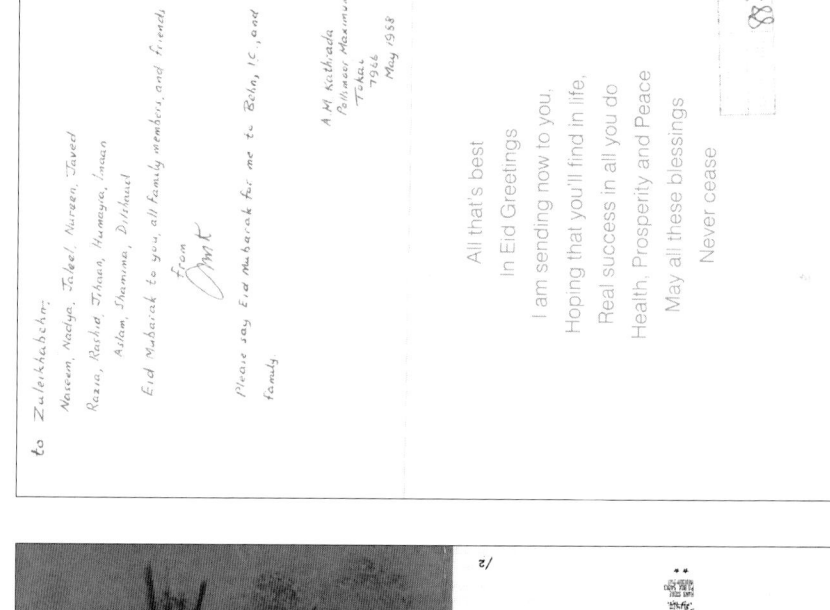

Two of the several Eid cards exchanged

Ahmed Kathrada after his release

30th June 1982

Prison Headquarters
Pretoria.

Dear Colonel Scott

I have tried during the past two years. to send some books to one of the prisoners at Robin Island. Viz; Ahmed Kathrada, but have met with no success.

The books are:

1) An English translation of the Holy Quran.
2) Nanima's Chest which is a book on Indian Antique costumes in the possession of Indian South Africans.
3) Indian Delights which is a cookery book on Indian Dishes.

The last two books have been edited by myself.

I have personally never met Mr Kathrada although I knew of him through paper reports during his trial. But three years ago when my husband died in a tragic car accident Mr Kathrada wrote to sympathise. My late husband was a well known Gynaecologist and Community worker and apparently Mr. Kathrada had known him while my husband was studying at the Witwatersrand University. Since that letter I have been corresponding with Mr Kathrada. My motive for doing so and for wishing to send him the books is based purely on compassionate grounds. I too am deeply involved with Community work and being a Muslim my Faith enjoins that compassion should embrace prisoners as well as free citizens.

You will guage from the titles that the books are not of a political nature, Is there any way in which you can assist in this matter? If required I can post the books to you for censoring before forwarding to Kathrada, or it can be sent through the Red Cross or any way that you suggest.

Colonel your help will be greatly appreciated and your reward will be with the Compassionate God in Whom we all Believe, even the misguided ones during their years of folly.

Thanking you.
Sincerely yours

*[signature]*

Westville 3631
25th November 1985

My dear Ahmedbhai

Assalamo Alaikum...

I am guilt ridden. I find your last letter dated 22nd July in my file of unattended matters, and all the time I was wondering why there was no letter from you! Normal practice is to attach a copy of my reply to your letter and then file that away, thinking that it would be good memorabilia someday when a student will want to do a pen sketch of Ahmed Kathrada.

My brother Abdulhak and Joan have arrived and are in Potch with my aged mother and family (mother is 86 – memory excellent and still does her bit in the garden even though she cannot bend down). The visit is of a very short duration, so if my brother does not come to Durban then I will go to Potch.

Sponsoring thirty students at university (last letter – re Cultural Group's activities) means at least R30,000 per year and that is besides the other welfare work we do. Currently we are responsible for the Islamic section of the exhibition at the Durban Art Museum. There is also a Buddhist and a Hindu section. Because Islam frowns on unnecessary expenditure, most of Islamic art is of a utilitarian nature. Mosques, orphanages etc. instead of sculptures or monuments. Instead of paintings (although Persian, Turkish and Mogul are second to none) there is exquisitely executed calligraphy on objects of use as well as for décor on wall. What did we manage to collect from our bourgeois, very materialistically orientated homes for the exhibition? You will be surprised. Apart from a wealth of textiles as appears in *Nanima's Chest*, there were the mashrabiyya screens (dove-tailing woodwork typical of India and the Middle East), Quran Riyads, tasbeehs, copper and silver urns, paan boxes, jewellery cases: all of these with the most artistic of calligraphy and arabesque detail on it. Then there is the jewellery and so forth. There is a saying of the Prophet "Allah is beautiful and he loves things that are beautiful." There is another that says that "a stone is a stone but two stones put together can become a mosque" and so on. Set around a fountain in a court yard, and with the low seating on oriental carpets and cushions, screened off with the see-through screens, the exhibition turned out to be just beautiful, serenely beautiful, I should say. We poor Gujaratis of trading and farming backgrounds have lost so much of that beauty and that repose that is really our birthright and heritage. Like Fatima Meer once told me "We are not caught between cultures, all culture has been crushed out of us."

With the rand worth only 37 cents against the dollar, not just the Lockhats but many old and established firms are going under. One now comes to appreciate the term that the world monetary system is a manipulated one. With South Africa still producing the best in agriculture, with the mines and (minerals, gold, diamonds, name it) at full production and with great future potential, the international community – in trying to knock some sense into us – have really knocked the ground from under our feet!

The Verulam Women's Group had asked me to launch a little recipe book for them at the annual rate payers meeting which was to have as its guest speaker advocate Skweyiya (I hope I have the name right but you will know that he was in charge of the Mxenge brief). In urging the crowd to buy copies, Mr. Skweyiya beat the whole lot of Indians gathered and gave R20 for a book which was to be sold for R5-00. That set the mood and the women collected over a thousand rand in a matter of minutes. Skweyiya's donation is treasured, for this is a time when the unrest areas unfold chapters of daily tragedies. In Claremont where he stays, Aubrey Nyembezi and wife Marina have lost a home. I feel frustrated in not being able to discuss these tragedies affecting so many of our friends, friends who I cannot even go and see. The occasional phone call is all that we have to hold on to precious bonds.

In between writing this letter I had to attend a dozen phone calls, and when I went to answer the last one, Mildred my efficient housekeeper, gives me a letter from you! No, as I explained I am the guilty party and nothing has gone amiss this time.

I will certainly give Bis your letters to read and I know he too will recall happy memories. Paul Hendrikse we met in 1962 when Mohamed and I toured Nigeria. We stayed with Ralph and Begum in Ibadan. Paul's wife was pregnant at the time and I recall him introducing us to her saying "This is the mother of my two kids and the third one in the box". Latter reference was to the pregnancy. Rustum Gool was also in Nigeria at that time and I wonder if he is still around? As you say so many have passed on.

Ismail will chuckle when I tell him that you find A.C.'s articles interesting. The only thing that I don't like about the series is the upgrading of that hick village called Waschbank. Why don't you jot down the inaccuracies and we can take the Meers down a peg or two.

Currently there is another exhibition on at the Local History Museum. The curator Ms Gillian Berning has really put together a lovely history of Indians starting right from the first load of indentured persons. The contracts, doctor's certificates, collection of old letters and the blown up photographs tell it all. Among the photographs are so many persons one recognises and I take a great delight in pointing these out to younger ones when they accompany me. There is a huge one of passive resisters at the Gale Street camp. (You saw the small sized one in the *Leader*) This one would fill half a wall of a goodly sized room. There clearly one sees Amina Pahad, Mrs Saloojee, Zohra Bhayad, Zainub Asvat etc.

There is another one of Durban women, and among these is my late sister Bibi who died with Mohamed in the accident; the two Mrs Meers; Mrs Monty Naicker; Mrs S. L. Singh; and others.

Mr. Poovalingham's little flutter in Tricameral spelt the end of the *Graphic*. Pat seems unsure whether he will continue in politics in the present set-up. The PFP may find a member soon.

Did you read the extracts from Van Zyl Slabbert's autobiography in the *Sunday Times*? He mentions someone who referred to you as daardie koelie. One does not hear that term being flung around anymore and naively I had assumed that it was not obsolete [sic]. Out of earshot it seems to be in vogue.

All those wild rumours of Nelson's impending release came to nothing. My salaams to him and all of you there and may your Christmas be blessed and your New Year full of promise and goodwill.

Nureen (daughter of eldest son Nasim) will turn 4 in January. Last week she started swimming minus belts and like the two others (Jaleel and Jihaan) she is demanding that I mark the occasion with a token. Material possession is chewing us all up and where is the trend going to take us I wonder.

Zuleikha

A.M. Kathrada
Pollsmoor Maximum Prison
Tokai
7966
5th January 1986

Dear Zuleikhabehn

Thanks very much for your letter of 25th November (which reached me on 6th December); and thanks also for clarifying the matter regarding our correspondence. Under normal circumstances I would have apologised to my prime suspects for holding them responsible for an "offence" of which they are not guilty. But you see in such matters we tend to take up an attitude on the basis of a gut feeling, with the idea of adding to the mountain of woes. I was fully expecting to get corroboration, but, instead, you have taken the wind out of my sails and exonerated the innocent suspects! However, please don't misunderstand me; I'm not for a moment trying to blame you for "letting the side down" or some such thing. In fact I'm only too happy that I've been proved wrong, and hope that in similar cases I can again be mistaken.

It must have been lovely to see Joan and Bis again. Did any of their children come with them? I wonder to what extent the South Africans in Canada keep in touch with one another. In 1984 I had visitors who are also settled in Toronto. They had heard of Bis and Joan, but they'd never met. Of course these are very young people and one shouldn't really expect them to be socialising with people of our generation. They were, nevertheless able to tell me about a number of other friends. I think I must have told you that Ouma Bhyat's son, Hamid, and Zaybee (who are also settled in Toronto) tried to visit me in 1984, but they were not allowed. They were already in Cape Town, and in fact came to Pollsmoor. I was most disappointed as they've been my friends for many years.

I'm happy to learn that your mother is well, and still manages to do a bit in the garden. Hers is really a hardy generation. Last year I persuaded a nephew of mine (who is 22) to visit Ouma Bhyat. He came away from the visit very inspired and enthusiastic. She is 93! Let's get back to the garden. I'm sure you couldn't have missed hearing about Nelson's garden which has been written about in local and overseas papers. Just before he went to hospital he left me in charge, with a one-page detailed instructions. With the assistance of a couple of kind young men we tried to adhere to the instructions, with some success. I of course know absolutely nothing about gardening, so the natural process of growth, and maturation must have taken their course accompanied by a lot of luck. We had a first class harvest of onions; and the spinach is prolific. We have a fair crop of leeks; a handful of beans; a couple of dozen berries; and a few other things. The beetroot and mealies look promising. But saddest of all, the tomatoes and cucumber turned traitor on us, and yielded some specimens which no self-respecting tomato or cucumber would want to publicly acknowledge as their kin. We nevertheless do manage to make a salad of sorts, which earn the praise of my colleagues. This, of course, does not mean very much. They may be good politicians but I don't think their testimonials in the culinary field can earn me a paragraph in *Indian Delights*.

In the midst of the greenery it is truly pathetic to see the dead and dying cucumber plants. If it were not for the fact that we really miss him, I'd have said it is just as well that Nelson has been unable to return to his garden. In the two visits we had with him since his return to Pollsmoor, fortunately the garden did not feature. He looked very well and appeared to have fully recovered. We have no idea when he will be joining us again. About the rumours of his release, we here have long ceased to take them seriously. They originated as far back as 1966 already, and have recurred with monotonous regularity. Fortunately most of our families and friends outside have on the whole learnt to ignore them. It is mostly the journalists who are responsible for keeping the rumours alive.

The Exhibition at the Local History Museum seems to be interesting. It is a pity that the *Leader* coverage was so scanty. Incidentally the fourth lady in the *Leader* photo is not Mrs Saloojee but Mrs Zubeida Patel.

While on the *Leader*, could I ask you to contact them for me? They seem to have a policy of never answering letters, not sending reminders re-subscriptions, not sending receipts, etc. My numerous letters to them have remained unanswered. I don't even know what the present subscription rate is but I sent some money in December hoping it will be enough to cover the next 6 months. Anyway what I actually wanted from them are the issues of the *Leader* which contained the first 5 of the series with A.C.'s historical articles. I wrote to them about it in October 1985, but received no reply.

About the upgrading of Waschbank, yes, I suppose it is a bit overdone. But then many of us are guilty of similar parochialism. I know I'm forever looking for little points which highlight Schweizer. For instance, I never tire of boasting about the fact that one of the most significant archaeological findings (if not the most significant) was the Taung skull, found by Prof. Dart in 1924. Before the Bophutatswana aberration Elizabeth Eybers was not only a "Schweizer girl", but their home was next to ours. The sculptor Irma Stern also hails from there. I could add quite a few more. I think I told you some years ago about Minister Le Grange's visit to Robben Island. He of course is your "home boy". When we were introduced he claimed me as his "home boy"; he was of course stretching the concept to cover the whole Western Transvaal. A bit of Potchefstroom imperialism!

About the errors in the history series, I should point out that I've not made a thorough study of the articles. For one thing, we do not have the necessary literature here to be able to do so. But as we go through them we come across a few errors. I think I can remember some; but I'm doing this purely from memory, and I hope I'm not doing injustice to the author. He for instance said there were no South Africans at the 1957 anti-imperialist conference in Brussels. In fact, James La Guma and Josiah Gumede (Archie's father) were present. He also referred to Dr Abdurrahman as the only Black of the Cape Provincial Council. In fact there were two: the first one was Dr Walter Rubusana. Then, he said that Yusuf Nagdee was a delegate to the Bandung Conference in 1955, with Kotane and Moulvi Cachalia. In fact, Nagdee was not a delegate; he went there merely as a tourist, but enjoyed certain facilities because he was a friend of Moulvi's. Recently there was an article on the 1956 Treason Trial (it was <u>not</u> part of the history series) which referred to a certain expert witness. It said that his evidence was so thoroughly destroyed by ADB Adv. Berrange in the Preparatory Examination that the State did <u>not</u> call the expert again at the Supreme Court trial. The expert was Prof. A. H. Murray. It is true that he was destroyed at the Preparatory Examination. But he again gave evidence in the Supreme Court and was again destroyed.

These are relatively minor errors; but as I pointed out to you before, this sort of material is going to be used as sources by students, and the inaccuracies are going to be perpetuated by future generations. If ever I'm allowed to do [an] M.A., I would strongly consider doing a thesis on historical inaccuracies in textbooks.

Yes I saw the bit about the "Koelie" Kathrada. The term has by no means disappeared; it has simply gone underground. I'll write more in this regard in a future letter.

I hope you and all the family and friends are keeping well.

    Fondest regards and best wishes for 1986, from
    AMK

Westville 3630
29th January 1986

Dear Ahmedbhai

December and January we reserve for our Transvaal relatives and this year we were kept especially happy with friends coming and going. Surprise – even my mother dropped in for a week and at her age travelling is no joke. Walking quietly around garden and home with her walking stick she left behind nostalgic memories of elegance and grace so difficult to come across these days. Coarse language is quite excusable in some of our old folks but I have never heard a word out of place from her. Unlike [other] old people she has not become garrulous but when you tap her memory for past decades, she astounds one, for she recalls vividly even childhood days in India and experiences since her arrival here. She fills in so many gaps in my knowledge – gaps that are crucial to the writing I one day intend starting. I am frittering away valuable time.

Does Nelson talk to his plants or does he, like my mother, listen to them? Each plant she says will tell you just what it needs in nourishment and care. The whole of Potch knows that no one can grow Karelas, brinjals and dodhi like Amina Khala. The karela secret was taught her by our Chinese neighbour in those days. How, when they reach a certain stage of maturity, they have to be enclosed in a brown paper bag.

The first Chinese family pulled into Potch after their disenchantment with Gandhi when he consented to give fingerprints for domicile documents. In those days the tales of Chinese eating humans were still going around and the Afrikaners steered away from their shops. But Muslim families accepted them as neighbours and opened their schools for their children, as they did to all children who had Indian fathers and Coloured and African mothers. When White school inspectors tried to object, samoosa diplomacy won them around. After all it is our school and we have certain rights as to whom we can accept. At times, white kids would get lost while their parents were shopping at Moosa or Abram's and it was a scene to remember the hysterical bouts the White mothers had, who thought that the child had been lured away by a Chinese. Our friend Pengy with her lovely sense of humour related lovely stories which would really highlight any fictionalised historical novel.*

Bis and Joan stayed exactly one week in South Africa. On the way to here they had stopped over in France to be with their daughter who is doing her Honours in French; another daughter, married and with one child, is in Austria and so the Austrian family had the grandparents for a week. My sister, who emigrated to Dublin when her son married an Irish girl, came down and so we had a sort of reunion with local and overseas members of the family. Bis insisted that I arrange a mammoth reunion this year (1986) for that was the year when my grandfather tiring of hawking took out the Dabhel House licence and started the business from where we were kicked out in 1981. Dabhel House however is still in business in the Indian Complex where the town council extracts heavy rentals from the tenants. My grandfather only paid rent for one year in Potch when he leased the land from the City Council and he had to stay with another Muslim family. Now most Indians in the Transvaal have become rent payers!

My intention was to highlight Potch like the Meers are highlighting Waschbank. That they have beaten me to it irks and I have said so to them. Another error (and I call it arrogance) was that only Natal Indians built their own schools. They thought that the

---

* Pengy and her stories feature in *A Treasure Trove of Memories*.

Transvaal schools were all built by the Provincial administration. I pointed out the schools in Potch, Klerksdorp, Rustenburg, etc. [were] all State aided under the pound for pound aid. Unfortunately I do not have the Transvaal figures but I can quote from the Orient School Brochures which I compiled last year and I can vouch that percentage wise, Transvaal can match their effort.

| Year | Government Schools | Community Schools (No of Pupils in Brackets) |
|---|---|---|
| 1912 | 4 | 35 |
| 1925 | 9 | 43 |
| 1945 | 20 | 116 |
| 1950 | 26 | 146 |
| 1967 | 45 | 204 |
| 1968 | (38,400) 51 | (68,110) 202 (Assumedly State took over 2 or they were demolished) |

After the year 1968 there is a steady decrease in Community Built schools so that by 1974 state has 96 and community 151.

Just like Yusuf Nagdee was made part of the delegation in Bandung while touring, my father was cornered by E. Randeree (also a tourist) and together they accompanied Ashwin Choudree and Sorabjee to Delhi to voice the South African delegation protest. How about us squeezing the old man into the pages of history without mentioning the tourist part? He used to laugh saying that Sorabjee worked on the principle that numbers meant strength even if the delegates were cautioned not to talk!

Ismail Mohamed wiped the floor with R.A. University expert on ANC affairs. He is as good, if not better than Berrange. I watched his "stage performance" during the State versus Fatima

Meer trial when she had purportedly broken her banning order by dining with Andrew Verster and being found to wander near the precincts of the Gandhi Settlement where a business course school had been set up for Africans. Ism. Mohamed's performance was worthy of a Hollywood film any day.

Nureen came to announce today that she will be attending nursery school from Monday. Like Bhai and Jihaan she is going to carry her lunch and her milk drink in her bag. My father in law cannot get over the fact that kids go so eagerly to school these days. He remembers when they had to be dragged to Madressa and school and the experience was so traumatic for both mother and child.

Talking of Madressas. At the time you became a state guest at Robben Island, the youth were completely disenamoured with the ulema class. Our jokes and discussions of the maulanas were full of disrespect and they were disregarded in virtually everything except that their presence was necessary for marriages, funerals, etc. These days, the priests are back in power and the younger generation hang onto their every word. Apart from the Cape Sheiks, the rest of the Maulanasseem [are] so anti-progress that it is frightening at times. Some of them are my friends and I discuss the trends with them. In private conversation, they can pin-point every wrong action but once they get on to the mimbar, it seems that they cannot emerge from their self-imposed grooves. They have established several schools/madressas. Young children are put into these establishments and the first priority is Islamic education or rather religious instruction (for in Islam education is supposed to entail every facet of life and not be compartmentalised into secular and religious). Every student has to become a Hafez. In the afternoons, teachers voluntarily offer their help in getting the students through Damelin College courses. You will be surprised that the students are performing very well and the J. C. results this year were astounding. Similar schools for girls are being set up and the primary requirement is that they arrive in overcloaks which they may take off once they are indoors. The girls' courses are domestic oriented for it is not expected that they pursue careers. The world is certainly not rosy.

We had a visiting Urdu poet from Canada (Pakistani emigrant) and he in his expertise showed how relevant Urdu poetry can be in these times. South African Urdu poetry remains very much escapist generally speaking, but I thoroughly enjoyed his poetry.

Salaams,
Zuleihka

P.S. Sonny Bramdaw is personally attending to your query re *Leader*. The first 5 A.C. articles will be posted to you, he promised.

Zuleikha

A.M. Kathrada
Pollsmoor Maximum Prison
Tokai
7966
22nd February 1986

Dear Zuleikhabehn

Thanks for your letter of 29th January, which reached me on 5th February. Sometime in January I received a very pleasant surprise, in the form of a Christmas card from Chota and Choti (P.M. Burg); it was really lovely to hear from them after such a long time. Shireen has been threatening to write to my colleague but so far nothing has materialised. I shall write to Chota and Choti when circumstances permit. In the meantime I'll appreciate it if you could please tell them how happy I was to hear from them. Please convey my fondest greetings to them and the other folks in PM Burg.

I must also thank you for contacting the *Leader* people. I expect the back copies to arrive one of these days. While I'm about it could I impose one more task on you? I should like to get <u>one</u> sample copy of the *Natal Post*, together with the subscription rates, address etc. Sorry for the bother.

I'm sure the mini-reunion of the Bismillahs must have been very enjoyable. Let's hope it was a prelude to the big centenary gathering of the Dabhel House clan. I still have an idea of how Dabhel House looked in the forties. What a tragedy, and disgrace, that after so many decades it was forced to move to rented premises. I wonder if the perpetrators of such callous deeds ever realise the extent of the hurt they have caused. A couple of years ago a brother of mine died after a massive heart attack. Although I have no medical evidence for it, but it is my belief that he started dying from the time that the family business and houses were forced to move. Letters and visitors from home indicated what a traumatic experience it had been for him, and how badly he had taken it. When the news of his death was conveyed to me this was among the first thoughts that went through my mind. I'm sure there must have been many similar and worse examples. I believe that the trauma of the removals has been well portrayed in a film made by a Cape Town man, whose name (I think) is Yunus Ahmed. Its title is "Grandfather, Your Left Leg is Missing." Capetonians know Table Mountain as "grandfather", and its "left leg" was District Six. The film received good reviews, and also won some awards.

For the centenary get-together, is it intended that all the family members – from Canada, Austria, France, Ireland etc. will come over? It will be wonderful. I suppose it will all be recorded on video? (You'll be interested to know that my acquaintance with videos is restricted to what I read in the papers, and what I hear from visitors). I wasn't aware that you had a sister in Dublin. I also have a nephew who is married to an Irish lady and settled in Dublin. He is a Kola from Ottosdal. I hope you did not forget to pass my greetings to Bis and Joan.

You mentioned that December, January is the time for Transvaal relatives. They couldn't choose worse months, from the point of view of the heat. "December in Durban" invariably takes my mind back to 1946, when I spent those weeks in Durban Central, together, among others with my former teacher, Mr N. Thandray (a very embarrassing, but interesting experience); and Pat Poovalingam.

This leads me to your reference to Sorabjee and Ashwin, two of the numerous colourful figures of yesteryear. I can picture a cartoon in the paper edited by Ismail in 1946/47, showing Sorab swimming to America. It was based on one of his flamboyant statements, after a rumoured threat to his passport. These gentlemen also passed through Flat 13, in the days of I.C. and J.N. and must certainly be included in my project.

Your reference to the early beliefs that Chinese ate human beings is a good example of how stereotyped ideas develop, and become entrenched, largely because of the lack of social intercourse and enforced separation. There are stories galore about the picture which Free State Afrikaners had of Indians. To many we were cannibals; to others we were thugs and crooks. Some believed us to be some sort of ogres; almost all were firmly convinced that all Indians possessed some mystical powers. In December of 1955 I was arrested with 2 friends, for being in the Free State without a permit. All 3 of us were as Indian as you and I; but because our laws applied differently to different peoples, one of my colleagues was legally a "Coloured." He was a medical doctor, and had the complexion of a white man. The other one was a French citizen! He even had a vote in France. The one and only time in his life that he visited France was in 1951. And he couldn't speak a word of French. Anyway, back to our arrest. The Jo'burg police knew us as "Indians", and arrested us, and took us to the police station, and handed us over to the Station Commander. Now our problems began. The Station Commander had never seen, or spoken to Indians in his life. He looked at these three specimen and simply shook his head, in wonder and disbelief, and perplexity. It struck him that these were just ordinary human beings like him – one, a bit fairer. He immediately confessed that he'd never had anything to do with Indians before and asked us where he should lock us. We told him to lock us in the "Non-White" section. After we settled down for the night, he came into our cell and sat down. His main interest now was the Indian doctor, who, he "knew" possessed mystical powers which would cure his ailing wife. So they talked and talked till very late at night. By this time he was feeling very embarrassed and ashamed about our sleeping accommodation and our food. Early the next morning, without discussing with us, he went to the "Coloured" location, and arranged for food to be sent to us. After a few days we were transferred to the Prison, and bailed out. But we had made a good friend. The state then withdrew the charges against my "French" and "Coloured" colleagues and proceeded only against me. My lawyer was Adv. Joe Slovo. We had to go to Bloemfontein a few times, and eventually won the case on a technical point. (Now 30 years later, I'm told that the Free Staters are inviting Indians to settle there!)

Yes Ismail Mohamed is brilliant. You may very well be right that he is as good as Berrange. I'm hoping to see him one of these days. We are hoping to test in court the refusal to allow me to do [an] M.A.; and the refusal to allow a niece and nephew to visit me.

Your mention of the former Pakistani poet reminded me of a visit I had earlier this month from a Jo'burg friend Khalil Saloojee and his daughter Shireen. Apparently Khalil's wife writes Urdu poetry, and in this context we got to talking about you. He seemed to have met you at one of these poetry gatherings. While still on Urdu, last week we saw an Urdu film "Noor-el-Elahi". My smattering of Urdu helped a bit, but luckily it had English sub titles.

I notice there is a new Islamic body in Cape Town to oppose the Moslem Judicial Council. It is called Tajad-Al-Islam, and formed by a Dr Hargey.

You asked about Nelson and his plants. When I last wrote to you we had been separated from him and I was "supervising" over his garden. Now we have been removed altogether from the section where the garden was and are staying elsewhere. The garden, therefore, is now officially dead. The 4 of us are still separated from Nelson, but have seen him. He is very well.

I'm sure you are not among the gullible persons who have been taken in by the latest "release charade". I don't believe it one bit, and remain completely unmoved by the media reports.

Healthwise everything's fine. Siko wrote to my colleague Walter* and mentioned some project of hers. I think it's a crèche or something.

Keep well. Fond regards to you, the children, and grandchildren; as well as the rest of the family and friends.

From
AMK

---

\* Sisulu

Westville
3630
17ᵗʰ March 1986

Dear Ahmedbhai

Checking with the *Leader* whether your back copies had been sent on, they tell me that they had mailed the copies subscribed for and want you to check at your end why there has been a delay. Should you not have received your copies they will compensate you with a fresh batch.

I have arranged with *Natal Daily News* to send you a copy of *Post* together with a subscription form. As a private person I cannot send this to you and [the] circulation dept will have to handle it.

Your mentioning Walter and Siko in your last letter made me phone her to ask why the silence these past few months. Result was she arrived yesterday (Sunday) with two grand-daughters in tow. Siko was dressed in a maroon silk Punjabi kurta and Ijar (do you know our Indian fashions?) and with her dark glasses she looked as no grandmother has a right to look! But it is really the two grand-daughters I want to introduce to you. Eldest one is 4 and the younger one 2. Their English was crystal clear and they expressed themselves so beautifully and clearly that I must admit that Humayra who is nearly two is nowhere near Isizwe, and Humayra is considered very bright. The elder child attends a nursery in a Coloured area and the younger one at a crèche where the majority of the children are White and English speaking.

This brings me to the point that I try and tell Afrikaners, how much talent has been aborted over the years from citizens who are not given an opportunity in life. A young man of about 25 came knocking on the Cultural Group doors asking for help with a musical course. With our financial assistance he made his B.A.

in music and two years ago Israel sponsored a musical troupe from here to perform in Israel. Pewa was one of the persons. On his return he came to see Fatima Loonat and said "while performing one evening in front of a full house I was overcome. The thought kept on recurring that it is because of your assistance that I am in Jerusalem today!"

Incidentally, Siko's short story on the medicine man in the valley has been published in a magazine. She has great potential as a writer and I am sure we will read much from her pen in years to come.

Joan and Bis sent their salaams. Bis mentioned that he had written to you on his return to Canada after attending funerals of Mohamed and my sister. I told him that you never received that letter.

Your Free State incident however pathetic was yet amusing. Reminds me of one particular incident. Soon after my marriage, Mohamed and I spent a month in Bulwer (Drakensberg dorp in Natal with breathtakingly beautiful hills and valleys) with the Kajee family. Horseriding was one of the big attractions of Bulwer and we spent hours on it. One day as we were going for our morning sprint, Mr Kajee asked us to call on a farmer some miles away and remind him to bring in the eggs. Mohamed had arrived there a few minutes earlier and he was chatting with the English farmer whilst seated on the horse. In his khaki shorts and shirts and his fair complexion and his good English, the farmer must have assumed him to be one of "them", but minutes later when I arrive – and no one can mistake me for anything but a child of Indian parents – the farmer cast looks which should really have killed me on the spot. His whole attitude towards Mohamed with whom he was chatting so amiably seconds earlier fell to below zero in warmth: Had I not been in the accident with him, would he have been taken to the White Hospital nearby? is a constant thought bedevilling my days and my sleep!

Khalil Saloojee's wife writes good poetry and he sings her ghazals at Mushairas, making it quite touching. Radio Truro was taken over first by Safee Siddiqui and when he could not make a go of it, Ketan Lakhani took over, but he too has had to dispose of it. This is most unfortunate for ventures like these are but too rare in the life of Black Communities, besides SABC now has no competition from this quarter.

You mentioned the death of your brother after they were forced to move from S[chweizer] Reneke. My in-laws were in Mansfield [Road] and my mother-in-law had worked out a beautiful life style with her friends from that base. On the Berea, with the Centre just a bus-stop away she could do her shopping, marketing and visiting to heart's content. What was also a delight [was] that visitors would constantly drop in for lunch, if they came from other parts of Natal, and locals would drop in for tea. When she had a stroke, these visitors were doubly welcome for as an invalid her movements were restricted. Then of course they had to sell their beautiful home, and mother and father came to stay with me in Clare Estate. This was such an out of the way, slummy area (and I remember one socialite who came to visit me one day saying "Julu, you haven't any pavements here?" "Oh aunty, I said, that's the least of my worries – I only hope they give me a proper sewage system for we have conservation tanks that need emptying out every few months!"

To get back to my narration. Mother was most depressed and it needed all our wits to keep her fairly happy. One day I got (at great expense) a gardener to transfer a magnificent magnolia tree from the garden of a friend who too had to sell out to Group Areas. Mother saw this tree coming in and she recognised it, for she was a lover of flowers. I shall never forget her poignant remark. "That tree is old. Old things do not transplant easily." I really pampered that tree for I had to prove to mother that old things or persons could adapt to a new environment even if not exactly to their liking. Next spring there was one solitary bloom on the tree and I with great joy took it to her room when it had fully blossomed out. Soon afterwards Mohamed and I attended some conference overseas and on our return the tree had begun to die. Nothing could save it. Some months later mother died. Father is still alive, and at 84 he still drives around in Westville on his way to Mosque or to see his daughter who lives nearby.

Talking of gardening. Nasim and Rashid (son-in-law) are busy trying to get the gardens in shape at their new cottages at La Mercy. They do the digging and planting and the wives the aftercare work. Jaleel, who is always envious that things grow so well in Nanima's garden, brought over some dodhi from La Mercy. The little fellow was cheating, for a neighbour who had trained his dodhi plants onto my children's fence had given some to them. This competition between granny and small ones gives them an interest in gardening.

With salaams to you from all of us
Sincerely yours
Zuleikha

A.M. Kathrada
Pollsmoor Maximum Prison
Tokai
7966
10th May 1986

Dear Zuleikhabehn

Thanks a lot for your letter of 17th March, which reached me on 25th March. Thanks also for arranging for the *Post Natal*; they sent me a subscription form and a sample. I've subscribed and have already received a few issues. I find it a useful complement to the *Leader* in our efforts to keep ourselves informed about Natal. Unfortunately the *Leader* with the first five articles of A.C. never reached me. I despair of even making enquiries, because I know what the answer will be. Anyway thank you for conveying my message; please tell them not to bother anymore. The issues are not all that important. In the meantime efforts to get the "Indicator" (of Lenasia) have been unsuccessful. I've been singularly unfortunate with Lenasia papers; I've been trying for the last 3 years and more, but have failed to get a single copy!

I've been listening for the past few weeks to the Radio Lotus programme on Sunday nights. I never imagined they'd be able to produce a programme that would be worse than the previous Saturday morning ones, even if they tried. But with "kaleidoscope", they have more than succeeded! Yet I continue to listen, hoping to pick up some interesting tit-bits. Some of the songs are nice of course but unfortunately my Urdu/Hindu is not good enough to properly appreciate them. It can be very frustrating.

While still with culture, I notice that Saira Essa's "Biko" has been having successful runs in Jo'burg and Cape Town. She appears to be quite a talented lady. I think you first mentioned her in one of your letters a few years ago.

It must have been nice to see Siko in the Punjabi attire. Yes I do know the Punjabi kurta and ijar, but I must confess it is not high up in my list of preferences. I have found nothing in Eastern or Western dress to beat the sari, provided it is properly worn. This does not mean that I find the Punjabi dress unattractive. Already before our arrest we used to see young ladies in Punjabi dress, and they looked quite nice.

In which magazine was Siko's short story published? For the past few weeks we've been getting *Fair Lady*, *Woman's Value*, *Sarie*, etc. If it was in any of these, I'll try and get the copy, but you'll have to tell me which issue. When next you see her and the family, please pass our regards.

You must have seen reports a few months ago of the visit of the Iranian President to Zimbabwe; there were articles about their refusal to shake hands with female cabinet ministers, and they apparently also refused to attend a banquet because of the presence of females, or the seating arrangements; I'm not sure. But, if the reports were accurate, I must say it was a very disappointing performance on their part. And earlier this evening I was reading about the separate campuses for male and female students in Saudi Arabia, and other discriminatory practices. Then there is this legislation in India to override a Supreme Court decision on the payment of maintenance to Muslim women divorcees. Having grown up in South Africa, in a Western orientated environment, I find it difficult to accept these practices. I wonder if Fatima touches on the question in her book on Iran.

While making these observations I don't wish to give the impression that I go all the way with some of the more extreme proponents of "women's lib"; you know the specimens who go in for things like wrestling and body building, etc. in the name of equality! On the other hand the attitudes to women in some of the Moslem countries (and now in India) appear to me to be carry-overs from bygone ages, and therefore unsuitable for today's industrialised societies. Of course I'm conscious of the fact that the little knowledge that I do have of the Moslem countries is derived almost entirely from media reports; which are not known for their objectivity, let alone sympathy for the Moslem world. Another disturbing feature is the sort of punishment meted out for certain criminal offences, such as stoning, cutting off the limbs, etc. I've raised this with a doctor friend, but his explanations were not convincing. I suppose I shouldn't really expect to receive comprehensive answers to my problems, considering the restrictions of prison correspondence.

Your description of the last years of your mother-in-law's life after the forced move from Mansfield Road, was really touching, especially the bit about how one cannot successfully transplant old trees. Is it possible to ever forget, or forgive, the undesirable hardships caused by the removals?

I didn't know that Mohamed's parents originally lived in Mansfield Road. I used to know the area fairly well, having been a frequent visitor at J.N.'s in-laws. In fact I think I stayed at their house on my very first visit to Durban; that is after spending a night in Pinetown at the Meers. That was in 1945!

This will be the lot for today. Life goes on much the same as usual. I've just been listening to the broadcast of the English soccer F.A. cup finals. Not that I'm exactly a sports enthusiast, but somehow I cannot escape the F.A. cup fever. I take a casual interest in the Wembley tennis; and every four years in the Olympics. Apart from individual events from time to time, both local and overseas, this is about the sum total of the interest in sports. Naturally I give rugby a wide berth; I have an intense dislike for just about everything connected with it. I simply switched off the radio when the commentary of the so-called test match started this afternoon.

Healthwise I'm fine. A few weeks ago I was taken to Cape Town for the annual check-up, as arranged by the Red Cross. The specialist said that I was okay. Nelson is also very well. Colleagues of mine saw him yesterday. I last saw him on Good Friday.

I'm sorry I never received the letter Bis sent from Canada. It's good to know that he did write.

Keep well. Greetings to all the family and friends, and Eid Mubarak to all of you, from

AMK

Salsabil
Ramadaan 20
30<sup>th</sup> May 1986

Dear Mr Ahmedbhai

Thank you for the Eid card with all its lovely greetings for each member of the family, friends and others. I should exclaim enthusiastically over the beautiful card, but then it is one that the Women's Cultural Group (of a series of six) had brought out some years ago and though soothing to the ego that it has reached as far out as Pollsmoor, for me to enthuse over its aesthetic features would be self-praise. However I send you another one from our series. It is the smallest one in the series and has an Urdu verse on it compiled by Farooqui Mehtar. May I translate?

> Eid has come bringing its glory
> And the dignity of Belief and Faith!
> Every pleasure of ease and happiness
> It brings from Haq (Allah) His Blessings!

I have phoned two persons to post on subscription forms of *Indicator* to you and I pray that the Eidy I send you with this letter will be able to obtain the newspapers that you want. Please accept it from my family.

Thanks! For your opinion of Radio Lotus Saturday programme. Some years ago I appeared regularly on that programme (before it was baptised Lotus) but out of frustration resigned after a year. The Jaatbhais (fellow-Indians) in charge there were more obnoxious than non Jaatbhais and bhens. I have also had my days with SATV. On three occasions the WCG (Women's Cultural Group, the logo can be seen on the back of our Eid cards) arranged sessions with them. The first one was done by a private producer who then sold it to SATV and with that we did not have much cause to object. The second was an interview with me as editor of *Indian Delights* and this they never showed on the screen. Fair enough. But the last one we were one of the organisations that helped with the Ramadaan programme. Our portion came out silent and just a flash of two scenes with no commentary. Hafez AbuBaker, whose interview a week earlier gave a true image of Islam was, in this programme, shown as part of Islamic fundamentalism (and whatever that means only the Western media knows) with pictures of the Iran revolution in the background. What has that to do with Ramadaan?

The Theatrical world in South Africa is heavily coloured with Indians these days. Saira Essa is most successful and so are many others. Ketan Lakhani is chief theatre critic for *Sunday Tribune* and Shan Moodley is producer of the very popular Prime Time programme on TV. Pleasant thing is that they are tackling very relevant subjects and not as in earlier days just sticking to the White Black confrontational ones. Attenborough's Biko will certainly bring the agony of Biko in[to] every man's home.

Ahmed, you do know that my family reads your letters and they all enjoy them. When Aslam read your last letter touching on the status of women in countries where Islamic Law prevails, he let out a yell and said "Shameema, this poor chappie does not know what he has let himself in for". Meaning that you had let yourself in for a good lengthy sermon from myself! Well as Aslam predicted here goes.

When you mention that you were not sure whether the media had correctly reported the Iranian incident, unlike most Muslims I am not going to say that they slanted the news deliberately, but there was another report in an Iranian newsletter which stated that the cultural differences were explained earlier to the Zimbabwean

Embassy but someone there boobed. The Western Media does slant things but often it is because they see things differently. By way of explanation let me mention one incident. A white woman from an audience where I spoke on Islam asked "But [is] it not cruel that you send these old persons away to Mecca. I saw them clinging and crying at the airport but it seems their children insisted that they go!"

How does one explain to an Occidental mind the emotional impact Haj has on old persons who leave home in a state of preparation to meet their end in places they consider Hallowed. Hence the asking of forgiveness and the tearful adieu's with loved ones?

Just as one has to toe the party lines of any organisation one belongs to, Islam insists that one submit to the Shariah (Law) and the success of the Iranian revolution can only be explained to their total application to a lifestyle they have chosen. How can their leaders then be seen, once outside the country succumbing to another way of living?

Since the Iranian revolution, young men and young women of the Islamic world have adapted living styles in keeping with their religion. Academics, business executives, field workers, students of both sexes quietly going about their work and the dignity of self assurance they display is lovely to behold. In countries like Algeria and Tunisia, and Turkey, young girls at universities [are] opposing the authorities who dislike the veils they have donned – burkhas such as my grandmother never wore!

These young people shun the headlines but in every distressed area in South Africa you will find them as social workers, doctors, running clinics and classes. Count the number of beards and knitted caps next time you came across a picture of some unrest situation in the Cape.

As far as the highly industrialised societies, after their factories have spewed out hightec objects to saturation point, they are coming to a grinding halt. Worldwide unemployment is one of the things we now have to face. When I read the statistics of sexual harassment of women in work situations I feel like joining the Gandhian call of back to the spinning wheel! It is not reforms we need in this world; it is a complete change!

You mentioned in one of your letters that the release of Nelson is just one of those things that make the rounds now and again. But our reading of all the English and Afrikaans papers bring to mind a picture of Nelson around a table negotiating with others and whatever anyone else believes I think the day is not far off when we will see you outside your present lodgings. Hope the censors leave this bit in!

I had Dilshad in a trolley at the supermarket together with bags of fertiliser and other goods. I bumped into a cement block and the trolley toppled over, Dilshad coming first and the heavies on top of her. An African gentleman nearby jumped so fast he managed to put his hands over Dilshad protecting her from the bags of fertilizer, which would certainly have caused a very serious accident. As it is she had a broken tooth and another loose one with a few bruises, on her body. That man was really an angel who helps children from getting hurt. He put parcels in the car, got granny and child up and did not wait for me to thank him sufficiently. After medical attention, when we came home she told her mummy. "Nani boom Dishaa".

This was written while Comrades Marathon was on and the first three Forsythe, Dela Motta and Hosiah Tjaale have just broken records again. A few Indians also undertake the run.

All the best for Eid from all of us.
Zuleikha

A.M. Kathrada
Pollsmoor Maximum Prison
27 July 1986

Dear Zuleikkabehn

Many thanks for your letter, the Eid card, and the "Eidy" – all of which reached me on 12<sup>th</sup> June, the day I "celebrated" exactly 22 years of my life sentence. Please don't blame yourself for the letter not reaching me before Eid; in fact it arrived at Pollsmoor in good time, but all registered mail, and letters containing money, have to first go through other offices (eg. Accounts office), before reaching the Censors Office. The consolation is that registered letters do at least reach me.

Since you have been an uncomplaining "victim" of our recollections let me take you back to that Friday of 1964. Just yesterday Walter and I were recounting the events to someone. We had been found guilty on the 11<sup>th</sup> June, and went to court the next day for the sentence. You may remember that there was widespread talk of a death sentence, and although our lawyers had done their best to assure us that there won't be any death sentences, I must confess that I wasn't feeling exactly relaxed when I went to court. The courtroom was packed, and there were thousands of people outside, which was most encouraging. The sentencing, which was broadcast live over the SABC, took only a few minutes. When the spectators heard "life sentence" there was an audible sigh of relief; which I suppose was a reflection of our own feelings. We were later taken back to the prison at great speed and non-stop. The convoy was led by traffic police, with sirens full blast. It was all very dramatic. Arrangements were made for us to see our visitors the next day, and we also made an appointment to see our lawyers the following week. In jail we had to change into prison uniforms, but were told we could finish all the "home food". We were moved into 2 communal cells, and after a few hours of small talk we went to bed. Then about 1 o'clock the lights suddenly went on, the doors were opened, and a whole group of wardens walked in. We were told to take our belongings and two blankets each. We were then handcuffed, and shackled, and put into a van, and driven to the military airport. At about 8 o'clock on Saturday morning 13th June, after a very cold and uncomfortable flight, the Dakota landed on Robben Island. Our life sentence had begun.

Since then I've been to the Transvaal once. That was in August 1966 when we went to Pretoria to give evidence in the civil action of Zeph Mothoping (P.A.C.) who had sued the Minister of Police.*
I had always loved Cape Town and the sea, but I never imagined that I'd be spending a whole stretch of 23 years, and more, in this city and its environs!

Anyway, back to 1986. Eid Day was once again very enjoyable. As it has now become customary, we were overwhelmed with goodwill and "goodies". So many people wanted to bring parcels that the authorities were obliged to refuse to accept. My day started with an early visit from Ramesh Vassen and his little daughter Priyadarshini. She brought chocolate and yoghurt. Then came Imam Cassim, who visits me every month. Then Enver and his 3 year old Nadia, together with Adv. Omar's daughter Fazlin. The afternoon was rounded off with a visit from two lovely young ladies from Athlone, who are friends of my nephew. So you see my Eid day was rather hectic, but welcome and exciting. Children's visits are always lovely. Nadia has been here a number of times and is quite familiar with the place. She is an extrovert, and has the

---

\* Zeth Mothopeng was the most senior member of the PAC after Robert Sobukwe. He was severely tortured. Kathrada was called as witness as he had seen the torture marks during his early imprisonment, and spoken to Mothopeng.

good looks, charm (and vanity!!) of her sex. When she learnt that her father was coming here she insisted that she had to show uncle her dress and shoes, which had been brought from India. Then she had to make Duwa, recite some nursery rhymes, and count from one to ten in Arabic, (which is more than I could ever do). She, like most children, is no respecter of uniforms, or iron grills, or regulations, and does her own thing, uninhibited, and unafraid. Not for her the need to resort to guile, or diplomacy, or bravado. How wonderful to live in a child's world! There is so much we adults can still learn from them.

Thanks for your efforts to have *Indicator* subscription forms sent to me. Nothing has reached me. In any case it does not seem as if I am going to be allowed to subscribe to it. I am waiting for the final decision from Pretoria.

Can I impose upon you to do me another favour? In the *Leader* of 6th and 13th June there were 2 photos which I would like to get. There was one with the late Dawood Seedat, Cissy Gool etc; the other was also a group photo with Monty, Dadoo, etc. They would be valuable additions to my collection. I would have written directly to the *Leader*, but as I indicated to you earlier, they appear to have a policy of ignoring correspondence. If the photos are available the best thing would be for you to send them with one of your letters, together with the account. I can send the money to them. There is no urgency about this; you can make the arrangements at your leisure.

There is yet another favour. A couple of months ago I read of the death of Professor Ramfol, and I wanted to send my condolences to his family. Unfortunately I do not know any of his family, nor their address. I mentioned to you some time ago that I had been in touch with him while he was at Westville; he was very helpful and sympathetic. It is very late, but I would still like to send this card to the family. Could you get it to them? Thanks a lot. I first met him in the fifties at the Hurbans' place in Tongaat. He was a school inspector at the time. He later stayed at the flat for a short while when he had to be at UNISA, either for a vacation school or in connection with his thesis.

I was sorry to read about the murder of Mohamed's cousin's wife and child. I also read of the death of a Goolam Bismillah in Potch, under mysterious circumstances. Was he related to you? Two of my nephews board at his uncle's place in Lenasia. They also wrote about it, but did not give any more information than what we've seen in the papers.

I've been reading about a Hashim Seedat, who is a historian. Is he the same chap as the lawyer? (I think he is in Thumba Pillay's firm).

Then there is a Durban lady, Kogila Moodley who is married to Professor Heribert Adam of Canada. Do you know her at all? She appears to be doing quite a bit of writing together with her husband.

This will be the lot for today. We are all keeping well. I saw Nelson for an hour about two weeks ago. He is fine. I like your optimism about our spending the next Eid at home, but I don't believe that's going to happen. Not for many years.

Keep well. Fondest regards to you, the children, grandchildren, and all other family members and friends.

From
    AMK

Westville
3630
12th August 1986

Dear Ahmedbhai

With Razia, Jihaan and Humayra, I have just returned after spending a month in London and Spain. Recollecting that my last letter to you was rather scrappy, it was my intention to post you a card from somewhere, and with that in mind I had taken your address along. The card was purchased, but never posted so please accept it now as an Eid card. I am not the best of correspondents when on travel and one letter per week to one family member does the rounds in Durban and the Potch family gets informed by one of the children. However I thought it would boost the spirits of Pollsmoor inmates to be remembered from overseas! My apologies.

Both Mohamed and I were/are great believers in travel as mind expanding. As early as 1966 we took all three kids and a niece to India and Pakistan. Later it was to Europe, Canada, States and Razia even made it with us to Thailand and Indonesia. Of course, Mecca, Medina, Egypt and Turkey were squeezed in between school vacations. Wishing to continue that tradition, and with Jihan turning 7, I persuaded Razia to come along. Humayra being too small to leave behind was dragged along. But she had returned a very grown up three year old. Knows the difference between double-decker, tube, train and understands that London and Granada are different countries, with different languages and currencies. The Gujarati phrase she picked up during travels (how is your Gujarati?) *Ketla hantha paisa* but then Razia and I used that phrase so often during the day when prices shocked us that the child had no option but to repeat the sentence.*

Jihaan needed no prodding to pick up value systems here and there. Menial work she realises is not reserved for any one colour group in other countries and that work done with hands is a public service rather than a messy task better left to others! When she saw white females cleaning stables, she exclaimed that she would help Jaleel when he pushed the barrow with the fertiliser at La Mercy! My generation has certainly done a lot of damage in many areas.

Mohammed would be shocked to see that my passport is valid for 7 years. In the years when we were blankly refused documents for a couple of years he knocked at the highest doors. At one interview the gentleman on the other side of the desk said there was no need to go for holidays overseas. Our country was beautiful and big, travel around here. Mohamed's retort, I always maintained, opened the gates for passports valid for 11 months for us. He said "What, use good money to travel in second and third class transport and have the hotels tell us they can't accept people with our skin colour?"

After Mohamed's death, I did not think that I would ever want to go travelling but seeing things together with this young generation has whetted my appetite. London was as intellectually fulfilling as always. However, this being the children's holiday, I did not gobble up all the things I desired but, between Razia and I, we showed them the usual sights such as Speakers corner (has lost all its fire!), Madame Tussaud's (which Humayra did not like), Toy museum, Covent gardens etc.

Wanting to show them something more relevant to our culture I went to the Moroccan Embassy and insisted that they waive the rulings against South Africans. The Ambassador-Consul himself attended to my pleas but said he could not take the decision

---

\* It is so expensive.

himself and would have to refer it to Morocco. This would take time. When after 10 days the reply had not come, we had to be satisfied with Andalusian Spain. Jihaan was so taken up with the Alhambra that I wonder what her reaction will be when she sees the Mosques of Turkey, the Islamic complexes of Samarkand, Bokhara, Afghanistan, Delhi, etc. I also wonder whether Jaleel will love travelling as we did and obviously as Jihaan and Humayra did, or will he be like his father? Nasim did not like travelling with us and even now considers it a chore.

Kogee Moodley and sisters are all highly talented. One sister is married to Mamoo Rajab and a younger one was leader of student protest at Durban-Westville in the early years. Professor Adam of course is an outstanding scholar and personality. Husband and wife were for some years at Cairo University. I am not sure of present location.

Goolam Bismilla is son of distant cousin but his aunt also happens to be my Bhabhi (wife of brother who died. She and her two married sons emigrated to Canada). Goolam's parents are not well off. His mother (Coloured, converted to Islam) is serious and hardworking and has been senior sales assistant in my brother's shop for many years. The son was well brought up but in matric year fell in with some bad friends. They got into some scrapes, one of which involved housebreaking. When another housebreaking incident took place, they were taken in for questioning at 5.00pm and by 7.30pm the police phoned to say that he had died. They had arranged for a private post-mortem but since my return I have not caught up with all the events. Young, healthy with no sign of any illness – what does one say to console parents at a time like this?

Hassim Seedat – a cousin of Zuby Seedat who was legal partner of I.C. Meer for many years in Verulam but who now practices in Durban – wrote a series of articles in *Leader* on [the] Ghandian era in South Africa. He is considered a historian and hopes to write a book at some stage. I have told him on occasion that collating material from already published materials is not good enough and he must interview persons in Natal and Johannesburg who lived in that era. There are still some around. I pointed out the error of Fatima Meer in *Apprenticeship of a Mahatma*, wherein she repeats errors of early recorders where Essop Mia is referred to as Essop Mian. Though Fatima knows Boy and Moosa Mia (who doesn't? Their house opposite New Town School in Bree Street and Moosa eloping with Parsee lady which incident jolted us Dabhelians out of our small Gaam skins) she never connected this historical figure as the father of this family. As Moosa angrily said, "Does she think he was some Mia-Bhai?" One does not laugh at Moosa when he is angry, but he marrying a Parsee (what a gracious woman) and still thinking in terms of Surtee and Miabhai.*

I phoned Johannesburg to enquire about the *Indicator* copies. Each one has been posted to you, these past few months. I have suggested that they send you a subscription form. Maybe that will help.

Photographs requested by you do not exist. The ones appearing in the papers were copied from old [Indian] Views and [Indian] Opinion issues. However someone has promised to let me have the positives of the negatives of the newspaper copies if that makes any sense.

Incidentally Abu Huraira sends his salaams to all of you. He dropped in unexpectedly a few days ago and read your letter that had arrived a day earlier.

I remain optimistic. Open any paper or magazine and there is something about the Mandelas. The latest issue of *Fair Lady* (and what I like about the article is that it does not romanticise or make

---

\* Surtees are Gujarati-speaking while Miabhais speak Urdu. Until recent times, it was considered taboo to marry across such ethnic lines.

of Winnie an object of adoration) has a straightforward story on Winnie. The plain facts themselves are heart touching. In a recent article on Nelson, Kierkegaard is quoted: "The tyrant dies and his rule ends: the martyr dies and his rule begins."

Hope that does not sound morbid. It's well for those outside to repeat these profound truths.

Enjoy a good Eidul Qurbaan and may the good Capetonian friends not forget you on this day of sacrifice.

Zuleikhabhen

A.M. Kathrada
Pollsmoor Maximum Prison
Tokai
7966
28th September 1986

Dear Zuleikhabehn

Many thanks for your letter of 12th August which, together with the card arrived on 20th August. I never cease to be amazed at the way people travel these days. They simply go off on foreign travels, and the next thing I get a card or letter casually mentioning their experiences in some distant land. Now, between your two letters, you have been on a month's trip abroad! Just like that. And, to fit in with my picture of the caring and kind granny, you took Razia, Jihaan and Humayra with you. Only difference is that in the old day's granny's treat for the little ones did not extend much beyond the proverbial cookie jar. I try to imagine what the little ones talk about among their friends. No more boasts about granny taking them for a drive, or to bioscope, or the beach, or giving a new dress. Now they must be talking about the plane trip and the wonderful experiences in London and Spain. A few months ago I received a letter from a niece who tells me that one of her unforgettable memories is of the time I took her to the Jo'burg Zoo! She must have been about 4 or 5 then.

Travelling was so unusual when I was young. I must have told you of the huge crowd that turned up at the airport when I went to Europe, in 1951. This had a sequel ten years later; and it was only then that I realised that just the fact of seeing one off at the airport was regarded as a special experience by some people. You will be patient with me for unloading some more of my recollections. In April 1961, after being discharged in the marathon Treason Trial,

I decided that I should have a break and get away from everything for a while. And what better place for this than Cape Town! But there was a snag: I was under restriction orders which, among other things, confined me to Jo'burg. Asking for permission was out of the question; they had already refused me permission to visit my mother in Schweizer. So the only thing to do was to take a chance, and hope for the best. I only informed one person of my intention, and that was the late Braam Fischer. He was a friend, a political colleague, and a lawyer; in case of trouble I would need all three. So together with two friends we left for Cape Town in my friend's brand new (and unknown) car. As luck would have it, by the time we reached Beaufort West the car started giving trouble, and we could proceed no further. It was Saturday morning of the Easter weekend and all the garages were closed. The prospect of spending the long weekend in that Karoo dorp was hard to contemplate. Seeing our plight, the sympathetic hotel manager suggested that we should try Mr X, who was a mechanic, but who refused to work over weekends. However, he was an ex-Joburger and might just relent, and help out. We were desperate and went along to Mr X's house, and introduced ourselves and explained our plight. I was of course travelling as "Mr Mohamed". He was very hospitable, and excited to see Jo'burg folks. In the course of the conversation he threw a bombshell, and asked, "Do you people know Mr Kathy Kathrada, who was recently discharged in the Treason Trial"? We were stunned, and gave some vague replies. When Mr X was out we quickly decided that we should tell him who I was, in the hope that this would influence him to fix our car. But also to save him from making exaggerated (and embarrassing) claims about his "friend". When we disclosed my identity, Mr X, turned round and asked "Don't you remember me? I was at the airport with …when you went to Europe." I later ascertained that he was indeed at the airport with a friend of mine. But I couldn't remember. Anyway Mr X became more enthusiastic. He was going to fix our car, but not before he could entertain us. So we spent a lovely weekend there, and then went on to Cape Town, where we spent about 10 days and returned safely. Just to complete the story. Do you know what? About 6 weeks after our return I was arrested; not for the Cape Town trip, about which they remained ignorant; but for having gone to Schweizer the previous December without permission. They refused bail and kept me locked up for over 6 weeks, mostly in Christiana jail. The Supreme Court eventually gave me bail. I was of course found guilty.

I'm very tempted to relate some incidents while I was in Christiana jail, but I'll save you the affliction.

You expressed the hope that our Cape Town friends would not forget us on Bakri Eid. Once again they were absolutely marvellous, and we had a most enjoyable day. They have really spoilt us. I don't know if the thought of Eid goodies is responsible, but I am suddenly feeling hungry. It is half past eleven (at night). I've just interrupted this letter, made myself a cup of instant coffee (water from a thermos flask), and had an Ouma Muesli. This sort of thing happens very seldom – about once or twice a year. Anyway I've now got enough energy to complete this letter.

Apparently the *Indicator* has been coming; but as I've indicated it is being withheld. I don't know the reason. It is strange since we've been receiving almost everything else, eg. *Cape Times, Burger, Star, City Press, Sowetan Weekly Mail, Frontline, Drum* etc. Anyway I have discussed the matter with an officer, and was told that Pretoria was considering it. So I'll have to wait.

In the meantime I've been reading the articles by Ameen which appear in the *Post*, etc. They are generally very good. He is competent, but unfortunately, as many of the younger generation, he is not strong on recent history. Once, after reading his article on the Fordsburg High School, I was tempted to write to him to correct some errors. But I changed my mind; he may have regarded my action as presumptuous.

While still on the media, I've been reading about Shan Moodley of the SABC. From your remarks, as well as other sources, he appears to be competent. Is he originally from Natal?

I saw a photo of the launching of Mewa's book. It was nice to see Chota, Vasu, Behn, Ismail Mohamed. There was a Mrs Barmenia among them. Am I right that she is the late A.I. Kajee's daughter? I must say I was a bit surprised to see her in this crowd.

I noticed in the papers that Kogila Moodley was teaching temporarily at the University of Cape Town. I will try to order their book from the library.

On coming back to Spain; I'm presently reading the autobiography of La Pasionaria (Dolores Ibarruri), who served as a Minister in the Republican Govt. during the Civil War. It's called *They Shall Not Pass*. It is fascinating.

Thanks for Salaams from Abu Huraira. Do greet him and family, and all other friends, who are constantly in our thoughts.

You asked about my Gujarati. I'm ashamed to say that at the best of time it was weak. These days it is much worse. I doubt it very much if I could conduct a 40 minute visit in Gujarati.

This reminds me. I assume you did manage to pass on my sympathy-card to Professor Ramfol's family? Thanks. He once sent me Beginners Books for Hindi.

Things are fine with us. If I hadn't been feeling old all these years, a visit I had earlier this month made me have second thoughts. A friend's daughter Shireen, came along to introduce her husband to me. I was present the night in December 1953 when Shireen was born, and I was responsible for her name. Thus I'm her godfather. Now she herself is expecting her first baby, and wants me to name the child! I wonder how common it is for one to be godfather to both mother and child! There is a related matter which I should discuss with you one day. Shireen has married a chap who is not Moslem, and is experiencing problems with her family. The couple are naturally very upset.

Sorry to come back to Hassim Seedat. Is this the same chap who was once in the firm of N.T. Naicker? In 1961 or so?

This is all for now. Keep well. Fondest regards to the children, grandchildren and all the family members and friends. All the best to you.

From
AMK

Westville
3630
12th November 1986

Dear Ahmedbhai

Nothing great but many little things occurred which prevented an early reply to you. Having just turned sixty, I jealously count the minutes ticking away, resolve firmly that each one must count for something and yet time is frittered away. What has one achieved one cries in frustration and in answer to that let me trace the life of a very ordinary citizen that died ten days ago.

Chota Saloojee (married to my niece who was involved in the accident with me) has a brother who had to leave on an exile permit to England, but Chota himself never made headlines. His father had died when he was very young and, with the elder brother a medical person and involved in politics, the widowed mother relied heavily on Chota to look after the family business in La Rochelle, see to the schooling and training of the four younger brothers and a sister and get them equipped to face life. All this and much more he did quietly, self-effacedly and with a gentleness that made him dearly beloved. His own family consists of four daughters. The eldest (married) qualified as a medical practitioner two years ago and with her husband works at King Edward Hospital, Durban. The second one is writing her finals and her marriage was to take place on the 29th inst. Cards already printed! Chota, who was only 50 and in excellent health, suddenly drops dead. The numbers turning up at his funeral and the people still coming daily from far and near to pay their respect to the young widow makes one wonder why this young man was known to so many. Remember he never hit the headlines, he belonged to no organisation and he never headed charity lists for he does not have that kind of money.

Let's start with Wilson. An African a few years Chota's senior. Wilson is one of those illegal residents of La Rochelle and having his work area near Chota's business (under threat of Group Areas for many many years) a relationship was established. On the day of the funeral Wilson wept like a brother. "The many times this man has helped me. Why just last week he put his hand in his pocket and said 'Wilson I haven't seen your family for a long time. Please take this.'"

There was the old Khala from Benoni who came as a stranger to weep with the widow. "I knew the Saloojee family way back when I lived in Johannesburg. Some few years ago I needed money desperately so I came with my little box of jewellery to Chota and said, son please keep this and give me so much. When I have the money to repay you, I will take my jewels back. Chota gave me the money and he gave me the box saying, I have no place to keep this. Why don't you keep it and pay me when you can?"

There was a young man who had just qualified from university and has started work. He said that in between studies he came to Chota for help with fees. "Aunty he would open the till, take out some notes and give them to me without counting. At one time it was over 300 rands."

I am only recounting a few incidents of which none of us were aware. Considering that Chota was constantly struggling to meet his many commitments, for his shop is small and the dependents all along many, he would have been quite justified had he only looked after his own family. My whole point is that this is the way our people lived, helping each other, looking after needs of others and the community, building schools and so forth without fanfare. Who will say that this man has not achieved? Definitely he made this world a bit better for some people and having done that he has earned his salt and his external peace. Like Alan Paton says, the obituaries of Indians makes one believe that the community is made up of saints. Sorry for this one!

It must appear callous that we send cards of our visits from all exotic places. I am in no position to judge what effect it must have on persons incarcerated as long as you have been. One can only hope that it colours your days slightly. Which reminds me that some time ago I wrote that the universal orchestration for Nelson and you others' release would pay dividends before another year has passed. I still hold thumbs!

The NGK having at long last conceded their sinful upholding of Apartheid had to find another horse to flog. Their adoption of the resolution declaring Islam a false religion and a threat to Christianity certainly brought the Umma together. Over 40 international organisations sent telegrams to the State President and newspapers have been flooded out with protest letters. With Mosques going up in Soweto, Kwa Mashu etc; no wonder the beleaguered feel threatened.

The anecdote of your surreptitious Cape Town trip made interesting reading. Do write about the Christiana jail incident. Did the Nanabhais, Mangera family look you up while you were government guest there? Once some friends went to our West Street Maulana and tried to nudge his conscience that he should pay visits to Muslim prisoners. I am told he stroked his beard and said "Yes, make appointments and send round your car. I will look them up." But to be fair to the old man when I asked him to accompany me to see the local chief in charge of detainees (after Timol's death there were 8 Muslim detainees in Durban) so that we could get Eid hampers to them, he willingly led our deputation and we were successful.

With salaams to all of you.
Sincerely yours
Zuleikha

A.M. Kathrada
Pollsmoor Maximum Prison
Tokai
7966
31ˢᵗ December 1986

Dear Zuleikhabehn

As each year draws to a close I seem to invariably run short of letters and visits, and I have to renew a resolution to plan my correspondence better in the coming year. But it never works out, and I'm obliged to delay my replies. My apologies for only replying now to your letter which reached me on 26ᵗʰ November. It is only 1½ hours to go before the New Year, so let me start off by wishing you, all the family members and friends, my very best wishes for continued good health, and success in all your endeavours. When twelve o'clock strikes I shall be waking up Walter to wish him a happy New Year, and to serve him a cup of coffee. I suppose we'll have a bit of a chat, perhaps watch some TV (if there's a good programme), and then to bed.

We'll be starting this New Year rather differently. As you've probably heard we've recently been given some new concessions, which among other things, have enabled us to acquire TV sets. We've got a big colour set in our cell. The invasion by this audio-visual monster into our lives has forced some radical changes in our daily routine. This, in spite of the fact that most of the programmes are mediocre, even trash. For sheer <u>entertainment</u> my favourite programme is the Cosby Show. I stress entertainment, because one cannot look upon the series as a reflection of the reality of the socio-economic conditions of Black people in America. I am aware of the danger that a superficial look at Cosby can easily foster the mistaken impression that all is well with the lives of American

Blacks. But I don't want to fall into the groove of seeking a social message in every film, novel, cartoon or comic. Reminds me: on days when the 1956-61 Treason Trial became very boring some of us devised alternative forms of entertainment. We used to bring along cartoon books ("Andy Capp", "Bringing Up Father", etc) and enjoy ourselves. One day my neighbour and I decided to circulate "Andy Capp" among all the accused, and observe the various reactions. Some obviously enjoyed it; others were indifferent; some simply could not fathom what was going on. A few hours later I received a note: "Comrade", it said, "what has all this to do with Marxism-Leninism?"!!

I also follow, and enjoy, Cagney and Lacey, but not necessarily for the content. We've seen some of the old films (War and Peace... etc). Shaka Zulu was lousy. I too was taken in by the press publicity which promoted the series, until I saw the thing. Fortunately we only saw the last 5 or 6 episodes, but those were enough. A word about "The Web of Persuasion". I hope I won't be crucified for saying this, but I found aspects of it interesting and even enjoyable. For instance, I liked Indira's acting, and her initially defiant stand. However, if I were to write a fuller assessment, naturally my criticisms will far outweigh any positive aspects. For news, I still rely mainly on the press, and the Radio Today sessions, 6–8.30am and 5-6pm. Of course I do watch a few sessions of TV news, but I find the coverage inadequate, unimaginative and unashamedly biased. A classic case of the abuse of this medium. Although the quality of TV2 news programmes is no better, I find it more interesting because it brings together township life, events, personalities, etc. closer to us. I also prefer some of the TV2 music programmes.

We are now also allowed to have wrist watches. We may write poetry, but no books or biographies. We can take up hobbies. And, we may keep pets – cats, fish, birds. My initial reaction to the latter still prevails. I cannot bring myself to imprison another living thing, be it bird, fish or beast. A very sensible and civilised concession is that our visits will no longer be in the cubicles where we were separated from the visitors by a glass panel, and we had to speak through a sort of microphone. We will now have contact visits. Unfortunately these concessions are not uniformly applicable to all prisoners; some of them are only for so-called "A group" prisoners. It took me 13 years to be "promoted" to "A Group"!

You will be pleased to know that I am now receiving *Indicator* (Lenasia). I've had a few back copies for 1986 and I hope to be getting it regularly in future. About half a dozen persons, including yourself, have been making efforts to get the paper to me. Now it transpires that the reason why I have not being given the copies is that it was thought that they were being posted to me by family and friends, and not by the *Indicator* people themselves. I have asked Ameen to ensure that my copies are always sent in the paper's official wrapper. Under the new concessions our people outside are now allowed to subscribe on our behalf; this fact too has contributed towards the relaxation of the prohibition by the authorities.

I suspect that my subscription for *Leader* should be expiring soon. I've already made arrangements for its renewal, and hope everything will be okay.

In one of A.C.'s recent articles he mentioned that in the 40s unmarried Moslem males and females did not appear together in public. Then I saw "Web of Persuasion". A combination of these set in motion a chain of thoughts that led be back a number of years to a letter of yours in which you remarked about my having been engaged to a certain lady many years ago. I did reply to that letter but it never reached you. This was when I was still on Robben Island, many letters were simply getting "lost". Many times since then I've been wanting to refer to the matter, but never managed to do so. I suppose I could not pluck up the necessary "courage".

On the other hand I knew I was conscience-bound to make an explanation. But who to? It was not too difficult to choose you. After all you have so willingly and uncomplainingly acted as a repository for the bits of information which I have been imparting over the years. The position is that I was not engaged to the lady in the formal sense, but for all intents and purposes we were as good as engaged and set to marry. We went to cinemas together, and also attended other public functions together. Our families, friends and the community had accepted our relationship. As you know (and as A.C. reminded us) in those years it was virtually unknown for unmarried couples to be seen in public. In fact even married couples in public caused raised eyebrows.

In 1951 I went abroad. We kept in touch for a while. Then, while I was still in Hungary, I unilaterally decided that I no longer wished to get married, and I stopped writing. The most despicable thing on my part was that I did not then, nor after my return, inform her of my change of mind. I caused her grave humiliation and embarrassment, and much pain. My family and friends also felt hurt by my disgraceful conduct, and virtually no one sided with me. I am not going to attempt to outline the reasons for my decision. But I want to very strongly refute the widespread rumours that it was because of a Hungarian girl. True I did have a girlfriend in Budapest, but there was absolutely no connection between that and my change of mind. Had my Hungarian affair been serious, I certainly would not have returned to South Africa some years before schedule. You see I was working in the offices of the World Federation of Democratic Youth, and it had been agreed that I would remain there for at least 3 years. I was enjoying every minute of my experience there, meeting and working with some fantastic people, and visiting different countries.

There, very briefly, you have the basic facts. Believe me, up to this day I have never ceased to curse and criticise myself [for] what I did. My only consolation is that the lady is happily married. Naturally there are a lot more surrounding facts which I have omitted because of restriction of space.

Having got that off my chest, let me tell you of our festivities. On Christmas day I had a lovely visit from Advocate Omar's wife and daughter. I may have mentioned that they are among the Cape Town folks who have been extremely kind to us. For Boxing Day, for the first time in all these years, we were allowed to order a full meal from outside. We sat down at table with a table cloth and serviettes and really enjoyed a well-prepared multi-course lunch. The menu could have come straight from the pages of *Indian Delights*! What really made our day was that Nelson was allowed to have lunch with us and spend a few hours together. He is very well.

I'll have to end now. I knew Chota Saloojee, and am sorry to hear of his death. My sympathies to his family. I was of course not aware of the philanthropic side of his life. As you so rightly observe these are the real unsung heroes.

Keep well. Fond regards to all members of the family and friends. All the best to you for 1987, from

AMK

Westville
3630
10<sup>th</sup> February 1987

My dear Ahmedbhai

The long overdue concessions – no doubt these will have brought some of the world outside to you and your colleagues. A world which is in a sorry mess for we have not, in spite of the many Prophets, reformers, religions and isms, yet learnt to share the goodies of life. What is mine by conquest, by subterfuge and wile and crookedness, remains mine and in the concrete jungles, it's not the survival of the fittest, but of the sly and cunning ones. What a theme to start off a letter. Sorry!

The Cosby show is excellent. Forget the colour and concentrate on the family that talks, and communicates and retains its sense of humour – as such the show cannot be faulted. If I were to analyse everything I enjoy, even my *Indian Delights* dishes would choke me, for while I am eating, millions are starving. Let me relate an incident.

So many years ago, in fact decades, we gave an acquaintance a lift from Johannesburg to Durban. It was Ramadaan and our friend was not fasting. Meanwhile we were carrying a small hamper with which to break our fast but told the co-passenger to help himself. Nearing Ladysmith it was time to break our fast but there was nothing left in the hamper, not even a morsel….. Two weeks later this person was seen approaching up Grey Street, but when he saw Mohamed (my late husband who had agreed to give the lift) he jumped across the road onto the opposite pavement and went on his way. Now he had suddenly remembered that as a member of NEUM he was not supposed to fraternise or socialise with the bourgeoisie and the sellouts! The idiosyncrasies of people does make life interesting.

Have you read any of Ahmed Essop's works? The Sufi or Haji and other stories are both well written in Naipaul's manner of highlighting the foibles of his characters and society. Frankly I find this tedious after a while but for a local writer he is good. What I find strange is that Essop views his characters rather superficially. The social institutions are dealt with very much as if a stranger or an outsider would deal without understanding the philosophy or inner perceptions. If a non-Indian had written it would be excusable but surely one of us would have deeper intuition? It's not the laughs at people and institutions that I am trying to criticise, it's the snide jeering (maybe not quite that bluntly) that irritates at times.

Abu Huraira came the other day and we were discussing the *Leader* articles. In between we regretted the fact that no paper had mentioned the death of S.M. Paruk that week. He was one of the few veterans of the Old School. Then we recalled the fact that in the 50s three veterans had died in the course of a few weeks and soon after that a leading (White) lawyer also died. The joke went around that the latter was quickly called and let through the pearly gates for the earlier 3 deceased ones needed legal representation. We thought of letting A.C. [know] of this so that he could include this in his articles. Are we now doing what I have just criticised Essop of?

In trying to come to the point or to show the difference between seeing an object superficially and deeply with understanding let me tell of another incident. Soon after setting up a home in Durban, Fatima Meer and I were interested in Bonsai. (Why do the Meers crop up so often?) What put an end to that interest was Ismail's furious remark "How can you desire to stunt healthy plants!" But in the 1970s when Mohamed and I toured Japan and we saw the gardens of the Japanese, especially those in Kyoto, we suddenly saw the difference between the Japanese style garden and the gardens of the Japanese themselves. The latter defined a culture and an artistry of the most profound kind and it was imbedded with their philosophy and view of life. Shortage of space had of course restrained their hands and so the bonsai was added to their culture.

The spirit and the atmosphere captured by the Japanese garden activates the mind to ponder on the link between the mundane and the supramundane. Material is not to be despised but must lead towards spirituality. Symbolism of the falling blossoms of the fully blown flowers reminding man of death while in the prime of life; the gnarled shape of bonsai demonstrating the struggle against the elements which often leave behind dwarfed, twisted and knobbly shapes. Nothing is ignored or discarded (as in current Western culture) but the mass is left nestling at the foot of a giant plant and allowed to creep up stones; the ground is raked in patterns emulating waves and fallen patterns and leaves raked and heaped neatly showing perhaps that the old and weary too have their beauty and place in life. Under those conditions and when seen through the eyes of the Japanese the Bonsai takes on a very deep meaning underscoring Universal Truths.

The Japanese in their communal baths do not shock. It seemed such a natural condition. What I found most impressive was their confidence in their own lifestyle. They, unlike us Indians with our inferiority complex, just do not go around explaining their culture or asking for an understanding of it, they just live it!

Thanks for the missing bits of the engagement history. Events have a manner of developing and not even the chief characters can explain the hows and whys but in the end they work out for the best of all. Imagine your remorse of having been taken in for all these years with a young wife left to care for herself. Also on the other hand the remorse of the other party having to break off things if she could no longer suffer the separation. There is a Higher Hand behind the scheme of things!

I have blabbered on and on. Please attribute it to old age. I have just begun to enjoy the pensioners' discount on internal airfares. Instead of the R250-00 return from Durban to Johannesburg, I now only pay R150-00. In August of 1986 I turned 60. I will be paying my mother the quarterly visit (she will soon be 90 and needs a bit more attention from her offspring) this week and Nureen will accompany me.

Salaams

A.M. Kathrada
Pollsmoor Maximum Prison
Tokai
7966
8th March 1987

Dear Zuleikhabehn

Many thanks for your letter of 10th February, which reached me on the 20th. I assume that by the time this reaches [you], you will have returned from your quarterly visit to the Transvaal. I hope you found your mother well; and also all the other members of the family.

Your paragraph on Bonsai was really an eye-opener for me. Up to now my knowledge of it did not extend beyond the fact that it had something to do with Japanese miniature plants. I had no idea that it had such interesting and fascinating philosophical as well as practical connotations.

I have not read any of Ahmed Essop's works; I ordered "The Haj..." from the Provincial Library, but never got it. All I've read are reviews and comments on his works. I noticed in the *Leader* recently that the "Haj" has been attacked for allegedly offensive observations about the Hindu religion. Is this the type of thing you had in mind when you wrote about the author's snide jeering and laughing at people and institutions? It will be a great pity if he has opened himself up to such criticism. Disputes based on religion are the last things we need.

The only book of Naipaul's which I've read is "The House of Mr Biswas." It was a number of years ago, and I hesitate to make definitive comment. But I found it enjoyable. Incidentally I think I met Essop once, in the mid-fifties. I don't wish to do him an injustice, but for some reason he reminds me of your Ramadan hitchhiker. Back to Naipaul; I notice he has recently published a new book, "The Enigma of Arrival". A reviewer described it as an autobiographical novel.

I can imagine how the late Mohamed must have felt about the boorish behaviour of this man who crossed the street in order to avoid greeting him. These types suffer from a surfeit of "principles". They live in constant fear that with almost every step, they may be transgressing one or other of their law of the Medes and Persians. They must basically be very unhappy individuals. One would pity them, were it not for the insults and hurt that some of their actions cause.

Regarding the Cosby Show, there can be no quarrel in general, with your advice that one should concentrate on the family situation – the relationships between the parents, between parents and children, between the siblings, the communication, the discipline, the humour. Perhaps the motive of the producers was to highlight these. But I still believe that one must always bear in mind that the affluence and general lifestyle of the Cosby's is not representative of the typical American Black family. Having made this point, I assure you that I thoroughly enjoy every episode; it remains No. 1 on my list.

In January a nephew of mine got married to a Cape Town girl; the Kathrada clan descended upon the city in droves. In the process I was able to see numerous family members, some of whom I had not seen for long as 15 years and more, and kids whom I had never seen. Perhaps the nicest moment was the visit by the bride and bridegroom, in their wedding attire! This nephew's mother is the sister of "my lady" of the fifties whom we have written about; so that part of the family was also here. I had a very pleasant visit from her mother, aunt, cousin and brother. It was good to see the old lady. Prior to the visit a story had reached me that the lady herself would also be among the visitors. I decided I was going to adorn myself in sackcloth and ashes and tender apologies albeit 35 years late. As it transpired, however, she remained outside, and we were only able to see each other as we passed her by car.

I must end now. I didn't know the airways gave such a huge discount to pensioners. But I suppose what you saved on your airfare, you had to spend on Nureen's. Or is she not yet liable for payment?

Healthwise all is well. Last week I was taken to Cape Town for the annual medical check-up. The specialist was quite satisfied.

Keep well. Fond regards to you and all members of the family.

From
AMK

P.S. Please do me a favour; check with the *Leader* if my subscription is still okay. I have made arrangements with attorney Ayob to attend to the matter; he informed me that all my subs have been paid. Please ask them not to discontinue if the money has not arrived. It should be on the way. I'm raising this because the issue of 27$^{th}$ February has not arrived. Sorry to bother you. I noticed the bits about Mohamed in the series of A.C.

[A sentence has been scratched out.]

This scratching out has been done by myself.

Westville
3630
9th May 1987

My dear Ahmedbhai

Like a "Warrelwind" as they say in Afrikaans, this election came and is over the hill. May we live to see the next one with more colour in it. Do you remember the "warrelwind" in the Transvaal? When during hot summer months, when the land was dry a gust of wind would visibly swirl the sand, building up like a miniature cyclone, and very swiftly dissipate its own energy. The only evidence of recent activity would be the disturbed sand patterns it had left behind. As children we had rather smelly Gujarati words to describe it, calling it the work of Satan.

The English press, having built up hopes of more liberal returns, had us all fooled. How we humans live in hope and perhaps it is better for what else is there that makes life worth living? There is so much happening in the country and yet, as a Pakistani friend who had recently visited here asked, what's happened? Where is all the action? On our screens and papers we have so much coverage of your country, and here I just don't see anything!

I have a new typewriter – actually it belongs to the Women's Cultural Group. We are busy with a new edition of *Indian Delights*. I have always used my typewriter for doing the Group's work and allowed whoever was helping with the work to use it, but currently no member is free to come and help with the typing, so we have had to engage a part-time helper. She does not like the new highly sophisticated bit of machinery that the Group has purchased and so she is using my older model. Please overlook the mistakes I am making. I too have to move a decade into the future when handling this one. Speaking of *Indian Delights*, I am enclosing your Eidy herewith, and perhaps you may be able to order a copy from Taj Company or CNA, P.O. Box 9, Cape Town, with it. Of course the cheque is for you to use on what you like, I just mention the book, because it remains a steady best seller. We shall manage to sell at least a thousand copies every month, and we will soon have to have a reprint of the current edition. The new one I am busy with will be *The Best of Indian Delights* and it will be a slim exclusive little volume.

Ramadaan started very smoothly. Days are short, in Durban the weather could not be any better and even Jihaan and Jaleel are keeping the odd fast. There is no way we can prevent them from attempting the rozas, for they have keen competition from schoolmates. My attention strays towards the two aloes outside my study window. They are in full bloom and the wise little birds know that early morning, when the flowerettes open up, it yields its best juices. At the moment three little birds with the most gorgeous plumage (black feathers highlighted with peacock and kingfisher blue streaks with long bills) are having their fill.

Did your mother and granny etc. also make the Kuwaar Paak from aloes each winter? That generation certainly believed in cooking their own vitamins for backache, for brain food, for confining mothers, and so forth. Maybe the old hakims took lessons from the little birds!

I have asked someone with more dealing with the *Leader* to check out your subscription. I forgot to ask them whether it has been sorted out but shall do so immediately after writing this.

Razia is expecting her baby sometime next week and we all hope it will be a little brother. Eid is soon after that so may yours be [word unclear].

Zuleikha

A.M. Kathrada
Pollsmoor Maximum Prison
Tokai
7966
14th June 1987

Dear Zuleikhabehn

Thank you very much for your letter of 9th May; it reached me on the 19th together with "Eidy". The cliché about there being a child in every adult is underscored every time I receive "Eidy", invariably my mind wanders back to those days many years ago when the chief excitement about Eid were the new clothes, the special food preparations, and "Eidy". Now, fifty years and more away from childhood it is still a delightful – albeit brief – experience just to momentarily re-live those days.

I must have mentioned to you before, that I had been living away from home since I was 8 years old, that is when I moved to Jo'burg to go to school. It was hard at first, but it certainly had its advantages, not the least of which was to be regarded as the baby of the family, and treated accordingly. Naturally it was the womenfolk (my mother, sister and sisters-in-law) who showered me with favours; but the menfolk didn't do so badly either. This not only continued throughout my school years, but also in my adult life. And believe me, to some measure it remains the same to this day. In fact more so since I have acquired additional "family members" like your goodself. Am I complaining? Not a chance; it is so nice to be pampered that I sometimes wonder if it is not better to remain in jail!

About ordering a copy of *Indian Delights*, I'm afraid it is not going to be possible. When the new concessions were made we had hoped that there would be some relaxation on the question of books. But there wasn't. So at present it seems that I'll have to wait until I come out of jail one day before I can peruse the book. In the meantime good luck for *The Best of Indian Delights*.

While on food, once again our Eid celebrations went off very well. Our only regret was that our colleague Nelson was not with us, and had to enjoy the goodies alone. We were last together on Easter Monday for a couple of hours.

You asked whether my mother made Kuwaar Paak; I can almost certainly say she did. I distinctly remember the taste, but somehow the name does not register. Is it known by any other name? But perhaps it is just my memory playing tricks again.

A couple of days ago I was telling Walter how my memory was letting me down. Throughout the years in jail, I have never forgotten the 12th June, and several other important dates. On last Friday, 12th June, we completed 23 years of our sentence, but it completely slipped my mind. Only at about 9 o'clock at night did I remember. Instead of expressing some words of encouragement, Walter, (somewhat cruelly I thought), simply reminded me that memory lapses do come with age. Yet, he at 75 (on 18 May) still has a fantastic memory.

I liked the way you invoked the Afrikaans "Warrelwind" to describe recent happenings. It is such an apt, and many will still say a farsighted summary of the prospects ahead. Yes I do remember the "warrelwinde" of the dusty western Transvaal.

You remarked about how human beings lived in hope. It reminded me of some writer who said that hope is what distinguished human beings from animals. Simple sounding words, but the more one thinks about them, the more one appreciates their profundity. In institutions such as prisons, hospitals, etc. perhaps more than anywhere else, one is able to see a mass of human beings constantly living in hope. I would have liked to expand on this, but unfortunately have to end now.

This sophisticated typewriter you mentioned, is it a word processor? I've long been reading about word processors but just could not understand how they operated. Dr Karim (of Bethal) tried to explain, but left a lot unanswered. Fortunately a couple of months ago we saw a library film which gave a detailed explanation. It is fascinating.

By now you must be a grandchild richer. Congratulations to Razia. I hope it was a boy.

Keep well. Fondest regards to you, and all the family and friends. If you are going to contact Vallabh soon, please pass my best wishes to him, Jesse and family. I recently heard that he is now almost totally blind. How very sad.

Best wishes from
AMK

Westville
3631
26th August 1987

Dear Ahmedbhai

A reply is long overdue and it would be senseless to apologise and say that I am far behind my set out schedule. Being a social animal, I cannot avoid the calls to attend funerals, weddings and so forth. In between I lost my eldest sister, lovingly called Bai, who with her husband settled in Dublin when their only son married an Irish girl and started his medical practice there.

Bai was 71, healthy, a workaholic like all us Bismillahs, and one who served whichever society she lived among with compassion and understanding. When her son-in-law died last year she spent three months here, helping her daughter to adjust to the loss. On her return to Dublin, she had a severe coronary and eventually succumbed to that ailment. For my mother, this was a sad blow and so I had to go and stay with her till she regained her equilibrium. Our close family system has a lot of merit, especially during tragic times.

Aslam and Shameema went overseas for a fortnight. Dilshad and I kept the home port going, but with bad bouts of flu, we were just too happy when her PARENTS RETURNED (sorry typewriter playing up again). No, it's not a word processor, just a very sophisticated machine, very light to the touch with some special built-in erasers, memory and so forth; incidentally much to everyone's disappointment Razia had another daughter, but now that she has arrived and is such an adorable baby, there is just love and enjoyment.

A distant uncle passed away last monthly. He was 103 years old. Eyesight, hearing, memory all in full working order. Of course he needed spectacles, but he read for hours each day; walking with a stick maybe and lots of aches and pains, but if that is old age I have no fear of it. Similarly look at my mother. 89 and still doing her bit in the garden! When she could no longer bend down, my brother raised a few vegetable beds to a height which would not need stooping and so she still tends her brinjals, papdi, mircha, patta. My father-in-law is 87 and we had to forcibly take away the car from him 18 months ago. Always a serious reader, he keeps it up and it is wonderful discussing historical matters with him, for he can fill up gaps in our knowledge in a remarkable manner. Recently a letter by Fatima Meer in the press over the Saudi-Iran issue brought forth the comment that she had erred in stating that the Saudi dynasty was put into office by the British. Fact is that Lawrence of Arabia, put up by the British, was helping the Sheriff Khan party. Later support by Americans and British for the Saudis is another matter. My point in all this is that if we can keep our wits about us, old age can be a lovely time.

I have to fetch my eldest sister-in-law (wife of my late brother Boetie) from the airport in a few hours. She has emigrated to Canada with her three sons and soon a fourth son will be joining her.

There are two visiting Shaers from Pakistan in the country currently. Both are eminent poets in their own poetic forms. Fortunately both are into relevant poetry, and do not indulge in the escapist forms of so many of our poets.

I forgot to mention that the baby has been named Imaan.

The Koornhof – Bobat* wedding caused quite a stir. If you had spent more years in Schweizer you would have known the girl's

---

\* (Johan) Koornhof, son of National Party MP and Ambassador, Dr Piet Koornhof, married Rashida Bobat, in defiance of the Mixed Marriages Act.

grandfather who used to be a traveller. The world has not come to an end with that episode in history.

With Salaams from all of us,
   Z.M.Mayat

A.M. Kathrada
Pollsmoor Maximum Prison
Tokai
7966
18th October 1987

Dear Zuleikhabehn

Many thanks for your letter of 26th August, which reached me on 10th September. For the past few weeks our attention has been focused on the tragic floods in Natal; our thoughts were constantly with you, and with all our friends and their families; and with all the victims who live in the disaster area. I tried to find out from visitors how the various friends were, but unfortunately I was only able to obtain information about a few. I can only hope that you and the family, and all friends, emerged from the disaster, relatively unscathed. I say "relatively" because I cannot imagine anyone who was not, directly or indirectly, affected in some way.

You wrote of the merits of the close family system which is still prevalent among our people. Its values pervade times of joy as well as sorrow. I can imagine its role in lessening to some extent at least the sufferings of so many of the flood victims. I wonder if any of our researchers have investigated the role of the extended family system among Indians in the country, since 1860? It would be most interesting, and valuable. To what extent do you think our young generations will be able (or willing) to preserve and perpetuate at least the more positive values of the system?

I am sorry to learn of the death of your sister Bai. She was presumably the eldest of the siblings. This, and the fact that she has been living so far away, must have made her demise particularly hard for your mother. I'm sure your spending some time with her must have comforted her considerably.

I have also learnt of the death of Moosa Mia, and Goolamhusein Ismail (who had taken over the Mia business in Schweizer). Unfortunately, I never came to know Moosabhai personally but from what you had once written, I gathered that he was quite an interesting person, and a repository of valuable information. Since then I had harboured the hope that I would be able to meet him one day, for I felt sure he would have been able to give me valuable information about the early lives of persons of our father's generation, and even before. I may have mentioned to you that I have a research/writing project in mind which would necessitate the collection of the type of information which Moosabhai possessed. Having been obliged to leave home at an early age resulted, among other things, in my deficiency in such knowledge.

The late Goolamhuseinbhai was also an extremely knowledgeable person. I knew him from my childhood days and was very attracted to him. I also greatly admired his intellect, his wide knowledge and humane qualities. During my High School days I would spend the holidays at home, and we often organised debates and lectures, in which all the menfolk of the community took part. An indication of his qualities (and of the other old-timers in Schweizer) was the enthusiasm with which they participated in debates, either in the same team as, or in opposition to, a mere schoolboy. There was no condescension or patronising. All of us made our preparations; we hit out hard, and also took our share of punishment. It was wonderful spirit. I disappointed him greatly when I left school in mid-1946, to work in the offices with Ismail, wrote matric (at the instance of Bis, Cas etc.) and decided to go to university. But alas, the wayward youth was going to disappoint him again; in 1951 I chucked up Wits and went overseas. In spite of all this, we remained close. I shall miss him a great deal.

While on the subject of education, let me tell you of a recent development here which may hold out some promise. After several years of effort I was informed earlier this month that the authorities will henceforth allow prisoners to do M.A. and doctorate. I have submitted my application to the Prison HQ for permission, and am hoping that it will be approved. The title of my proposed thesis is:

"A Historical review of Political movements, workers and peasants, organisations; and other social groupings among African, Coloured, and Indian South Africans, from the 19th century; with particular reference to policy trends, and methods employed for the achievement of objectives."

If permission is granted I can see myself having to make radical readjustments to my routine. For one thing I will have to reduce the time I spend on TV; which I suppose will really be a blessing. Otherwise, it will be back to the 1984 days, when I was still studying.

It was interesting to see that Saira Essa was chosen as the Woman of the Year. I hope I'm not putting my foot into it by hailing her selection. Apart from press reviews I know nothing about the various plays she has put on. They appeared to be relevant, and convey an image of her as a committed person. What I admire about her is her independence, her courage, and her willingness to defy and discard antiquated and expendable traditions.

This brings me to the Koornhof–Bobat wedding. They seem to be a lovely young couple. How ridiculous that what should have been a normal, every day, private affair had to be engulfed in a blaze of publicity. I knew a Bobat family in Fordsburg. In fact I am almost certain that the girl's father, Solly, and I were in the same class at High School. The boy's sister and father became well-known to us through the media, and naturally won our admiration and respect. I believe the professor occupies quite a respected position in the medical field.

My congratulations to Razia and Rashid on the arrival of Imaan.

Jihaan and Humayra must be quite excited over their new sister.

I notice that a namesake of mine, Miss Hassina Kathrada, from the Stanger Secondary School has got herself into hot water over the play, "Look at Yourself", that she has written. Perhaps Saira Essa will be interested in putting it on at the Upstairs?

This week our attention will be focused on Mpho and Mphonyana at Bara, and on Baby Paul in America, who has just had a heart transplant. We hope the babies will pull through the crisis, and be able to live their full, normal lives.

This will be all for now. We were shocked to learn of the death of Siko's son. If you see her some time please convey my sympathy to her and the rest of the family.

Keep well. Fond regards to you, and to all the family members, and friends.

AMK

Westville 3630
1st December 1987

Dear Ahmed Bhai

Will you believe it – both typewriters not functioning and at this time of year, they hold one to ransom when it comes to repairs – especially if it is done under guarantee period! One thing the typewriter does excellently is to spoil one's hand writing and mine was never good to start with! When I read your neat script I must hide my face in shame!

As for the floods, there was not a home that had not suffered leaks or damp walls. One home (European occupied and owned) not far from us collapsed as the soil underneath gave way – and this was a beautiful double storied, landscaped home!

My aunt in law 6 doors away had a newly erected fence of brick lying in shambles – But as always the better homes are always insured. It is the poor and the needy who may first have managed to build one, or are still paying off; or those that live in ruins anyway – these suffer most for to begin with the areas they occupy are disaster prone, they are not insured, they cannot pull the strings that will set the state machinery working for such disasters, the hire purchase furniture and gadgets whether washed away or damaged beyond repair still has to be paid for at each month's end. The wolves are always at the door!

Most of the younger generation desire to live on their own in nuclear family units. They can afford to do so for with their education and expertise they earn enough. However, there are still lucky ones like myself. After my husband's death the children decided for me that one of them would stay with me and it fell to Aslam's lot. I have no doubt that Nasim will do his bit if circumstances warrant it.

Moosa Mia – like most of the Mia clan whether here or back in India – though rich, lived very simply. His car, home, possessions were sturdy and aesthetically beautiful but never went beyond necessities. People think of the Mias as puritanical. I find them philanthropic, most warm and loving, giving more to life than taking from it, and most endearing of all they have never lost touch with the common. I will not say that of the G‑‑s.

For your field of study (and we rejoice with you that you are able to take it up again) you will need the latest info from Cosatu, etc. This last 5yrs trade unionism etc among Africans especially has leapt forward like the genie from Alladin's lamp.

Saira Essa has truly achieved it – her commitment or otherwise plays have also an entertainment value that excels. There are no bludgeon statements there! As for your remark over antiquated and expendable (?) traditions, I will let it pass for the moment.

Spoke to Siko – she is bearing up wonderfully.
Salaams,
Zuleikha

[note by Mayat added at the top]

Most students doing interviews for their thesis start off with a prepared questionnaire and this inability to speak in the vernaculars makes the older generation clam up. Should you ever want to (or are able to and this is not meant pessimistically) use my notes, you are welcome. I will also have reached the age (presently 61) when instead of writing I will be giving interviews!

A.M. Kathrada
Pollsmoor Maximum Prison
Tokai
7966
10th January 1988

Dear Zuleikhabehn

Thanks a lot for your letter which arrived on 9th December. Let me begin by wishing you, the family and friends my very best wishes for 1988. For my own selfish reasons I wish that at least one of your typewriters will be returned before the weeks and months make substantial inroads into 1988. I say this because your last (handwritten) letter once again confirmed my belief (superstition??) that once one gets used to typing one's letters, in the course of time the typewriter virtually takes over the thought-process; and consequently the letters are fuller and more informative. Now, I'm not complaining about your last letter but when I <u>compare</u> it with your "normal" ones, it looks a bit anaemic! Please don't take this as a criticism. It may just be that sub-consciously I'm merely trying to validate my "superstition".

In spite of what I have just said above I must immediately assure that even in its "anaemic" state your letter did not omit interesting bits of information, and observations. Your description of the late Moosa Mia's life-style fits in exactly with my impression of him, and of the wider Mia clan. At the risk of repeating myself I must tell you of a visit to Moulvi Mia's place on their farm in 1953. I was taken there by Moulana Cachalia, and accompanying us also was an architect friend. The memory of the few hours we spent with him remains with me to this day. I had of course heard of him before, but this first face-to-face meeting surpassed my expectations. He was erudite, extremely knowledgeable in a variety of fields, well-spoken, and a good host. My friend's attention was drawn to an overseas architectural magazine and this led to a discussion on the subject. Moulvi Mia's authoritative remarks really amazed our friend. We talked about plants and flowers, politics, business, education ... and on everything he was well informed and made valuable contributions. It was really an eye-opener for me. The simplicity of the house and furniture, his mode of dress, his modesty, and his virtual anonymity – all belied the man's real qualities. Of course our political views and outlook differed radically, but that did not prevent us from spending a most fruitful and enjoyable few hours together.

I hope you haven't abandoned your plans to write a book about the old stalwarts of the community. I must be boring you with my constant reminders; you must forgive me for it, but it's become almost an obsession with me to get every aspect of the past to be written up, political, cultural, social, economic – of all the Black communities, African, "Coloured" and Indian. I'm pleased to say that my efforts are meeting with some success. I recently heard that a friend's daughter in England has got her M.A. for her dissertation on the history of the Naidoo family in Jo'burg. I'm sure there must be many doctors around who boarded with the Naidoos while they were at Wits. It's a family with a tremendous record of service, dating back to the years of Gandhi in South Africa.

Now about my own studies. Although I applied 3 months ago, I still have not had a reply from the Prisons Department. I just cannot understand the reasons for the delay. I hope the delay is not an omen for unfavourable news.

Unlike previous years – we did not end 1987 on a happy note. I wrote to you about our Christmas festivities of 1986, how we enjoyed a lovely lunch together with our colleague Nelson. This time the authorities refused to allow Nelson to join us; instead we were permitted to see him one at a time for 40 minutes each. The whole happy atmosphere was spoilt. We did send him some food – to eat alone. We too ate alone.

A friend of mine, Dr Jassat applied to visit me on Christmas Day, but a day or two before Xmas I was told that the visit had been refused. No reasons are provided, but I assume it must have been because of his politics. Yet about two months ago I was asked whether I had any objections to receiving a visit from members of the House of Delegates*! Not being my political colleagues, nor my relatives or friends, I said I was not willing to have visits from them. I still have no idea why they wanted to see me.

Last January I wrote to you about an "invasion" of Cape Town by the Kathradas for a wedding of a nephew. This time, in December, the clan descended upon Durban also for a wedding, of another nephew. I believe the bride was a Moolla girl, whose parents were originally from Volksrust. Then there was an engagement of yet another nephew, to Dr Momoniat's daughter in Jo'burg. If I get out of here one day, I'll find the family having grown by a few hundred per cent! With the prevailing housing shortage, I think it's better for me to continue to take advantage of my present accommodation!

This is all for today. Healthwise all is well. Fondest regards to you, and all members of the family and friends.

From
AMK

---

\* The House of Delegates was the section of the Tri-cameral Parliament designated for Indians.

Westville
3630
29th February 1988

Dear Ahmedbhai

December always had an influx of visitors, mostly from the Transvaal. This past one, we were inundated with cousins from India, niece from United States and with them of course came other family members. When Layla came it was a good opportunity for a family get together so we brought over my mother and my sister Rokayya. Three weeks went like 3 days so full of reminiscences and recollections were brought around the dinner table for us to chew over. Cannot remember having laughed so much in years. One thing about the Bismillahs, we can when on our own laugh at our foibles, but let someone else point it out and the chilli-hot tempers flare up. Opposition is soon devastated in the resulting conflagration. Once the visitors leave it is time to start paying bills and squaring accounts with receiver of revenue. The auditors want the minutest details and the insurance premiums, etc. somehow manage to stretch out their hands at the same time. How we complicate our lives. For peace and tranquillity Robben Island seems to present itself as a possibility.

You will have reacted at the last statement by exclaiming that you would not wish it [on] your worst enemy. Sorry but somehow our lives are so tied up that one thinks of Khankaahs (hermitages) under some sufi guru, living on what one's own hands raise and wearing what one sews and stitches with one's own hands.

You are so right about a typewriter taking over and running ahead of one's thoughts. I am completely lost without one. The Olivetti is still anaemic – same ailment recurring over and over again, so I am back to the one Mohamed bought for me some time before his death. My husband had a sadistic side to his nature and I was often the one that had to suffer at his cockeyed sense of humour. A representative of the Hermes (typewriter firm) came home one day with a few machines and asked me to select one for Shifa Hospital. This on instructions from Dr Mayat. I had a niggly feeling at the back of my mind that there was something amiss for why would the typists there not choose and why me, a self-taught three finger typist? Anyhow I made the selection.

Three days later the selected machine was delivered to our home with a note written by Mohamed and signed (under duress I was told later) by some of his colleagues that this was a Birthday present, but the colleagues wanted to know whether at my age it would not be more sensible if a second hand typewriter was chosen, well, seeing ... that I was getting on in years? Mohamed and two of the colleagues have passed on and I am still here battling with the typewriter! You may ask what was the joke? Well Mohamed believed like many others that a woman always hides her age and this was his way of telling me that all his friends now knew how old I was. A silly little incident, but that is what life with him was – one long hilarious situation, making light of every situation, getting others to join him in climbing mountains just because it was there!

No, I have not abandoned my plans to work on a book on our contribution to this country. That is at my age (62 in August) I still hope to do so. Currently I am busy with the last cookery book (or so I say) and this should be in print before Ramadaan. *Indian Delights* is still such a good seller that we dare not abandon it (have sold nearly 200,000 copies to date). Prospects of launching it in America seem great. Two agencies are at present negotiating with us on this score and we are seriously looking into it, since the offers have come from them without any approaches by us.

How can I abandon those plans? I have just recently heard that

Essop Mia (Moosa's father) who was instrumental in bringing many a Gujarati Hindu craftsman from India when there was a dire need for blacksmiths, iron mongers, book keepers, etc. in South Africa [and] played a vital role in getting these people adjusted to conditions here. Among the services rendered to these new immigrants he helped establish a crematorium.

Ahmed, the typewriter is making too many mistakes today. Please ignore them. I am sorry about the delay in your studies, do hope there is some decision soon. After [Govan] Mbeki's release we were preparing to see more of you others from out there, but with the new clampdown......?

I had to answer the telephone about 6 times since commencing this letter. 3 were from students who wanted help with their university fees. So many African students now study at Durban-Westville and are in residence at the university. As can be expected there are some adjustment problems on both sides. We will have to learn to get along with each other. This world is just too small for racial prejudices on racial lines. Which makes me feel that tolerance like the one displayed by the late Mr Mia in helping get a crematorium off the ground, when as a Muslim he would have believed that it was very wrong to cremate persons, is most remarkable.

The Schweizer elections will show the trend of Afrikaner Politics. We will watch the debate between Treurnicht and De Klerk this evening. Do you read Afrikaans? Something made me buy the latest novel "Fiela se Kind" and I enjoyed it thoroughly. It's all about a Knysna Forest Boskapper family who lose a child when it wanders into the forest. No trace is found. Nine years later the white census officials came across a Coloured family who had brought up a child that was abandoned on their doorstep. This was in a dorp beyond the mountains and by no stretch of imagination could a child that small have wandered through the elephant land of the forests and survived. Besides it would take a grown up three days to walk that distance. However officialdom and 'Die Volk' decide that this must be the child that had wandered off and so it is consigned to the Boskapper family, who in terms of economy and social refinement are well below that of the Coloured family. The fight by Fiela for her kind, and the child's unhappiness in his White home, the attitude of officialdom and race attitudes are all well defined in good old – no holds barred – Afrikaans. Three letter words abound which is Afrikaans as I know it but would be reluctant to use in company. Knowing a language gives you an insight into a community as no other thing can.

I am not thinking what I am writing today, so both typewriter and thoughts are racing!

Salaams

A.M. Kathrada
Pollsmoor Maximum Prison
Tokai
7966
10th April 1988

Dear Zuleikhabehn

Thanks a lot for your letter of 29th February, which reached me on 16th March. I must first of all sympathise with you and with all members of the family on the death of your father-in-law. Fatima's tribute gave me a glimpse of the man – a veritable pillar of the community. He is yet another of the stalwarts whose life and work needs to be recorded.

A.C.'s series makes passing reference from time to time to numerous individuals from different walks of life whose contributions should not be allowed to be forgotten. A truly mammoth task awaits our historians. The series do not purport to be an academic history-thesis on the community's past, so it will be unfair to assess it from that perspective. Yet every now and then I am struck by a feeling of disappointment when some event, or personality, is either dealt with cursorily, or not even mentioned. When A.C. dealt with the 1946-8 period I eagerly looked for a paragraph or so on a man by the name of N. Thandray. I think I mentioned him in one of my letters to you. He was my teacher in Std. 3; by the mid forties he was a school principal, which position he gave up to come and work full time in the offices. Oh yes, now I remember telling you how embarrassing it was for me when we went to jail together in December 1946. He was a wonderful man. A puritan, strict disciplinarian, honest to a fault, courageous, unassuming; a man of high moral standards and principles. Somewhere someone will have to record his contribution.

Coming back to your father-in-law. In the photo he was holding one of his "great-grandchildren", according to the caption. Was this one of your progeny? Which set me thinking of Mohamed and his fellow doctors of that year. I was surprised that I knew all of them, though not well enough to speak to. As with photos of this nature, one thought leads to another, and soon we were back in the forties and I found myself telling my colleagues about the medicos. In the process I remembered and made a mental note, of a few more persons who were visitors to Flat 13. I recently heard that Limbs was not well at all, and that his wife had passed away. I knew the late Cassim Ismail quite well since the days when he was boarding at the Bharoochis. I think I must have mentioned Abe (Advocate Gani) who was Mohamed's fellow boarder at the Dayas. He stayed at the Flat until he left the country in 1963. He married Cassim's widow, and they're settled in England.

Let me move away from my reminiscences before I fill the whole letter. The anecdote about Mohamed's birthday gift of a typewriter was quite amusing. With respect, I have to agree with his contention that ladies do tend to understate their age, or refuse to disclose their years altogether. I base [this] on a certain amount of personal knowledge, but more on observations made by numerous eminent persons. For the present, however, I'll just agree with the sentiments expressed by Oscar Wilde: "No woman should ever be quite accurate about her age. It looks so calculating." My favourite quote is: "A diplomat is one who remembers a lady's birthday, but not her age." I hope my few remarks will not condemn me to the ranks of M.C.P.s?[*]

You asked whether I read Afrikaans. I read the *Burger*, *Rapport* and a few Afrikaans journals. But unfortunately I seldom get around to reading an Afrikaans book. I have, however, read *Fiela se*

---

[*] Male Chauvinist Pig

*Kind*, and have tried to follow the press reviews of both the theatre production and the film. I've already been trying to hire the film, but it is not yet on the 16mm circuit. I wish they'd make a video of it. Although the story is set in the 19th century it does succeed in portraying the tragedy and heartache of racialism, which is still very relevant. A book which highlights the contemporary situation is Elsa Joubert's *Die Swerfjare van Poppie Nongena*; it is based on a real life experience of the woman whom the author calls Poppie. Do try to read it. I remember the comments of an Afrikaner academic who stated that after reading the book nobody will have the right to say "I did not know".

Much to my shame and regret, I do not read Afrikaans with ease. I do not have to explain to a fellow Transvaal plattelander like yourself that in our childhood years Afrikaans was the second home language. But like Gujarati I have forgotten much of Afrikaans, and speak it with difficulty. Luckily I can still remember parts of Afrikaans poems, and every now and then recite them to myself. Let me tell you of a little incident which took place in 1963, while we were under 90 day detention. The police officer interrogating me was the well-known "Rooi Rus" Swanepoel who, you may remember, stood for the Conservative Party against Pik Botha in the 1987 elections. Anyway he interrogated me several times, trying to persuade me to give information about my colleagues and other matters.

At one of the interrogation sessions I decided to recite a verse or two from an Afrikaans poem, and asked if he as an Afrikaner was not ashamed to ask me to betray my colleagues. The lines of the poem go something like this:

Ek hou van 'n man wat sy man kan staan
Ek hou van 'n man wat 'n slag kan slaan
'n Oog wat nie wyk,

Wat 'n bars kan kyk
En 'n wil wat so vas soos 'n klipsteen staan.*

I like to think that I detected a tinge of embarrassment in his face.

Before I leave the subject of Afrikaans I want to just mention some interesting discussions and debates that are going on about the language and its users. Firstly, there is the contention of Achmat Davids that Afrikaans really originated with the so-called "Cape Malays"; and that the first Afrikaans book appeared (I think he says in the 1840s) using the Arabic script. If proved to be correct this will knock the wind out of the sails of those who claim monopoly of knowledge about its origins, development, usage etc. But even a bigger blow awaits the "purists". The first shots have already been fired by Afrikaner historians and genealogists, who by means of meticulous research have produced incontrovertible evidence to show that a large percentage of Afrikaners are descendants of Black and White unions. There was big talk of damages actions against the publishers running into tens of thousands of rands. But they seem to have decided it would be better to play it low, and hope that things will fade away. But historical facts have a strange habit of cropping up at most inopportune and unexpected moments. Incidentally, I'm certain that most white South Africans will be surprised to know that Simon van der Stel's mother was an Indian! Finally a relatively recent discussion has started on the usage, prospects and status of the so-called "Kaaps" Afrikaans, which is spoken mainly on the Cape Flats. A very welcome development

---

\* I like a man who can make a stand
I like a man who can strike a blow
An eye that does not look away
That is steady
And a will that stands as solid as a wall.

has been the shift away from the viewpoint which appears to have peaked in the mid seventies that rejected Afrikaans as a "language of the oppressor".

How I've gone on about Afrikaans! I still wanted to comment on the "adjustment problems" at Westville University, and other matters. I'll leave it for another letter. You are wrong in thinking that I would not wish a stay at Robben Island or Pollsmoor "for my worst enemies". In fact I have said to a number of my correspondents and visitors that our prison life has somehow helped to arrest the ageing process and kept us in good health. We often lightheartedly remark among ourselves that if only people like Dadoo, Nokwe, Marks, Monty ... had been with us, they would have been still alive. Of course there are unhappy and unpleasant periods, but on the whole our prison life has been, relatively speaking, tranquil and almost free of prolonged tension.

I must end now. Both the Prisons Department and the UNISA History Department have not approved of my topic for M.A. So it's back to October 1987 for me.

Keep well, and good luck for the new cook-book and for *Indian Delights*. Fond regards to all the family members and friends. All the best to you.

AMK

Westville
3630
2nd May 1988

Dear Ahmedbhai

By the time this reaches you it will be nearing Eid, so a Mubarak Eid to you and your colleagues and perhaps you can use the cheque I am sending to celebrate.

A.C.'s series is a Meer saga more than anything else and it is all culled from extracts from the [Indian] *Views*, plus *Leader*. It concentrates on Natal personalities especially those around Waschbank and district, which was the early Meer stronghold. In so far as Transvaal is concerned there is only Dadoo and sometimes Nana but of the pioneer families who were the backbone behind the Gandhian struggle, there is bare mention. Possibly because most of their letters to the press and comments about them appeared in the Gujarati section of the *Views*. Though A.C. was totally conversant with Gujarati, I suppose it has become easier to extract from the English section.

Since Maureen Swan's reference to Gandhi being a leader of the merchant class, who used the working mass of Indians just later to give impact to his movement, more people are climbing in on that wagon. Nowbath of Fakir fame is one. Uma Mesthrie (Gandhi's great grand-daughter) has finished her thesis on P.S. Aiyar and from the newspaper blurb one gathers that this was the true leader of the masses and the one who opposed the authorities of the time rather than the Congress led by Gandhi.

Of the medicos you remember so well: Limbs lost a teenaged daughter in a car accident some years ago. His wife died last year and Limbs, who was Bis's and Mohamed's colleague and with whom I got on famously, I saw only once after his exit to Zambia. This was some 5 years ago at the wedding of my nephew in Botswana. Limbs and Bibi had come down for Bibi happened to be a sister of my bhabi whose wedding we attended. His surviving son now runs the huge farm that was Bibi's pet project.

Ismail Kajee settled in Estcourt and is still practicing there. Zuly Christopher married Enver Hassim and they went out on exit permit to Toronto. Enver has a flourishing practice – believed to be one of the best criminal lawyers.

Whereas all my contemporaries walk around with beautifully dyed black (and some even dark brunette which is the latest trend among our women) hair, I flaunt my silver grey tresses. To add to your collection about women and age, I hugged my granddaughter when she came to my defence when Jaleel commented that "Dadima is old". Jihaan promptly corrected him "Nani is not old, only her hair is." I am of course hoping that someone will associate my grey hair with wisdom.

I would never apologise for my Afrikaans if I could quote "Ek hou van 'n man wat sy man kan staan…" That episode of yours should certainly be recorded for posterity. The impact of *Fiela se Kind* and *Die swerf jare van Poppie Nongena* is because this is Afrikaner literature. Similar writing has existed in English literature and the work of the Black Sash women deals with Nonnie type of problems all the time.

Achmat Davids's proof (not contention) about the Malays being the first to write in Afrikaans is beyond doubt. He has over 70 manuscripts, children's exercise books, religious kitaabs etc, written by hand and printed in Holland which he brought to show at his lectures in Durban last year. The Afrikaner academics at Durban-Westville University did not like it and examined the material very critically. In the end they could not object to his contention (at this stage this part of it is) that Malayalam and Arabic played a greater part in the structure of the grammar than did Nederlandsch. One Academic then got him to concede that Flemish played a greater part on the technicalities of Afrikaans grammar than did Dutch but the way this question was put, one could feel the white lipped anger behind it.

However, in so far as printed evidence goes, written and published Afrikaans first appear in these religious books of the Cape Muslims. For a lecture I prepared for the monthly Buzme Adab lecture (years before Achmat Davids's publication) I drew the parallels between Urdu and Afrikaans. How each developed in its milieu out of the dire necessity that the rulers and the masses had to communicate. Whereas local words slowly creep into the Persian language of the rulers and eventually displace it, similarly Nederlandsche remained the official language of the masters but in their dealings with the slave and servant population they had to communicate in the 'taal'.

Miscegenation was not just between White and Black but also between the various ethnic slave and servant groups and the latter grew very fast. The Malay slaves being nearest the Masters, their company was sought by the other deprived groups and many found refuge in their quarters. In his Mosques of the Bo-Kaap, Achmed Davids from birth and marriage certificates shows how many of Sara's daughters marry into the eminent White families. When Heese starts from Simon van der Stel and even brings in Treurnicht into the contemporary picture of 'tainted blood' few Afrikaners can ignore the historical proof of 'other blood'.

I am going to scribble a few lines in Arabic (and give the transliteration to make it easier to read) and you will see the indisputable proof of Arabic letters writing the first Afrikaans words.

Sorry about your topic not being acceptable for your Masters.

    With salaams
    Zuleikha

A.M. Kathrada
Pollsmoor Maximum Prison
Tokai
7966
2nd July 1988

Dear Zuleikhabehn

Many thanks for your letter of 2nd May, which reached me on 17th May. Thanks a lot also for the "Eidy". Happily we are not affected by the Eid-day-controversy; we celebrate on the day the goodies are delivered. I suppose we should be hanging our heads in shame for putting our emphasis on the culinary aspect of Eid! But I do assure you that we are never unmindful of the manner in which Eid day unites us in spirit with all you good people who constantly have our welfare at heart, as shown by the cards, letters, Eidy, visits, prayers … and so many other things.

Our Eid fell on the 18th May, which is also Walter's birthday. So we had a double celebration. Outside, we hardly ever celebrated our birthdays, but Eid days often saw us getting together at the late Aminabai's place; Diwalis we'd be together at Jasmatbhai or Nassibhai's places, while at Christmas time we'd go to Nelson or Walter's place in Soweto. So, to some small extent we are carrying on an established tradition. Oh yes, on Christmas day we'd also be popping in at Mrs Helen Joseph's place. It was wonderful; throughout the day friends would call at her house, convey wishes, have some refreshments, and depart. What a grand old lady! I'm happy that this practice still continues. The numerous visitors cannot fail to be inspired by that indomitable lady. We are saddened by her recent illness, and hope that she will once again conquer the setback

Helen is now 83. In one of my letters I teased her about an

incident during the Treason Trial. There was a brief period during that marathon trial when we dismissed our lawyers, and conducted the defence ourselves. We called Helen as our first defence witness, and we had to help prepare her evidence. Nelson and Advocate Nokwe were, fortunately for us, the two lawyers among the accused, which was an advantage. In taking down her statement, Nelson asked what her age was! And, typical woman that she is, her reply was curt and final. Nelson simply moved on to the next question.

Walter turned 76, and Nelson will be 70 on 18$^{th}$ July. I knew them from my teen years, and have come a long way together. The three of us were co-accused in 3 major trials – the Defiance Trial 1952; the Treason Trial 1956-1961; and Rivonia. Apart from the legal aspects, there were literally scores of incidents that we recall, and of course a lot that we can tease one another about. I like to rag them about their Youth League days, particularly about an incident when we found ourselves on opposite sides of a dispute. I wonder if Abu Huraira will still remember it? Nelson and I happened to meet in Commissioner Street (in 1950), and, what began as a friendly exchange, developed into an argument during which I, with the "wisdom" of my 21 years behind me, made certain utterances to which Nelson took umbrage. This I was to discover later when at a formal get-together of senior men from all over the country, Nelson complained about me (I was a doorman cum messenger-driver at the gathering). I was shocked and shamed by the accusation. As if this was not enough, Ismail got up and asked Nelson and the gathering to dismiss my behaviour as an intemperate outburst of a "youngster". My humiliation was complete. Today we are able to joke about it.

I think it is appropriate for me at this stage to say something concerning the UDW "adjustment problems" to which you made reference recently. It is always painful to read reports of ethnic tension and friction; it is much worse when the reports relate to problems in a supposedly enlightened environment such as a university campus – and a campus of underprivileged students at that! However, in the background of the socio-economic-political situation, such problems are virtually inevitable, and understandable. The surprise should be that they are not worse. When ideologies and lawmakers have ordained that from the cradle to the grave, human beings be nurtured to accentuate so-called differences among them, what else can one expect? Your positive approach is most encouraging, and one hopes that it reflects the attitude of the students. The University of Western Cape is systematically educating students and staff alike about the oneness of human beings; in the process they are resisting and eradicating dangerous concepts such as "minority rights" etc.

This is not to say they deny the existence of a plurality of languages, religious and other cultural traits. When I reflect on the fashionable practice of certain people to harp on "fears of Black majority" and the need to "protect minority rights", I always wonder if these persons are simply not repeating, parrot-like, some unfounded and certainly unsubstantiated assertions made in times gone by. Please forgive me for trying to refute the arguments by invoking my own experiences. I know it is not scientific, but I believe that experiences such as ours should be taken into account. Apart from my social and political association since childhood (which I have referred to above), for the past 25 years I have been part of so-called "minority groups" among an overwhelming "African majority"; for the past 6 years I have been in a "minority" of one. A prison environment is by definition tailor-made for all sorts of frustration, jealousies, suspicions, envy and tension. An aggravating factor was the differentiation in the diets, clothing etc of the "Coloureds" and Indians on the one hand, and Africans on the other; the Africans of course receiving the less favourable treatment. (Happily this differentiation has since been done away with). I would not be truthful if I claim that "racial" tension was completely absent; it must be remembered that the Island had inmates from a number of political groups, at least one of which was known for its extreme narrow "nationalism", and a generally "anti"-outlook. In spite of this, and especially considering the time period, and numbers of inmates, these periods of tension were so brief and far between that at most they can be included as footnotes in the story of our imprisonment. And they came nowhere near physical confrontations between groups. Never did we feel threatened or insecure. In fact, with the passage of time these aberrations virtually disappeared. The important thing to bear in mind is that there is no secret or complex formula for the maintenance of harmony, and good fellowship. It is basically a question of having mutual respect for one another; the relinquishing of misconceptions about cultural traits, customs and practices that are different from one's own, and the willingness to learn about them; the absolute avoidance of any suggestion that one particular culture is superior – or inferior – to others. I could add a few other do's and don'ts, but they are superfluous. To put it simply: all that is needed is for one to behave naturally; it will be found that the basic values and behaviour patterns learnt in the course of upbringing are universal, and are sufficient to transcend all barriers in the path of friendship and understanding.

Let me turn to a couple of other matters. Sometime last year I mentioned the wedding of my nephew, in Cape Town, but I left out the bride's name, thinking that it would make no sense to you. Imagine my surprise when in the course of a conservation, Kader Amien asks me if I knew "Mrs Zuleikha Mayat" of Durban! He then told me of his friendship with Aslam, and how he was in and out of your place while he was at university there. My nephew is married to Kader's sister Rabia, who incidentally is in Cape Town at present for her confinement.

We have avoided going to court on the question of allowing my niece to visit me; the Prisons Department allowed her to come, after refusing permission for 14 years! The question of my studies is not yet settled. I have submitted another topic, and am waiting for an answer.

I'll have to leave other matters for a future letter.

Fond regards to you and the family from
AMK

Toronto – Canada
7th October 1988

Dear Ahmed Bhai

I owe you a reply and I shall attend to that once I return home but meanwhile this card to inform you that my sister Rokeyya and I are visiting our relatives in the States and Canada – There are actually six family units out here and we are being spoilt with lots of love and warmth from all quarters. Bis and Joan are so entrenched on their 120 acre holding (a hundred acres of the original 220 was sold last year) and to think that 4 generations of Bismillahs could never buy land in South Africa! Both of them enquired about you and said to give their salaams when I next wrote. I thought a letter or card from overseas would break the routine where you are!

I have been interviewed on 3 TV stations in Washington and yesterday for 7 minutes on the multi-lingual channel in Toronto. "Voice of America" has asked for another when I return to Washington just before my return home on the 14th. Meanwhile I am in a dilemma – The Islamic Institute (IIIT) executive (Washington based) wants me to go to Trinidad for a week – they will make necessary arrangements. But I am missing my 7 grandchildren so I will vacillate between the mental urges of "should I or should I not" till the 11th – for then is when I have to commit myself – what a chance and what a fool to hesitate! Our South African Ethnics excelling themselves here. Zubeida Barmania – Top management in (legal) Labour Problems. Summaya Bismilla – Vice Principal of Danforth Garden School. Zubeida Vahed – officer overseeing special needs of Ethnic Communities in schools. Etc. – The slots are so specific – we have no South African equivalent of these posts.

Salaams,
    Zuleikha

16 Leander Crescent
Westville
3631
3rd January 1989

Dear Ahmedbhai

I am shocked to note the date on your last letter to me (2nd July 1988). In September when I left for the States and Canada, it was with the conscience of that unanswered letter, and so I remembered to write to you from the States. It was unregistered, I do hope you received it?

I may be repeating myself (in case you did receive that letter) but it was most reassuring to see friends and family members, well settled overseas; contributing to society in whichever field their talents and inclinations led them; being accepted as worthwhile citizens with no extra nor less privileges than any other ethnic group around. Problems are there, for life is made up of problems to live out and to cope with, but this needless petty frustration that bedevils one's every step is mercifully missing.

My trip was overwhelmingly successful. Friends and Islamic societies went out of their way to give me media exposure, so necessary for the persons who sell *Indian Delights* in the States and Canada. I had 4 TV interviews, had to turn down 2 more, and several newspaper interviews. I was pressurised to go to Trinidad to an Islamic Conference but did not do so because of my promise to my mother that I would return within a month.

Bis and family are very well. In our nostalgic recollections you too featured and I was asked to convey greetings from Joan and Bis. Their home situated on their estate of over a hundred acres is something Indian South Africans can only dream of. The land is wooded with nature trails and of rabbits, squirrels, birds etc.

there [are] plenty. Since last year (1987) Bis has established a 7 round golf course and the bunkers and greens and pools of water etc. makes it look like the golf course at Sun City. Bis won't allow the daily help to touch the greens for this is his own baby, 2 more holes were in the offing and then others across the road leading to the home are planned for the future.

Since my return I have had to make three trips to Potchefstroom to look after my mother. Old age has caught up (90 plus), the heart is failing, as a result other complications arise and she has to make use of a wheelchair that she hates. Seeing her robbed of her independence is painful but she is a fighter, my mother. The day she feels better, she is up and doing rounds around the house again.

All were awaiting the release not only of Nelson but you others as well. Actually we were told to be on standby – this not officially but along the bush wires – and now another year has gone by. I can only pray, like so many others do, that we will now be counting not months but days so that society's conscience can be eased, families can be together again, and perhaps one can begin to start building a new nation.

The *Best of Indian Delights* which is the latest addition to the *Delights* series is selling very fast. Since September when it first saw the market we have sold over 5000 copies. Of the older Encyclopaedic *Indian Delights* we are negotiating another impression. The girls are happy at the success of both babies. Talking of babies, Aslam and Shameema have a son named Asif Muhammed. Six weeks old and so there are now 8 grandchildren.

Fatima Meer was hospitalised for a fortnight [with] suspected gall stones. Due for surgery once the infection she developed clears up. One can only admire a person with her energy and total devotion to causes. I could only pay her a brief visit but there is a promise of a full day in each other's company. She attended my wedding and we too have come a long long way together. Old friends like old shoes are too comfortable and precious and if anyone objects that I treat [hand written from here] shoes or friends as an analogy then they should step into a pair of tight fitting shoes for a day!

With Salaams,
    Zuleikhabehn

A.M. Kathrada
Pollsmoor Maximum Prison
Tokai
7966
5th February 1989

Dear Zuleikhabehn

Your unregistered letter from America did reach me, on 25th October; and I received your latest one on 10th January. I'm sorry for having taken such a long time to reply. I'm sorry that your mother has not been well; I hope she is up and about again.

Congratulations on your successful overseas trip. You certainly managed to put in quite a bit of work combined with visits to various family members. They must have been very pleased to meet someone from home. I assume they all still regard South Africa as home?

It was nice to hear about Bis and Joan. I take it that his interest in golf is in addition to tennis, for I just cannot imagine him abandoning tennis altogether. During December I took a trip down memory lane, and Bis featured prominently in my reminiscences. You see December was exactly 40 years since we first visited Cape Town. It was Bis, Cas, Hoosein and myself. We came in two cars – Bis's Austin and Cas's Morris. Enver and his wife travelled in their Cadillac, but they were not really in our holiday group. In those days, as you know, there were very few Black doctors in South Africa – or university students for that matter. So my three prospective doctor-friends were enormously popular, and I think I was the main beneficiary of their popularity. Our original plan was to spend a couple of weeks here, and then move on to P.E. and East London. But things turned out to be so good here that the 4 weeks we spent in the "mother city" proved to be too short, and we reluctantly returned to Jo'burg from here. During this last December, as if to jolt my memory, Radio Good Hope played a number of songs which were popular in the late forties, and with which we became familiar in Cape Town.

Looking back, if I were to select a single factor which was responsible for our enjoyable stay, I would without hesitation say it was the couple whom we affectionately called "Moms" and "Pops". The only person I knew in Cape Town at the time was the late Cassim Amra, who was at university here. I had written to him to arrange accommodation for us, and he introduced us to "Moms and Pops". We took an instant liking to them, and, for me it was the beginning of a long and happy relationship. My 3 friends soon qualified and went their separate ways; my friendship with the couple grew, until Moms became for me almost what the late Aminabai Pahad was – a mother figure. In August 1962 (during a period of respite between banning orders) I especially came from Durban to Cape Town to attend her birthday party. That was the last time I saw Moms and Pops in "freedom". They visited me on Robben Island. Pops died in the early seventies, and Moms continued to visit. Until she was "visited" and warned that she would lose her passport, and other dire consequences, if she continued to see me! The poor lady was thoroughly intimidated. But we kept in touch, indirectly, through friends and family members. You'll be wondering why I am boring you with all this. You see towards the end of 1988 Moms passed away. I had been aware of her deteriorating health as a result of breast cancer, so the news of her death did not come as a surprise. But the full impact of the loss came a few weeks later, especially in December. I suppose I am still suffering from the after-shock. This lengthy expression of my grief must be a sort of catharsis.

I learnt of Fatima's illness (I call her Behn) from visitors, and from the Press. I hope she has fully recovered and is able to resume her various activities. My warmest regards and good wishes to her, and the family. Shehnaaz and Joel applied to visit me, but were refused! No reasons given. Yet they allowed Dr Essop Jassat to visit me in November! He had been previously refused. What is puzzling is that in 1987 the prison authorities were prepared to allow members of the House of Delegates to visit me. Since they are not family members, or friends, or political colleagues, I of course refused to accept the visit.

In the light of the major policy-switch towards Nelson regarding matters such as visits etc. one wonders if they will continue with their restrictive practices towards our visits. At present I am entitled to 30 visits a year, of which I can take a maximum of 5 in any one month. As you know Kader is getting married on the 19$^{th}$, and the folks from home will be coming down. I don't know how I will be able to fit in their visits.

You have no doubt seen reports of our visit to Nelson on 23$^{rd}$ December. It was a pleasant surprise for us, and we spent a little over 7 hours together. We had last seen him for about an hour on 4$^{th}$ August last year. He was already ill then, and we came away quite disturbed about his condition. A week later he was admitted to hospital. On our recent visit we were happy to see him almost fully recovered; I think he said that the treatment would be for 6 months. I won't bother you with details about the furniture, the high-tech kitchen complete with a white prison official as chef, the swimming bath etc. It is spacious and luxurious. He no longer wears prison clothes. As a "special category prisoner" he enjoys numerous facilities and "privileges" which the ordinary prison population can only dream about. For the 7 hours we too were accorded "special-prisoner" treatment. We were served with a complete banquet-style meal, with crockery, glassware and cutlery which I was nervous – and in any case had forgotten how – to handle. For some of the items I had to resort to the good old fingers. Anyway, having said all this, one can never forget that he remains a lonely prisoner in a luxury prison. In this respect at least, we, although we are only 4, are better off. After 26 years we have exhausted and repeated ad infinitum, just about every anecdote, biographical detail or joke, but we are still able to discuss our visits, our letters, the news, TV programs etc. etc. About two weeks ago Walter (who is my cell-mate) spent 4 days in hospital for an eye operation and I had already begun to feel lonely. How much worse with Nelson! I came away from Victor Verster with mixed feelings; very happy to have seen him in good shape, but sad to leave him behind in his loneliness.

My congratulations to Shamima and Aslam on the arrival of Asif Muhammed; and congrats to you on becoming granny for the 8th time. Last August my niece Rabia brought along her 2-week old Khatija to visit me. I had made extensive preparations for several days to learn how to hold a mite of that size. I even resorted to the British monarchy for lessons. Princess Beatrice had just been born and I studied TV shots of Prince Andrew holding her. I also got detailed advice from my experienced colleagues but when the moment arrived all my preparations proved of no avail; I was too terrified to hold her. However, last week the young lady returned, almost 6 months old. Her mother simply placed her on my lap, and there she remained for a full minute or two! Unluckily that is as much as my "charms" could hold her; she let a yell and went straight back to the safety and comfort of her mother's arms. From there she gave me a toothless smile.

Some time ago – I think it was in August – I read of the phenomenal success of *The Best of Indian Delights*. Congratulations. Some day I must get it.

This is all for today. Best wishes and regards to you and all family members and friends.

From
AMK

Westville
3630
1ˢᵗ March 1989

Dear Ahmedbhai

Though reason dictated that State guests too must age, somehow in my mind the image of the young man that was taken in years and years ago, lingered on. Reporting to the many persons who enquired about you on my return (surprising what an active grapevine we have) I said "well there was this well built, full of vitality and zest for living, but ageing man with grey temples, who has that admirable quality of putting visitors so quickly at ease, that they have not the time to think about the place nor circumstances surrounding the visit."

It was only after we left, that Aslam and I, in the silence that ensures when two minds are travelling along avenues of similar thoughts, that the agony of the situation struck us. Some lines of Iqbal's famous poem of the bird in the cage lamenting over freedom kept on recurring. Once home I have looked up my Urdu collection of Farooqui Mehtar, Iqbal, Faiz Ahmed Faiz, Zafar (last Mughal Badsha imprisoned and exiled by British) and all of these indicated that behind smiles lurks many a sorrow. Iqbal says "Do not be misled by the smile on the lips of the rosebud; it has been newly washed by the tears (dewdrops) of agony."

What an elegant and gracious language is Urdu. Recently a friend of the children, doing her doctorate in Paris came home for a visit. A French student had come down with her and when she heard us all speaking in English she remarked "I told Reyhana's Granny, how sacrilegious of you to talk to your children and grandchildren in English." That's been our tragedy. Our language, customs, traditions have become foreign and our youth like Aslam etc; often do not even understand our languages, which thought brings me back to Salman Rushdie.

A Kashmiri boy, educated and nurtured in a British environment and who even had to learn his religion through Orientalists in a British University. An existentialist groping for philosophy from the luxury of his surroundings.

The title *Satanic Verses* derived from an incident recorded in the life of our Prophet, Period when Quraish persecution [was] becoming intolerable and [the] first batch of refugees [were] sent to seek asylum with the Christian King of Abyssinia. When the Quraish Fat Cats were seated in the Haram in Mecca indulging in their favourite pastime of how to turn fast bucks, the Prophet who was meditating there, stood up and boldly started reciting a Revelation as it was being revealed. Normally they would have pelted him, but on this occasion they were so taken aback that they sat listening in silence and when at the end of it and Prophet prostrated, all but one of them (being too fat to make Sajda) fell down in Sajda. They were heavily criticised as sellouts by those that were not present and so had to come up with explanations such as (I) Muhammed eulogized Lat, Manat and Uzza (deities Arabs worshipped) but when told that the verses belittle these they said Muhammed changed it for it was interpolated by the Satan in the original rendering. Early Muslim narrator Ibn Hisham recorded it like they recorded every incident during time and life of Prophet, but Muslims always treated it as the Volte Face of the Quraish. However, when Christian Orientalists picked this up in their studies of Islam (for purposes of criticising and renouncing) they went to town. During my course of study at the School of Oriental and Islamic Studies in London, I discussed similar incidents with Professor Jaffar and he said Islam is big enough to stand up now as it has in past centuries.

Rushdie is no philosopher. Nor is he a mystic. In his surrealistic approach he blasphemes every character. In his book "Shame" when he could not find any sexual transgression by Benazir Bhutto, he calls her Virgin Iron Pants. All the political personalities are retrogrades of worst order whose wives jump out from one bed to another.

Rushdie is not a mystic but he mystifies the reader no end, with his usage of literary gimmicks. He talks of a dream sequence, no doubt alluding that Quran is nothing but what Muhammed has dreamt up. In Islam Allah is such an abstract entity – no physique therefore there can be no physiognomy; Does not occupy space and beyond time, yet is Alpha and Omega and All-Pervading. Though man has sensible perceptions, imagination, vision within and much besides, the Essence of Allah cannot be understood or comprehended and we can only know Him though 99 attributes, attributes which humans too share such as power, majesty, justice, honesty etc. One very eminent classical Mystic Ibn Araby who penetrated many veils beyond those accessible to man, comes to a certain station (Makaam or destination of man's approach to the Highest) throws up his hands in despair and says: "Beyond this remains only Revelation. Man can proceed no further." Rushdie depicts God as an old, balding man, with dandruff. The veil which many Muslim women adopt is as much worthy of respect as the veil of the nuns of Xtianity; Rushdie names his brothel Hijab (veil or burkha as we know it) and the mates within named after the wives of the Prophet; and the bums that visit there have the names of the Prophet's disciples. If this is free expression then the West and its disciples are welcome to it. My Quran says "Revile not the religious Beliefs of others". This is why we get so angry with Mr Deedat of the Islamic Propagation Centre. His sneering and deriding other religions wounds sensibilities deeply. Our world is better off without it.

After all that outburst, please believe me that we in no way agree with the pronouncement of the Ayatollah or the reaction of the masses. The Shariah is clear that a proper court of law, after a fair trial alone can pass judgment, and in instances like Rushdie, fair period of rehabilitation offered. My friends and family maintain that once provoked, my onslaught becomes unbearable!

Sikosi Mji came with 2 granddaughters on Thursday for dinner. She shamed me in that I had neglected to enquire about Walter. She has brought out a health series of books aimed for the teenager, hoping that they will stay away from smoking and drinking. The first one in print is [the] biography of a lung. Well illustrated and it tells its story well.

I had not told my mother of my impending visit to Pollsmoor knowing that it would cause needless anxiety. Nasim and family looked after her while we were in Cape Town. When told by Nasim that I had seen you she said "Is that why she left me while I was a guest here? But no, it's good she went to see him". Tradition bound, she had wondered why I was leaving houseguests – it's bad manners. She was greatly touched by your Salaam and asked me to reciprocate when next I wrote. She left for Potch; the day I returned Dilshad wanted to know who is uncle Kathie who sent the chocolates for her. Why does she not remember him? What do we tell her at 4½ and with the stories she hears and sees only bad people are in jail! Jihaan of course was another matter. She questioned me so minutely over the visit, that I marvelled at the grasp of this 10 year old child of the situation in our country but then I am reminded tragically of how many ten year old ones have become old and wearied in their violence and involvement.

Sincerely Yours
Zuleikhabehn

A.M. Kathrada
Pollsmoor Maximum Prison
Tokai
7966
25th March 1989

Dear Zuleikhabehn

Your letter of 1st March (unregistered), much to my surprise reached me on 7th March!! Record time! This, plus your American letter makes me want to suggest that we revert to unregistered letters; but I'm hesitant. Having in mind the long history of "lost" letters I think the old saying is still valid, namely; two successful unregistered letters don't make a Pollsmoor summer.

I must thank you for taking time off to visit me. After all the years of contact-by-letter it was a real pleasure to meet you in person. Luckily the authorities processed your application in record time; and some Transvaal folks who had booked to come decided to postpone their visits, thus leaving space in my quota for February. Pity the 40 minutes passed so quickly. One cannot even contemplate discussing any particular topic at length; one is obliged to jump – often incoherently – from one thing to another and try to absorb a mass of information. Fortunately in our case this problem is somewhat mitigated by the letters we have been writing. Partly as a result of a habit since childhood but mainly because of the prison situation, there is a greed for all sorts of information, and I have to impose on you, and other friends to be my constant sources.

Under the circumstances, your "onslaught" on the Rushdie affair is more than welcome. I am not exactly enthusiastic about reading lengthy articles and books on complex issues that require mental effort, hence my knowledge of the Rushdie imbroglio has been peripheral. I doubt it very much if I would go out of my way to read his "Satanic Verses" even if it was not banned. Your observations have greatly helped my understanding of the issues. You know in the sixties and seventies we had on Robben Island several very outstanding intellectuals, and I could always turn to one or other of them to enlighten me on just about anything. People like Dr Neville Alexander, Mac Maharaj, Dennis Brutus, Andrew Masondo, Leslie van der Heyden, Kader Hassim, Fikile Bam, Nelson... There is Walter who to my mind is <u>the</u> expert on the history of the liberation movement. I have just named a handful; there were many more. With the influx of the youth after the Soweto uprising there came a huge crop of bright and knowledgeable young men, who had so much to impart, and to teach. Here at Pollsmoor we are only 4, and the range of expertise has consequently dwindled. I often find myself frustrated by the absence of persons I could turn to, and I have to rely on visitors and correspondents.

Your mention of Iqbal took me back to my childhood years. It was in 1940 or so, when I was in Std. 4 and befriended a classmate, Cachalia. Through him I met his uncles Moulvi and Yusuf and I soon became a regular at their home. Soon Yusuf decided to take me in hand and gave me lessons from the Hadis. He also felt it was necessary for me to learn some Urdu poetry, and one of the poems/songs he taught me early on was Iqbal's "Sarê jahan sê accha – Hindustan hamara..." Planned indoctrination? Perhaps. But not one bit to be regretted. The temptation is great to write more about those years, but I have to move on.

Your reference to Iqbal's poem about the bird in the cage lamenting over freedom reminded me of the well-known song "Pingrê kê panchi rê, tera dard ne janê kooi." Let me try out my Gujarati. (For Censors: "No one knows the agony of the bird in the cage".

I suppose there is some merit in the poets' observations that behind the smiles lurks many a sorrow. When I last heard of him (many years ago) Faiz Ahmed was himself in jail in Pakistan. From what I've gathered, the prison conditions there were such as to cause [a] great deal of suffering and sorrow. In addition to the generally known universal complaints of prisoners, it would be most surprising if every prisoner did not have his own private agony and suffering. Some have much to agonise about, others less; some manage to disguise or hide their problems; others are less successful at concealing. Like all prisoners "security" prisoners are not immune from personal problems. If anything, because of their generally longer sentences, they should be more vulnerable. However, our experience on the whole (especially on Robben Island) has been that affected individuals have not allowed themselves to be plunged into prolonged periods of gloom, sulkiness or dejection.

In my view this is because in times of trouble there is always someone to turn to, some older inmate to boost up the spirits, and provide guidance, and comfort. You see the great advantage we have over common-law prisoners is that all of us share certain basic ideals, and we are all sentenced for similar offences. There is a harmony and sense of oneness among security prisoners which transcends superficial parochial differences; a relationship which is unfortunately absent outside.

I think I have previously written about my regret at not being able to speak Urdu. At Madressa we spoke only Urdu and got along well. Then I went and forgot it, it's inexcusable. Now, after 26 years of not speaking I'm also in difficulty with Gujarati. I don't think I could satisfactorily go through a 40 minute prison visit in Gujarati. One would have thought that after all these years of opportunity I would have been fluent in one of the African languages. But I failed. I was doing quite well when I was doing Special Xhosa for

BA. After getting through (21 years ago), I neglected it, and made little progress.

I'll stop now with my catalogue of failures, and proceed with something else. I notice that Mrs Thatcher has once again spoken about Nelson's release; I just hope we don't have a repetition of 1985 and 15 November 1988 when waves of expectation and excitement swept through the country – followed by the inevitable disappointment. The powers that be remain as determined as ever to derive maximum benefit for themselves by continuing to hold out the carrot of release, while having no intention to release us. It's a charade that started way back in 1966 already, and therefore we remain unimpressed by the goings on. Oh yes after every few years they will let out an individual or two – on grounds of illness or old age; eg. Mbeki, Mthopeng, Gwala. Walter will be 77 in May, and we won't be surprised if he is next. On the other hand there is Oscar Mphetha; he is older, has had a leg amputated, and is bedridden in hospital – he has finished over 3 years of his 5 year sentence, but they won't let him go. Yet they continue to proclaim that "security prisoners" are treated the same as common law prisoners!

I hope I don't give you the impression that I'm being embittered by these things. I think I have learnt quite a bit about the workings of the system, and am able to take a realistic approach to things.

A few weeks ago the Prison authorities informed me that I could proceed with my MA, but on condition that I do not quote banned literature, or quote the words of listed persons! That sounds like no permission at all; my lawyers are looking into the matter.

This is all for now. Yes it is difficult to explain the concept of imprisonment to a child; yet their reaction can be most interesting. A few years ago 2-year-old Shameez came along with her mother, and during the visit informed me that she did not like police! I was quite encouraged by her remark but alas – a few minutes later she looked at me, and said; "I don't like you"!!

Good to hear about your mother; about Sikosi, and all other friends. Oh yes, I had a nice letter from Jesse and Vallabh. I will be replying.

Fond regards to all family members and friends.
AMK

Prisoners are expected to be rather pre-occupied with matters culinary. Don't be surprised, therefore, if I express fascination with Durban's giant samoosa. From the dimensions given, it can occupy half the floor space of our present cell! Wonder what it tastes like?

Westville
3630
28th April 1989

Dear Ahmedbhai

The first Eid card received this year is from you. Thank you very much and may we from here just wish you a very Blessed Eid Mubarak – the word blessed is of course redundant for Mubarak means just that. All Allah's Blessings on you. Your Gujerati is excellent, the writing as neat as your Roman Latin script and the spelling cannot be faulted since you know the subtleties of the ણ and ર. Krishna Somers must be told about this. Do you know h[im?] Eminent in the medical world – expatriate who was dean of medical faculty in Kampala right from the inception of that institute; escaped during Amin's days, not that he was in any danger, but he had been made to understand that unlike the Europeans on the staff, he would not be allowed to resign. So when attending a medical conference overseas, he did not bother to go back. For a while he was based in Papua New Guinea, and we teased him saying that he was now in the midst of the head hunters. Currently Prof at Medical School, Perth. On his annual trips to South Africa, he never fails to pay his duty call on me (we correspond off and on, and he being a friend of Bis, and my late husband). His knowledge of Asian arts and culture is remarkable for a South African, but then he did his first medical degree in India, and his many conference attendances in Pakistan, India gives him a sound basis for this. Before this diversion, I was telling you that Kris once remarked that he was surprised that my brother Abdulhak wrote to mother in Gujerati, since so few Indian South Africans care to know the vernacular.

Yusuf Cachalia was only doing what we all do for our friends.

That is introduce them to the things we find interesting. I am sure you must have talked to many of your acquaintances of the movements that you were interested in. Hadith literature is often confusing. One can find a Hadith to suit one's views virtually on any subject, so that confirms the allegation of many a scholar that much interpolation has occurred by interested parties during the centuries. However the Sahih Bukhari, the Muwatta of Malik and so are very close to Guidelines in Quran and lifestyle of our Prophet. I find the commentary on Hadith by eminent scholars such as Maulana Shabbir Ahmed Uthmani invaluable; and as for the Urdu translation and Tafsir of Maulana Maududi, it's become such a habit that if I skip a day of my reading, I feel I have lost out. It runs in 6 volumes and it outlines a lifestyle that is completely integrated, in harmony with all creation, and ethical even in every aspect of life, be it material, political, educational, social. Have you a copy of Muhammed Asad's translation of Quran? Please let me know. I am sending you a copy of *The Best of Delights* (latest of my cuisine series) for Eid. I pray the authorities will allow it. If so then do try some of the newer recipes such as cabbage, carrot, rice, Lagan. It can be cooked on the stove, although an oven is the ideal.

Incidentally "pinjre ke panchhi" ("The Bird in the Cage") has become a classic. Reading Benazir Bhutto's biography, the picture of stark inhumanity to political prisoners, detention without trial, house arrests and so forth is spelt out in vivid terms. Which brings me to Faiz Ahmed Faiz's poems on the subject of prisons. Victor Kiernan has translated some of his works most ably but as all translations go, it is far from the beauty of the original. This one is on solitary confinement and you will note the difference between the English and the Urdu.

Subject : Solitary Confinement.

Dūr Āfāq pě lahrā'i kobī nūr kī lahr
Khwāb hī khwāb men bedār hūā dard ka shanr.
Khwāb hi khwāb men be-tāb nazar honě lagī
Adam ābād e judā'i men sahar hone lagī
Kasa-e-dil men bharī apnī sabūhi main ne
Ghol kar talkhī –e-diroz men imroz kā zahr<sup>*</sup>

Far on the horizon a tremor of light flickered
still plunged in sleep, pain's citadel grew conscious,
still plunged in sleep eyes grew once more restless;
Yes, Yes, ever more restless.
Over the ghostly house of exile, a dawn.
In my heart's cup, I poured the morning light
Stirring in yesterday's gall, today's poison.

Without bothering about the Urdu, the rest of the poem goes:

Far on the horizon a tremor of light flickered
harbinger of a still invisible daybreak.
Some melody, some perfume, some siren face
strays alike a careless passer-by through the ghostly
house of exile, bringing all hope's torment.

Stirring in yesterday's gall today's poison
I made an offering of my homesickness
To friends in this and all lands who have drunk with me
To earth's beauty, to the charm of cheek and lip.

---

\* Beside this verse, Mayat writes "Never noticed typing space was running out – Forgive the askew lines. Hope that no one thinks this [Urdu] is some sort of code."

My sadistic streak shows up when I copy this out to you. But I do miss the late Moosa Mia with whom I corresponded and most of our letters were extracts of Urdu poetry we came across. Moosa lumped us all South Africans of India as devoid of culture and in his letters he was educating me out of the goodness of his heart. He knew your family well and your brother in Lenasia was a friend. Moosa died last year.

As for the giant samoosa, by the time they had blow-torched it into an edible stage, the vegetable filling inside had gone off. Imagine if it had a khima [mince] filling. Talking of cooking, I have to answer a lot of queries from persons who run into difficulty with their cooking. One letter from Los Angeles from the editor of World Cook Books wanted to know what to do with tukmewia seeds, you know, the small black seeds which became translucent and which flavour Ramadaan falooda milk? Sorry if this makes you nostalgic and makes the juices run, (may be again the sadism showing up) and what the properties of it were. I recalled a conversation with my late father-in-law. He mentioned that when Khwaja Kamaluddin had toured South Africa he had mentioned that those seeds cool down the body heat. In hakim or traditional medicines effect of food on blood, nervous system etc play a great part.

Some interesting films are being shown during the film festival and Aslam has booked for World Apart. While in the States I saw Cry Freedom. What an impact it makes. Critics have of course said that it is more about Woods than Biko, but what was important to me was the face of the system that it portrayed, in all its stark nakedness.

I was so taken up with getting the books ready for the auditors (society's books) that I neglected writing this letter. And now I am hurrying through it so fast, that the thoughts come out all mumbled. Better grammar next time I promise.

Meanwhile salaams and the best for Eid.
    Zuleikha

A.M. Kathrada
Pollsmoor Maximum Prison
Tokai
7966
15 July 1989

Dear Zuleikhabehn

Your letter of 28th April reached me on 19th May; many thanks. Thanks also for the Eidy; Gorima's magi and mithai and the *Delights*. The "Best..." with its glossy paper, printing and photography makes it extremely attractive; the very appearance is sure to win new converts to the delights of the Orient.

I'm writing this letter the day after Bakri Eid. We didn't have our usual Eid celebrations; we were taken on a little trip to see Nelson. We celebrated his birthday four days in advance. He is very well and fully recovered. He especially remembered you and other friends; he even knew that you had visited me. We spent over 4 hours together, not nearly enough time to even exchange news about our families and friends. Yet every minute of it was worth it.

Yesterday we moved one notch up in our status as prisoners; we are now allowed to wear civilian clothes, so we were all togged up in our suits. My niece Zohra was here a few weeks ago, and after making clear what I don't like, I left the choice of clothing more or less to her. She hasn't done badly; but when it came to wearing which tie with which suit I think I could detect signs of shock in the faces of the Cape Town friends who delivered the stuff. They were very polite, but their opinions were unmistakable – I belong to an age which has long gone by. Anyway they were not around when I dressed for our outing, so I had my way; I put on my red tie with a brown suit. You see, they don't understand that I grew up wearing a red tie.

This latest dispensation raises our prisoner-status to somewhere between that of Walter and Nelson. I should have mentioned in my last letter that Walter no longer stays with me; he was moved to another part of the prison on 15th March. We have been with him a few times since; we celebrated his 77th birthday together on 18th May, and yesterday too he was with us. He is very well. I miss him a great deal, and only hope that his removal from here leads to better things for him.

Back to our clothes. It is wonderful to be able to shed our prison uniforms; it helps to some extent to assert one's individuality. Zeke Mphahlele has written about the tyranny of time and place. In prison there is the tyranny of colour – the green uniforms of the prisoners, the grey walls, the monotonous wardens' uniforms, the grey concrete. Now we have the "freedom" to look different, which of course makes one feel different.

On our way to Victor Verster prison we passed Stellenbosch, and once again my thoughts wandered back to my childhood days. In a popular song the Afrikaans singer powerfully expressed his longing for his birthplace – Stellenbosch. We grew up associating Stellenbosch with Afrikaans and Afrikaners. And not entirely wrongly. After all was it not Stellenbosch University which has spawned Prime Ministers and other eminent Afrikaners, many of whom fathered the race policies since Union, and before! As our vehicle passed the pride of Afrikanerdom I thought of the paradoxes and incongruities which the race-obsessed volk prefer to sweep under the carpet. I think of the Tricameral system and wonder if its authors (who included Stellenbosch graduates) ever considered how Simon van Der Stel would fit into their constitutional dispensation. His father would have to sit in the House of Assembly, his mother in the House of Delegates; and he would be consigned to the House of Representatives! Or, would it be too far-fetched to suggest that the Tricameral was specifically designed to meet such a situation?

I think you are being over-generous in describing my Gujarati as "excellent". Even in pre-prison days it could not have been rated as "good". Now after 26 years of not speaking it I'm sure I am unable to go through a 40 minute-visit in Gujarati. The situation almost arose last month when I would have been able to test myself. A cousin of mine from India is presently on a 3-month visit to S.A. He speaks only Gujarati, Urdu and Arabic; he was to have visited me, but unfortunately he could not make it. I could have practised my Gujarati on Robben Island with Lalloo Chiba who was with us for 18 years, and who could read, write and speak it fluently. But we hardly ever spoke it.

Thanks very much for the verses by Faiz Ahmed Faiz; I tried to understand the verse in Urdu, but failed. I understand a number of words but not sufficient to make sense of the sentences.

Yes I do remember Dr Somers. I must have met him through Bis and them. I think I last heard of him when he was at Makarere.

Oh yes, some time ago I told you about the Afrikaans poem I recited to my interrogator, Mr Swanepoel. You thought the incident was worth recording. In fact the matter was brought up during the Rivonia Trial, when Advocate Berrange questioned him about it, after reading out the poem. The incident was part of the Trial record.

There are interesting developments in the Afrikaner cultural world, among academics, writers, artists, musicians, churchmen etc. The increasing number of "rebels" have made a significant crack in the Afrikaner monolith, and things can never be the same again. At the time of our arrest it was just Bram Fischer and a small handful of "communist traitors". Now every sector of Afrikaner society is daily spawning its "rebels". It is one of the more positive developments in recent years.

I'm sure you must have found "A World Apart" very interesting.

All the reviews have been favourable.

This will be all for today. I was very sorry that Fatima and Ismail were refused permission to visit me. Please pass my greetings to them. Nelson is expecting another visit from her soon.

One of these days I am going to take a bash at making chevda here; I've asked my niece Zohra to send me the recipe. If I don't succeed I shall have to seek your advice.

As you know Cape Town had 2 Eids. Since we couldn't have ours yesterday, Enver brought along the goodies today. As usual we thoroughly enjoyed ourselves.

Keep well. Fond wishes and salaams to you, the children, the grandchildren and friends. I hope your mother is well.

All the best from
AMK

Westville
3630
27th August 1989

Dear Ahmed Bhai

It is nearing the end of August and I yet have to reply to your letter dated 15th July. The guilt is all the deeper knowing that the nation was celebrating your birthday and sending you cards – but then I am no one for celebrating birthdays. Incidentally Jaleel, Aslam and myself are all August born. No cards but lots of duas for them, for you, myself included! May the next August see us all celebrating in an air of freedom.

Fatima is very busy and she has something else in the pipeline. It will be my pleasure to join her in the venture. I am trying to collect a lot of old correspondence together, go through it. You know once every few years I go through my collection of papers, letters etc; and the amount I discard has to be seen to be believed. Recently a Maulana Pandor visited Durban. Ex Johannesburg, he has spent some three decades at a library in India but will now return home. We hope he will help us at the proposed Activity Centre we intend building. Our Centre is projected to be one where three generations of women can relax, educate or gratify their particular skills under one roof at the same time. This way grannies will not feel left out of activities. The activities themselves will revolve around the improvement of minds, hands, bodies so there will be class and lecture rooms, Jamaat Khana, Gym, swimming pool, Library, auditorium, even a Ghusal Khana to wash and shroud the dead. Dwellers in flats always complain that it is very difficult to perform ghusal of the dead in their tiny spaced rooms.

My Nasim, Aslam and son-in-law Rashid do not possess suits. When they have to attend formal functions and if they really can't get away with it, then they have navy blazers and Aslam is the only one that has plenty of ties. The other two come and rummage among their father's international collection of ties (I mean it, we collected ties and topis – for namaaz so don't think I am referring to wigs – from all the countries we visited. The one that he purchased in Bokhara, black with white embroidery is a prized piece) and somehow present themselves and pass off. I can imagine a red tie with black, navy or grey suit, but with brown!!!! Anyway it must feel like the child's first long pants suit to be back in mufti.

I am sorry that you only have the *The Best of Delights* and not the encyclopedia *Indian Delights* that has an excellent chevda recipe. Incidentally I received a huge volume (over 500 pages) of "The Encyclopedia of the Cultures of India, Pakistan, Bangla Desh and Sri Lanka" from the Cambridge University Press (who are the publishers). This is in payment for allowing them use of our spice transparency. It made my day to see among the credits to various museums, libraries, universities, also the credit to "Women's Cultural Group". To be chosen from among so many excellent cookery books on our cuisine is I think a singular compliment.

I met Molly van Loon the other day. She has a rare collection of Buddhist art and religious artifacts. Born in Burma and later travelling with her husband to Tibet since both converted to Buddhism, they have a collection that is unique. She re-iterated the remark you make in your letter that there are interesting developments in the Afrikaner cultural world. She is [...] exhibiting her collection at the Pretoria University for some weeks and they have come out with a 30 page catalogue for it. Saying that though the very founding of South Africa was because of the spices and riches of the East, the White rulers turned their backs on the cultures of Asia. The blanket of lethargy being snatched away from them, they are only now discovering the cultural and exotic riches of the Asians who live among them. Curry and rice and koelie drie hoekies* (samoosas) have at last done their work.

We are all awaiting the day when you will be a guest at Tuinhuis – the new incumbent should follow the precedent set by the predecessor. "Over my dead body" statements just do not apply in the South African situation. From Danie Craven to State Presidents they have all had to volte face. I remember our sports administrator, [in the] period when anti-apartheid agitation overseas had started. Well a tennis complex was quickly set up in an area which would be accessible to Blacks and Browns and somehow I got landed with my kids to witness the opening. Oh yes, the Sports administrator had come that day to observe the finals and when it ended and prizes had to be presented, his wife was to do the honours. It is Western etiquette that you remove gloves (unless it is Royalty) when shaking hands, but lady quickly donned hers when she had to shake the hands of the winners. Nowadays I see a lot of kissing when it comes to congratulating winners. Can you imagine what she would have done? Perhaps borrowed some artificial lips from a plastic surgeon!! I can laugh at the foibles of such restricted minds now, but when younger one could just about explode.

I have a good mind to get in touch with all the persons that you have corresponded with. I know Dr Karrim is one and then maybe your family members. Anyone else? Would it be possible to give me a list?

Before I forget and it may read like a bizarre note out there but on Wednesday evening I am speaking at a very posh dinner hosted by the YPO (Young Presidents Organisation). One has to be under 49 and either possessing or in a high administrative capacity of a financial institution worth at least 7 million (could be a higher figure but my mind stops at some figures). Anyway

---

\* Literally "little coolie triangles".

the Indian gentleman who inveigled me into this is a well liked acquaintance and the subject he proposed right up my alley, it is "The spice of life". The blurb introducing me reads – come and travel with her to the exotic lands of Kashmir and Spain and get a whiff of the fragrance of saffron…. "I hope I do not spoil the YPO appetites for I will dwell on the macabre story of the spice trade which brought mighty Empires down on their knees and gave rise to the Colonial powers who plundered, murdered, committed arson, conveyed human cargoes and since the trade was so profitable even established half way stations to the Spice Islands." One such victim of this rush for wealth lies buried in Robben Island, His karamat is still there I believe, did you ever see it? Will I get invited again – well I will tell you in the next letter how my talk was received.

With Salaams

A.M. Kathrada
Pollsmoor Maximum Prison
Tokai
7966
17th September 1989

Dear Zuleikhabehn

Thank you for your letter, which arrived on 8th September. Congratulations to you and the Women's Cultural Group for the credit you received in the "Encyclopaedia of Cultures". I must apologise to you about the chevda recipe. I do have the *Delights*; I missed the recipe when I hurriedly looked through it. Now I am waiting until I have the energy to take a shot at it.

All success to your Activity centre project. The bit of information you gave sounds interesting, and valuable. This Maulana Pandor, is he not originally from somewhere on the East Rand?

The news that Nasim, Aslam and Rashid do not possess suits has jolted me into the painful recognition of my sartorial ignorance, or backwardness. Ever since I donned my first items of civilian clothing in 26 years I have met with more or less an equal measure of compliments and criticism, but in retrospect I find that the compliments are more from fellow prisoners than from visitors. The latter have been very polite, but their messages were unmistakable – fashionwise I'm still living in the dark ages. The latest in a series of shocks came a few days ago when I turned up at a visit in a suit and my very beautiful jersey; only to be told that jerseys are just not worn with suits! The in-thing is to wear a waistcoat! Good heavens, under no circumstances do I want to wear a waistcoat; how then should I keep warm, I wanted to know. They then enlightened me about some garments which go under the name of "thermal underwear". They brought these things the next day; but to me they seem to be no different from the humble vest which has helped to keep me warm for 60 years. Besides, the thermals are white; for which colour I have developed a pathological hatred. You see through the years of prison labour – which included chopping stones, pick and shovel, chopping wood, collecting seaweeds, weeding – the one thing I learnt to really hate was to do my washing! And the whiter the garment the greater the need to expend more energy. I must confess I don't exactly have an inclination or enthusiasm for this chore. So until such time as I have access to a washing machine (in the old sexist days I would have said, or a wife) the whites will remain unpacked.

Yes the lowly masala has made a tremendous impact on the history of geography of the world; in their selective amnesia the whites seem to have conveniently forgotten that it was the search for these ingredients that brought Dias, Van Riebeeck and others to the shores of South Africa. I hope that your talk on the "Spice of Life" will make some contribution, however small, towards establishing the rightful place of masala in our history. As for the present day popularity of [the] samoosa I have yet to meet a single white person who has not tasted and enjoyed it.

About the Karamat on Robben Island; yes I did visit it. In fact it is not far from where we stayed. When we arrived in 1964 it was in a pitiful condition. I understand the Prisons Department thereafter took the initiative to build a solid, attractive structure, which was completed by the late sixties. I made representations to be allowed to go regularly to keep the place tidy, but this was refused. Groups of Moslems from Cape Town go out on Sundays to spend a few hours there.

Some points now about Behn's proposed project in which you've also been drawn in. Firstly, as to the advisability and/or necessity for it I feel I should state my general position. The best persons to decide are the folks outside jail, who are able to take into account all the pros and cons; if they feel that a project of this nature can make some useful contribution I have to accept their judgement. Having said this, I nevertheless feel that I should restate some of the points I made when similar suggestions were put to me previously, on Robben Island and here.

I very strongly feel that there is a great dearth of historical literature about our people, and biographies can be invaluable in filling the gap. I was personally involved when Nelson and Walter wrote their autobiographies on Robben Island. Because these were illegal, I was deprived of my studies when the authorities discovered Nelson's original manuscripts. (The manuscript had some comments suggestions etc. in my handwriting). I was most disappointed when I recently found out that these were never published, as they contained not only the first-hand account of their lives, but a lot of valuable historical data.

While I hold a strong brief for biographies I am not convinced that I fall into the category of persons whose lives should be chronicled. True, I have had a long innings of activity during which I have experienced and participated in interesting events. I do not believe this qualifies me as a suitable subject. These events definitely need to be written about, but not by focusing on a single individual. I have stated to numerous friends that one of my primary aims is to personally write, or to get someone to write about the period in which I was involved. But my idea is to approach the project by centering it around Flat 13. In this way we will be able to cover the events, and, perhaps more importantly, numerous individuals who were the real backbone of the events, and who are virtually never mentioned. It is absolutely essential that their contributions be recorded. Naturally aspects of my own contribution will not be excluded, i.e. insofar as it deserves mention. One of the things I fear is that writers tend to be a bit too generous about one's role, resulting in a picture which the subject finds it difficult to recognise himself. When I read a few things recently in the press, and in letters, regarding the birthday, I remarked to someone: "I wish I could meet this person they're talking about."

When Behn's project was brought to my attention I asked that she should check and co-ordinate with friends in London. I am aware that something was being planned there, but I haven't any reports of what in fact was done. Nelson told me that something had been published or was about to be published. I'm sure Behn wouldn't want to duplicate things. I don't know to what extent the friends in UK have used letters.

I must emphasise that I am not trying to put a damper on Behn's plans. I have briefly tried to bring my views to your attention, but as I have earlier said, in this and similar matters the final decision is yours.

Under present circumstances there is hardly anything that I will be able to do by way of rendering assistance. A couple of 40 minute visits will not even scratch the surface of our problem. This aspect will require more thought and attention.

It was very heartening to receive good wishes and duas from you and other friends at home and abroad. Let me reciprocate, albeit belatedly, by wishing you, Aslam and Jaleel – my fellow August babies – everything of the best. I spent very pleasant hours with Walter and my other colleagues. We were allowed to order food from outside. Unfortunately the authorities did not accede to my request to allow my other Rivonia colleagues – Nelson, Motsoaledi and Govan Mbeki – to be with us.

However, on 5$^{th}$ September I was given a pleasant surprise when I was taken to spend a few hours with Nelson. My colleagues were not taken with. I had a nice lunch with Nelson, and was there for over 4 hours. Although I was not given the reason for this unusual trip I suspect this may have been the Prison Department's way of dealing with my birthday request. After our Eid-visit to him we as a group were with him again on 2nd August. These visits are very nice.

Let me end with an interesting coincidence. I listen every Saturday morning to Shirley Veale's radio programme "The Gentle Alternative." Apart from music, the programme, consists of humour and quotations. As if she knew the contents of my letter, she mentioned the following quotations, which I offer to you without comment.

"Fashion is something so intolerable in its ugliness that it has to be changed every 6 months."
– Oscar Wilde

"A biography is like an embalmed body with its guts taken out."
(I can't remember the author of this)

This is all for now. Keep well. Best wishes to you and the family and friends.

AMK

Salsabil
Westville
3630
[October 1989]

My dear Ahmedbhai

This morning, due to a slight cold, I failed to get up for my fijr prayers. In walked Aslam in my room with the morning paper at 6am saying: "Today you can read it first."

There was this wonderful news – awaited for many a long year – of the release of the detainees, and all I could murmur was Shukar Alhamdollillah, Shukar Alhamdollilah.

At 8pm a friend (member of Women's Cultural Group) phoned saying "I feel I owe you a present for keeping us in the Group informed these past ten years of Ahmed Kathrada and his fellow detainees. But for that, we would have treated their detention as but one more bit of news. Thank you for sharing an essential part of history with us."

I hope you are released even before this letter reaches you. However I make haste in adding that having been wrenched away from the outside world for 27 years, the entry into it will be traumatic. Adjustment problems tremendous. Party and people will want you to do what they decide for you. Through the 10 years of our correspondence and from that brief meeting, I have personally no doubt that the quality of resilience, also those of self-reliance and confidence that you exude, is for me sufficient guarantee that you will be your own man, that you will take obstacles in your stride.

May Allah guide you all along your march into the Future.
    With salaams and duas
        Zuleikha